Advance Praise for *Surviving Deep Waters*

"Exceptional talent, prepared, frank, tenacious, fair, honest, and trustworthy."

—**JAMES BROWN**, Host, the NFL Today and
Special Correspondent for CBS News

"Bruce inspires me to this very day as I continue my own career journey that hopefully enhances opportunities for others to be a real difference maker through actions—not just the superficial chit chat I tend to dislike at the various journalism conferences. Bruce Johnson is a winner. A winner against cancer. A winner against those who tried to change his approach to covering news, no matter their rank on the corporate ladder. Bruce is the ultimate winner Because he always learned and grew, thrived and inspired so many in journalism to make a difference, especially African Americans who still need his help every single day."

—**DAVE ROBERTS**, Senior Vice President, ESPN

"At a time in our history when newspapers are dying all over the country, when many radio stations are building audiences by embracing alternative realities, and when more and more local TV stations are in the hands of corporate entities devoted to ever increasing margins of profit, who will cover City Hall? Whoever they are, wherever they are—on social media or standing on street corners with megaphones—Bruce Johnson is their model."

—**GORDON PETERSON**, Retired Washington TV News Anchor,
Host *Inside Washington*, PBS

SURVIVING
DEEP
WATERS

—

*A Legendary
Reporter's Story
of Overcoming
Poverty, Race, Violence,
and His Mother's
Deepest Secret*

—

BRUCE JOHNSON

Post Hill
PRESS

A POST HILL PRESS BOOK
ISBN: 978-1-63758-182-7
ISBN (eBook): 978-1-63758-183-4

Surviving Deep Waters:
A Legendary Reporter's Story of Overcoming Poverty, Race, Violence, and
His Mother's Deepest Secret
© 2022 by Bruce Johnson
All Rights Reserved

Cover Photo by Ronald Gilbert Baker
Solid Image Photographic Service
www.solidimage.com

PRESS
Post Hill Press
New York • Nashville
posthillpress.com

Published in the United States of America
1 2 3 4 5 6 7 8 9 10

Isaiah 43:1–2

"When you go through deep waters, I will be with you.
When you go through rivers of difficulty, you will not drown."

TABLE OF CONTENTS

THE NEWS

"FBI! I'M ORDERING YOU TO MOVE NOW!"

A day I will never forget. It was a Friday, midafternoon and I'm staring down the FBI in a motel parking lot just outside Washington, D.C. I had been on the trail of one of D.C.'s biggest stories; the takedown of Marion Barry. D.C.'s renowned Mayor for Life had been arrested the night before while smoking FBI-provided crack in a downtown hotel.

The combination of fear and determination in standing up to that FBI agent will always be easy to recall. I was a reporter for WUSA9, the CBS affiliate in Washington, D.C. I felt somewhat protected by my celebrity, earned from years as a reporter on the city's meanest streets; but I was still a black man, and this was the FBI.

"Get the fuck out of the way," the agent ordered. He was clearly angry at having been caught trying to move his star witness from her motel safe house. But I had been tipped off!

Was his right hand on his gun as he stared me down?

Tall, handsome, and White, he could have played the lead actor in the CBS series *The FBI*, but this wasn't fiction. He had placed the woman he was escorting into the back seat. Anybody watching these scenes unfold had to be asking, "If she wasn't a prisoner, who was she?"

It was Rasheeda Moore, Marion Barry's former girlfriend.

The FBI agent slammed the car into reverse. With tires screeching, the dark-colored vehicle backed toward me.

"Show me some identification!" I yelled back. "How do I know you're FBI?" Where the hell did that smart-ass response come from? What was I thinking? The truth is…I wasn't thinking about the consequences. I was prepared to take a bullet if it came to that. What a story that would be!

In reality, I was only trying to buy some time for my cameraman, Greg Guise, to get into place. Guise had seen and heard the commotion from the far end of the motel lot. He was already in a full sprint with the video camera on his shoulder and pointed at the car with the tall attractive woman inside.

Rasheeda Moore was the FBI's prized witness in their case to send Mayor Barry to prison for smoking crack during a sting operation they had set up to nab him after years of rumors, police investigations, and grand jury probes that led to others going to jail but not Barry.

Rasheeda would take the stand and testify that she and Barry had used cocaine or crack at least one hundred times. Is that recreational drug use?

A positioned source divulged only to me that the star witness and her children had been under guard at the Renaissance Hotel, on Lee Highway in Falls Church, Virginia. The bureau wanted her out of D.C., away from family, friends, Barry associates, and the media. The Renaissance hotel was in Northern Virginia, across the Potomac River from D.C.

It was over my dead body that I would let the FBI hide its prized witness without getting her image and his on videotape.

My exclusive report of what happened in that parking lot aired on our eleven o'clock newscast that night. The video was brief but dramatic. It confirmed my confrontation with the FBI. Rasheeda was captured on camera for a few seconds. We had to slow down the video, which actually added to the suspense. I thought while watching the scenes unfold on TV, why not two agents on such an important assignment? One might have stayed behind to arrest me for hindering an FBI investigation. An arrest would have been a boost to my incipient reputation. I was closing in on fifteen years in Washington. But it was never my intent to be just an average reporter collecting a paycheck: I wanted to be a difference-maker.

⌁

On so many levels there had never been another one like me. When your journey starts as far back as mine and includes the critics and abettors, Black and White, that I had, it takes more than a lawman or a racist or a life-threatening illness to stop you. My story has never been about just me: this African American has been carrying the aspirations of a mother, a grandmother and entire communities of black folk. They had done the heavy lifting long before I was born.

CHAPTER 1

Early Life

THERE WAS NOTHING IN MY early life that would suggest I'd find myself in that parking lot staring down an FBI agent. Or was there? I was born angry. Probably got that from my mother.

Decades ago, when I started researching and filling notebooks for *Surviving Deep Waters*, I couldn't find one single photo of myself—not one image of me or my siblings from our childhood. Who was there when I was brought home from the hospital? No first communion, no grade school or high school graduation pictures. Nothing. No faded images of a bronze-colored kid squeezed into a Polaroid frame with his siblings.

I did have memories, good and bad. And the more I wrote, the more they came back to me.

"Junior, Michael, Bruce, and David!" That was the call that would come from the screen door in the Louisville public-housing project when Ma wanted her four boys to come in from playing outside.

In the 1950s, the area was still being called "Little Africa" by some. We were among the 700 African American families moved into the Joseph S. Cotter homes, named after a local Black poet and educator. Located west of 32nd Street and south of Garland Avenue, we were public housing tenants surrounded by better off Black folk in Louisville's segregated west end.

Although we were poor, legalized segregation made sure that upward mobile Black people were never too far away. Within a few short blocks we had plenty of examples of the bootstrap self-help ethic that prevailed in much of Black Louisville.

Educators, physicians, lawyers, business leaders, even funeral directors shopped at the same stores and frequented the same parks and places of worship. White people in Louisville seemed okay with our progress as long as we didn't try to live next door or send our children to public schools alongside their children.

I was but four years old in 1954 when two White newspaper reporters turned-activists were arrested for trying to integrate a White suburban Louisville neighborhood. Ann and Carl Braden were charged with sedition after they purchased a home in Shively only to turn that same house over to a Black couple, Andrew and Charlotte Wade. Carl Braden was found guilty and sent to prison for seven months. Ann's case never went to trial. All charges and convictions against the couple were eventually dismissed or overturned. Carl Braden died at age sixty. Ann continued to fight racism. She was commended by Martin Luther King in his 1963 Letter from the Birmingham Jail. Ann Braden was a key advisor to SNCC, the Student Non Violent Co-ordinating Committee which included the late Congressman John Lewis.

There was nothing threatening about the Wades. They were merely a Black couple who wanted a piece of the American dream: a house in the suburbs with a yard, driveway, and perhaps some peace and quiet.

The Wades were never allowed to move into their new home. It might have cost them their lives had they done so. Angry White people picketed. Guards were posted, but that didn't stop someone from firebombing the house one night. No one was ever held responsible. Andrew and Charlotte were forced to sell what was left of their home at auction. They moved back to Louisville's west end with the rest of us Black folk to spend their remaining years.

Unlike the Wades and Bradens, my parents were not ones to challenge the system. Few Black people in Louisville back then could afford to step out. There was always a price to pay. I recall an interview with The Reverend Andrew Young, a lieutenant to Doctor King. He told me, "None of us in the movement retired rich or even with a pension."

My mother complained a lot about "those White people." She had a separate list of complaints about some of the Black people she didn't like.

Ma was born Mary Pearson in 1928, a year before the start of the Great Depression. Her own mother Ivory Bell had little to do with raising a young daughter and even younger son, Jim. That responsibility fell to their grandmother, Millie Bell.

The threesome was so poor they would move from place to place, not bothering to unpack because they were always getting evicted. They would go hungry. At the railroad tracks they waited for the trains to come by. When crates of vegetables and fruit fell off the speeding cars, they were there to scoop up their dinner.

I didn't hear these stories early on. It was only after I had become a news reporter and started asking questions that my people, sometimes reluctantly, started filling in the empty scripts of their lives. They saw no need to burden us with how bad off the family had been.

My mom would be the first in her family to graduate high school. It was a big deal in a Kentucky family where some people never learned to read or write. But Ma had bigger plans for herself and her children and maybe a special plan for me. Who could have imagined that at age fifty-two after raising her children, practically singlehandedly, Ma would graduate from the University of Louisville? I learned perseverance from my mother.

There was no dad to teach me anything. It's not because Mary didn't try. She had gotten married at age nineteen to Leslie Johnson, Senior, a drop-dead handsome man; I could see why Ma fell for him. Les was a smooth talker. Brown skin, a shade darker than my caramel color and he stood at least six feet; taller than I would ever be. I can still smell the Old Spice cologne that he splashed on to complement the neatly pressed starched shirts and trousers. He never owned a car, and I couldn't say if Les had a job. I don't recall my "natural" father ever living in the same house or apartment with us. I know that Les only came to visit my mother and "his" four sons; he never gave the impression that he would be staying. I didn't know him, and he certainly never got to know me. Les Junior, my oldest brother and his namesake, was clearly his favorite and, it turns out in the end, the most like him.

Our history of growing up with no dad was more common than rare among my Black friends.

"You need a dad to play baseball,". I got that proclamation once from a young White friend after I accepted his family's offer of a free ticket and a ride to a Washington Nationals baseball game. They had season tickets. Baseball, basketball and all sports had been a lifelong bonding experience between the dad and his two sons.

Growing up in Louisville, I didn't experience any advantages to not having a dad around. We envied the boys with fathers especially the ones who were present and seemed interested in us too.

In the 1950s and early 1960's in Louisville, it seemed every colored adult was trying to look less like a Negro and more like White folks. The men added pomade or strong chemicals to their hair that would leave it hard as a brick but resembling White men's hair.

I recall stealing bleaching cream from a dresser jar and rubbing it on my face and arms to lighten my own skin.

Any visible defect could be reason for ridicule. Neighborhood influencers with bad intentions insisted on giving people embarrassing nicknames. Names other than what our parents had given us. Names like "Peanut, Hammer head, Retard, Midget, or Smoke".

We were already at bottom. The goal was not to be at the very bottom. A nick name helped keep people down, their self-esteem below yours. Athletes and entertainers escaped the scorn. They were held in high regard from the time we were able to walk and talk. Sing and dance.

I am my mother's son. Quick to smile, her high-pitched laughter became my laugh as I grew attached to her sensibilities. Her anger was sometimes more fear than anything else. She would say mean things at times because "It made me feel better," she explained.

She was short but not small, maybe five feet tall. Shapely, tight figure, probably from all that manual labor and walking everywhere. Ma drank only on weekends or at picnics and rarely seemed drunk. The woman could throw a punch like a man. She could slap you so hard you thought you had been shot. If she really wanted to hurt you, Ma would ball up her first and throw a roundabout blow at your head. We learned quickly to duck such blows because if she connected upside your head, there would be bells ringing between your ears for days. She could be really loud when she wanted to make a point or issue a command. Her laugh was infectious—high-pitched and full of delight, much like mine. Her dad was Lonnie Pearson, a Louisville barber who never married her mother, Ivory.

Her one constant growing up was Grandma Millie. She was everything a poor southern black grandma was destined to be: burdened, always needing to sit or lean on something to rest awhile from what had to be a lifetime of trials and tribulations, which she was never willing to share. Despite all my efforts when we snuggled to learn more and get her to tell me a story or two, she never did. Maybe Grandma Millie didn't think her inquisitive great-grandchild could handle it.

Millie didn't live on a street. By the time us kids came along, her home was an old grey wooden duplex hidden away in an alley behind large single-family homes that faced the affluent Floyd Street in Louisville's east end. White people lived in those big houses. Some of the families had slaves before the civil war which would have been the age of Millie's parents. My grandma Millie and a handful of other poor black people had addresses that said "rear Floyd Street," to let mail carriers know they presided out back in the alley. By the way, that same alley was gentrified over the years. The shacks were torn down or rehabbed with indoor plumbing. Whites now live on the front and back side of Floyd Street.

On weekends, Ma let my younger brother David and me board a city bus to travel to Grandma Millie Bell's house. My job was to get my little brother there safe and sound. There would be no "call me when you get there," since Millie didn't have a phone. No one would drive out later to check on us either. We never owned a car and Ma didn't learn to drive until after her second divorce.

After boarding the bus and hearing our change drop into the box, David and I took our seats up front as instructed, behind the driver. I checked out every other passenger on the bus and memorized the stops as we traveled along Hill Street from west to east. If the bus ever broke down, I would decide if we would continue our journey to Grandma's on foot or return home.

After disembarking, we'd walk the four or five blocks to Millie's house. We passed Bloom's Grocery Store on one corner. A bar sat on another corner.

We would make a left turn off a neighborhood street onto Grandma Millie's alley. We might yell "Hi" to Mr. Tom Titt and his buddies who often huddled across the way in front of a fire in a steel drum. There was always some drinking going on around the fire. Tom had a wooden wagon that he had built to haul junk, discarded tires, bottles, anything he could collect and convert to some petty cash. He lived in a nearby shack and did odd jobs for the White folks when he wasn't flirting with Grandma. "Y'all get out da street," he would warn us, as cars came speeding through the alley where we played nearby by day and under the streetlight at night. If he was sober and having a good day, Mr. Tom Titt—and we always called him by both names out of respect—would invite us kids into his shed, where he would produce packages of stale Hostess cupcakes as rewards for being no trouble to anybody. We'd take one bite and then toss the stuff.

Grandma Millie Bell had no running water. The toilet was in a small unheated shack built off the back porch. Imagine having to use that "powder" room in the dead of winter. She brought a bucket with a cover into the house, in case we had to get up to pee in the middle of the night.

Like a lot of poor Black people in the 1950s and '60s, Millie lived in what was called a shotgun house: you entered her three-room house via the front room, which led to the middle room, which led to the kitchen. You could fire a gun through the front door and the bullet would travel undisturbed through the last room of the house. Wood and coal stoves in each room provided the heat.

We had to take baths after playing outside all day in the dust, dirt, and abandoned surroundings behind well-to-do White people's homes. Water was pumped from an outside well that we then hauled inside to fill up the round metal tub.

Once a week, a middle-aged White man who called Millie by her first name would knock on the front door and collect some coins that Millie had religiously been depositing in an envelope that she hid behind the front door. This was Millie's burial money. She didn't want to die leaving my mother with the burden of paying for a funeral.

Millie was born Millie Buckner in 1865 or thereabouts, roughly two years after Lincoln signed the Emancipation Proclamation. The town was Pembroke, Kentucky, not far from the Tennessee border in Christian County, Kentucky. Millie's mother was named Unc which could have been a misspelling. The census taker wrote down what he heard. It wasn't always what the Black person was saying. Millie's father was named Jim. Both her parents were born in Kentucky. I am the descendant of slaves brought to the United States between 1700 and 1808. My people likely were captured and transported across the Atlantic to Virginia. Ancestry.com says I am 32 percent Nigerian and 16 percent German. Like President Barack Obama, I've visited slave houses in Western Africa, specifically on Goree Island off the coast of Senegal, and these visits filled me with anguish and pride—anguish for what my people had been put through, including my great-grandma Millie and my mother, but also pride in their perseverance so that I could be to stand on their shoulders.

Although now free, Unc and Jim Buckner had not left their shack by the summer of 1865, when Millie was born. They were said to be free to leave the Buckner plantation; but where would they go? The former slaves had no financial means to set out for places unknown with lots of danger lurking. A Census record showed they remained in place tending the same fields. If they were paid it couldn't have been much. They continued to live in the same slave shack. There were no reparations to slaves. President Lincoln had actually allowed compensation to go to the slaveowners to make up for their losing slave labor.

I couldn't find a record of Millie living in her parents' home, which isn't all that unusual given the times. At age twenty-four, Millie married James (Jim) Bell who was from nearby Tennessee. I obtained their marriage license from 1898 at the Christian County courthouse, in Hopkinsville, Kentucky. James Simons and EW Glass were listed as witnesses to the marriage.

The Bell family was still living in Pembroke a couple decades later. Jim Bell, at age forty-three, was working as a farm laborer. Millie was a housewife. The U.S. Census says they could both read and write, although I don't recall Grandma Millie ever reading and saw no evidence that she could write. They had children: Virgil, Douglas, Mary, Catherine, Marcellus and twins, Ivo and Ivory who died at birth. Ivo later took her twin brother's name as her own.

Millie moved to Louisville after Virgil returned from military service. He sent for the family, or Millie simply decided the family would move to the big city up North. It's unclear why her husband didn't follow his family North.

By the time I came along, the house in Louisville on rear Floyd Street had become a crowded place as grandma Millie's adult children came and went. My favorite great uncle was Marcellus, a tough talking, pistol packing hustler who lived with his girlfriend Jean in the front room of Millie's house. He called me "Red", because of my different skin color. I didn't mind. Took it as a sign of affection. Marcellus Bell had been to prison. I felt protected and enjoyed tagging along as he tended to his several illegal business enterprises. He fenced stolen goods from the barbershop where his legitimate job was shining shoes. He proudly introduced me and my brother David to his clients before reaching into his pocket to produce a few coins, a handful of dimes and nickels for each of us. Uncle Cellus was also a notorious numbers runner. The pistol, a 22 caliber, was assurance that people who bet a number, paid up when their number failed to come up. Finally, on Sundays when most Black people were in church, my great uncle was pushing illegal pint size bottles of whiskey from the front door of grandma Millie's house. Jean was always asleep in their bed a few feet away when strangers would knock on the door. I would peak from the middle room, a backup set of eyes, in case of trouble. The gun made sure the people at the door didn't try to force their way into the house to rob us.

I never told my mother about her uncle's illegal activities. I know there was lots of stuff she knew but never shared with me.

By the time she was twenty-two years old she had been married, divorced, and left with four young sons.

She had a high school diploma and a determination to provide a better life for her boys. She had tried living with Leslie Johnson's mother. When applications went out for some new public-housing that was being built for Black families. She put her name on the list. There was separate public housing for White families.

It was also about the time she met Frank and Catherine O'Callahan, a rich, White Irish Catholic couple who were looking for a young woman like my mother to cook and clean for their family. The O'Callahans lived in a rich community outside of Louisville called Saint Matthews. I don't recall how a poor negro teen from Louisville's west end first met this Irish Catholic family, but it changed my mother's life and subsequently mine too. Saint Matthews is still 90 percent White, with well-to-do Blacks making up just under 5 percent of the population.

My mother never felt she was part of the O'Callahan family, but she was affected in a positive way during all those years while cooking, cleaning, and babysitting at the family mansion and later in the homes of their children. Several of the O'Callahans showed up years later for my mom's funeral.

Frank and Catherine were devout Catholics, which meant my mother became Catholic and that meant her first four boys were going to be baptized and raised in the Catholic church.

"Mary," as the O'Callahan children called my mother, would take the bus out to the grand white house that sat on a sprawling green lawn. I was sometimes allowed to accompany her when she went to work, but I wasn't allowed to use the pool. Was that because of the liability, or because I was the help? My mother never bothered to explain. I should have been grateful just to tag along to see how life was in a world I could hardly expect to live or thrive in someday.

I did tour the big house, every floor and room. The basement would have been enough space for all of us. I was allowed to watch TV all day while Ma moved in and around carrying baskets of clothes, frozen food, cleaning supplies.

She stayed in the basement while ironing, and we were often glued to the television with its antenna and three over-the-air black and white channels. Broadcast news had not yet caught my attention. Why would it? Looking back, there was nothing on TV that resembled my world nor my limited space in the O'Callahan's world.

Bonanza, Gunsmoke, The Rifleman—all great cowboy shows— and of course there was Superman! Only White men could be heroes and protectors of pretty White women against all that was unfair and evil. They became my heroes too. *Leave it to Beaver, Father Knows Best, My Three Sons.* The sitcoms seemed innocent enough, but I watched them with a child's filter, mistakenly thinking I was watching depictions of a life that could one day be mine. There was nobody on any of these shows that looked like me or my no-show dad. My mother didn't have that kind of husband and I certainly didn't have a father figure like any that I saw on TV— caring, soft-spoken, smart, and always present with a man's hug or reassuring smile.

I could have used a dad to help me handle Donald Brown, the grade school and neighborhood bully. My bully problem was solved in the grade school boys' bathroom: it was just me going toe to toe with Donald, fear and anger becoming one as I punched him in every part of his body from head to his waist. There was no dad in the bleachers for my youth basketball and baseball games, no man for me and my brothers to see showering his woman with love, respect, and support during tough times, like Robert Young did on *Father Knows Best.*

I would have been fine staying forever in front of the TV in the O'Callahans' basement, but at one point, Ma stopped taking me to the O'Callahan's and she never explained why. But I overheard her sharing a story with one of her girlfriends. Turns out, I didn't know my place while visiting the rich White people.

As Ma tells the story, Mary Ann, the youngest of the O'Callahan children, came to her crying. She explained, "Bruce slapped me!" Ma says she insisted on the spot that I apologize. Instead, I offered this explanation: "She slapped me, so I slapped her back!"

The O'Callahans had a yardman. He was an older Black man named Allen. He cut the grass, trimmed the shrubs, and took care of the pool. Allen and his wife lived in the Cotter Homes, just like we did. The fortress-looking complex was built just for us Black folks. Poor White people had their own projects across town. The same company built their fortress.

After all these years, I still recall the address, 1627 South 34th Street. The homes were built beginning in 1952. Grey cement and red brick on the outside with maybe a dozen apartments in each building. No way us poor people were going to tear down this place. Us four Johnson boys shared a bedroom. We had bunk beds.

Roaches were a problem. One day we would trap them in jars treating them as pets. Other days we were torturing and killing them by the dozens. We were at constant war with the roaches.

Poor people always make do, and that meant sharing what one had with neighbors. There was government-issued milk powder, cheese, and peanut butter, which everybody on our block divided up. We put mayonnaise and sugar on bread for sandwiches. Shoulder bones, white beans, or pinto beans for dinner. Fried chicken on Sundays.

Once a week our poor people's food monotony was broken up with scraps from the O'Callahans' table. We would get excited as we waited for Ma's bus to bring her home at day's end. If she was tired, if her feet were hurting, she always seemed to find another gear as she stepped off the bus and into that familiar soulful strut toward home. We kids had to skip and run alongside just to keep up. If we had been inside the house fighting and breaking stuff up, it was all cleaned up by the time Ma got home, or she was going to be throwing some haymakers of her own.

How I loved this woman, our everything! I recall wanting to just touch her, but as I write this, I don't recall getting many hugs from Ma. Did I ever get to just crawl into bed with her, smell her perfume? Even so, I never doubted her love for me or my siblings. The woman often worked two jobs to keep her family together. She had felt the sting of a mother's abandonment.

What's in the bags? There was always anticipation as to what she was able to pack into those two or three bags. Did she steal this stuff, or did the O'Callahans let her have what they certainly wouldn't need or miss? I recall eating steak cooked medium and burnt at the edges. I like it cooked that way to this day. I didn't like the barely seasoned string beans.

We were on a fixed income and should have gone to the free neighborhood public school like our friends and neighbors, but Ma wouldn't have it. The O'Callahans had converted Ma to their faith. She had us baptized Catholic at Saint Philip Neri in Louisville's east end, just blocks from Grandma Millie Bell's house.

Ma worked out a deal with the priests at Immaculate Heart of Mary Catholic Church and School, just blocks away on 34th Street. She would pay what she could in tuition. In exchange, we were offered up to be at the church seven days a week to help clean the school and sanctuary and to sell raffle tickets and candy to raise money for the school. Cleaning the gym and classrooms was the same: spread some sawdust on the floor, then brush it up. Straighten up the desk and chairs, clean the blackboards, empty the trashcans, and I'm done. After school, the priests often would drive us to far-off White communities in the suburbs to sell World's Finest Chocolate Bars or raffle tickets. We showed up for mass during the middle of the school day and on Sundays, and any evening that Mary Johnson decided we should be there. I was a lead altar boy at those church services. My younger brother David would help, at my insistence.

Sports were huge among Louisville Catholic schools, beginning in grade school and reaching near obsessive levels by high school. I played on every team in every sport.

I also got involved in theatre and at age twelve or thirteen, I was encouraged to write an original script for a play depicting the fall of the Holy Roman Empire. It was awful. There were maybe fifteen people in attendance. They laughed throughout. It wasn't meant to be a comedy.

Meanwhile, life was looking up for Mary and her four sons. I'm not sure when my mother started dating James Marbry: I was still in grade school. He was a tall skinny guy with a good job at the nearby American Synthetic Rubber Corporation. We were about to say farewell to the Cotter Homes for a single-family house with a front and backyard, still in the west end, but near the great Chickasaw Park and the Ohio River.

For my family, James brought a good job and a steady paycheck. It wasn't always the safest work. James was assigned to clean out dusty chemical bins. The American Synthetic Rubber Corporation was one of several giant factories in Louisville's west end that were fined for releasing thousands of pounds of cancer-causing chemicals over the years.

I'm not sure what chemicals ended up in the nearby river but that was the same water we kids learned to swim in. We'd swing out across the river on tree limbs. We'd drop like rocks into the deep waters. Before we learned to swim, we would paddle quickly and long enough to get back to shore. If you didn't pay attention, the river's current could sweep you downstream to God knows where. It was thrilling and a little scary too.

In addition to the river, there were the ponds and streams that cut through Chickasaw and Shawnee Parks, which doubled as our family play and picnic areas. Nobody thought about pollution in those days or what it might do to us.

Reporters for the local newspapers made names for themselves documenting many cases of cancer in our west-end communities. The saying became, "If Rubber Town doesn't kill you, the booze and smokes and drugs certainly will."

Black people, men and women, also found work alongside White people at Brown & Williamson, the tobacco packing plant on Hill Street that paid well long before we learned that cigarettes cause cancer. Employees were encouraged to grab a handful of free smokes at the end of their shifts as they headed home. Later, during summer months when we were off from school, my brother David and I worked at B&W. My brother Michael would retire from the plant years later.

Eventually, James and Ma got married. I don't remember where or when or if us four kids had been there. Here's what I do recall: We were soon moving on up and out of the Cotter home projects into our own single-family home further into Louisville's west end surrounded by other Black families with big backyards, pet dogs, chain-link fences, and driveways for cars!

We lived on Kaiser Court between Virginia and Hale Avenues. One day the neighborhood was buzzing because Ann and Carl Braden had moved in with their two children. Jimmy Braden, their son, became my playmate. The civil rights family was conspicuous from the beginning because most White people had already joined the exodus out of the west end. In hindsight, I'm thinking this might have been the safest place in the world for the Bradens after they were prosecuted for helping a Black family buy a home in a segregated Whites-only subdivision outside the city. Louisville and the State of Kentucky eventually came to their collective senses about Bradens. They were heroes. Anne later taught at the University of Louisville and at my alma mater, Northern Kentucky University.

James Marbry was the first Black man I got to observe up close. I grew to like him and fear him at the same time. He treated my mother well, in the beginning. He was dependable, in the beginning. A skilled craftsman at carpentry, plumbing, you name it. He built two bedrooms in the attic for the boys; but started a utility room addition on the back of the house that he never finished. There were a few unfinished projects. Every year, James bought a new station wagon. A shiny new car was a status symbol for working Black men, maybe even more so than a first home. You could take that new car everywhere to show it off.

For us, that meant a summer drive from Louisville to Newark, New Jersey, to visit my grandmother Ivory. We could hardly contain our euphoria as we piled into the Mercury, jockeying for a seat in the very back as far away from our mom and step-dad's conversations. Ma had brought sandwiches, snacks, even a large jar in case we had to go pee. James wasn't comfortable stopping except for gas during the night. I learned much later through the *Green Book* that it wasn't safe for Black people to be on the road in a nice car at all hours.

I could never be sure if I wasn't more than a bother to James Marbry. He clearly wanted children of his own, and he and my mother went on to have four kids: Philip, Ordette, Don, and Doug.

That's three more boys and only one girl in the whole bunch of us. The Johnson-Marbry kids now totaled eight in all.

Needless to say, neither parent had time for my school activities. No one checked my homework. Food on the table, roof over our heads: that's what mattered most.

For reasons I still don't understand, James sometimes felt the need to ridicule me in front of my siblings. Especially when he had clearly been drinking. *Why me?* "You think you're better than the rest of us," he would charge. I would reply to no one but me, *No. but I do think I'm better than this.* Better than his ridicule, his verbal abuse. What did James see when he saw me that I wasn't aware of? I wanted to punch James for talking to me this way, but I knew it would give him an excuse to administer an immediate beatdown. Better judgment told me to just sit there and take it. I was pissed but never told my mother about these incidents. It could only lead to more confrontation. She couldn't help me.

Eventually I learned to stay out of his way so as not to get on his bad side. My oldest brother Les seemed to have that place reserved. James would whip Les, or Junior, as we called him growing up, with a leather belt. Curfew violations were the usual offense. The punishment left welts over his body. For years we Black kids would share horror stories of those horrible beatings from our angry parents. Were those vicious beatings learned behavior, passed on from slave masters to punish runways and put the fear in bystanders? It worked for me. I swore to never beat my children.

On most days, including holidays and birthdays, life was good for the Johnson and Marbry kids. But when Ma and James' marriage started to fall apart, we kids were caught in the middle.

James and Ma would fight on payday. The Fridays after he stopped at the liquor store to drink outside from paper cups with his friends from the plant, he'd fail to pick up my mother from her second night job at a fast-food restaurant, just outside town on Cane Run Road.

A typical Friday would go like this: It's near midnight. James was home, passed out in their first-floor bedroom. We kids were upstairs and only pretending to fall asleep as we knew what was about to go down. At about midnight after her shift ended, Mother began to call home. James didn't answer the telephone and that left me to announce the bad news. "James is asleep and I can't get him to wake up." She'd order me again to wake up my stepdad. He'd refuse. She'd call back and I again gave the bad news.

Her cousin, Mary Louise, eventually would pick her up, and all hell would break out. She'd walk into the house, drop her keys on a table, take off her coat, and then let loose with a series of profanities that any tough woman growing up in the hood could recite when provoked. Then came the sound of her pushing and shoving her husband who was now pretending to not hear her. He had no answers to any of her questions.

I'd be wide awake, afraid for both of them. When I heard glass break, I knew the fight was on, and with a single leap I'd fly down the stairs and order my oldest brother to call the police. One time, James' gun, the 22-caliber that he kept hidden in their bedroom closet, went off as he struck my mother in the head with the weapon. "You've busted my eardrum," she screamed. I was between them and easily could have been shot with his 22-caliber weapon and killed.

Police arrived. James was arrested. In those days, police were a godsend for this child. The White men in blue were the only authority who could stop my parents from fighting, beginning with their knock on the door. When they entered the room, there was dead silence. The cops would decide which parent was right and which parent would go to jail.

When a child becomes the adult in the room, there is no family order. I was the adult when Ma and James went to war. In another incident, I was trying to separate the two when the three of us hit the floor in the center hallway. James ended up on the bottom, suffering a broken wrist. Police had been called and this time, they had no choice but to arrest my mother for an alleged assault. She was crying. Cousin Mary Louise and her husband, Lee Faye, were called to bail out my mother. The charge eventually was dropped. Neither ever wanted to pursue charges the next day.

I prayed for peace.

My prayer went something like this:

I want to be anywhere but here. I won't survive this!

Ma and James had four children of their own in the years they were together. Philip, Odette, Donald, and Douglas. There was always a big difference in ages between the Johnson boys and the Marbry siblings. We never considered ourselves half-siblings. I still am the big brother and they are my little sister and brothers.

Ma eventually took the kids and left James. Years later, I was stunned to learn that James Marbry had been shot to death outside that liquor store parking lot. He was sitting in his pickup truck when someone came up from behind and shot him in the head. The gun was the standard concealed weapon. A 22, like the one he kept in the bedroom closet. There were witnesses to the slaying, but Louisville police never made an arrest. His life mattered to me, and especially to his four children.

CHAPTER 2

The Good Son Is Going to Become a Priest

I BEGAN WRITING THIS CHAPTER more than twenty years ago. It's the only way I could have recalled all the detail you'll find here. My recollection of my seminary days and the impact of that life-altering experience had been profoundly positive.

Then, as a veteran reporter in Washington, I was assigned to cover the sex-abuse scandal in the Catholic church. That included interviewing alleged perpetrators in the clergy and their victims. One of those victims actually found me. He was my best friend at Sacred Heart Seminary. None of my journalism credentials or experience could have prepared me for what I learned while researching and writing the following chapter.

Back in 1964, on any other Sunday afternoon in Louisville I would have been outside leaving the rest of the Lord's Day for a lazy trip to Chickasaw Park along the Ohio River. It's where every family in the west end gathered to play, picnic, and watch other people. Young girls pointed and smiled as guys leaned on their freshly polished cars before driving them for inspection on the winding one-way park roads.

We might have been swinging on the tree limbs that took us out high above the Ohio River, which flowed alongside the park.

My mother insisted that we be back home in time for Sunday dinner, which was hands down the best and biggest meal of the week. Sweetened iced tea, fried chicken, mashed potatoes, mac and cheese, and green beans cooked in bacon fat. We ate every part of that chicken.

Us working poor folks loved to eat! Every Baptist church in the hood was serving up soul food, sometimes seven days a week. And the Friday fish fry at Immaculate Heart of Mary brought out the faithful and nonbelievers alike. To this day I can't explain what went into the "lard" that church ladies used to deep fry that fish.

Good eating was one of our few entitlements. Good food and lots of it, was part therapy and assurance that we were not that bad off. We measured not just the quality but the quantity.

When they were still together, not even my stepfather James was allowed to miss the family's Sunday dinner.

But this particular Sunday, there wouldn't be enough time for seconds at the dinner table. My ride was on the way. My mother was sending me away.

Prying neighbors watched the shiny black car slowly pull up to our front yard, driven by a serious young White man in black short-sleeve shirt and trousers. The neighbors must have been suspicious. Usually when a White man in uniform found his way to 1119 Kaiser Court, it meant someone was in trouble: my mother, stepfather, or one of my brothers.

"Are you ready?" the man asked, probably realizing that I had been waiting for that moment.

"I'm ready." I had just turned fourteen on June 5, but was that really old enough to be leaving home? Some Black kids in Louisville's west end only left home to visit relatives down south. I had no relatives that I knew of outside Kentucky. I had never been away from my mother and siblings.

Ma stood behind me. Her silence communicated her nervousness and fear. If she cried, it wouldn't happen until we were out of sight. My mother was a master of disguise and a wizard at camouflaging her pain and fears. She would have made a great poker player. I don't recall my siblings having a reaction—whether they were concerned, indifferent, or excited about my leaving.

The man in black put an arm around me as he gave my mother a reassuring look that she was doing the right thing. She and I hugged each other. Then he led me to the car. The neighbors hung out on their front doors in bewilderment. "Where is that White man taking Bruce? He's never been the one to give Mary any trouble."

I had not shared my fate with anyone outside my immediate family and the parishioners at Immaculate Heart of Mary. The man who was leading me away was a priest. Father Joe Bragotti was taking me to a seminary. I was going to begin my studies to become a missionary priest.

There wasn't a specific moment or an epiphany when I determined my future was in the priesthood. My turn to the church at the age of thirteen or fourteen was more incremental. I embraced what I believed was a calling from God. My stepfather, James had been right, at least partially. He would say, "You think you're better than us, don't you?" I was just different. Not better than anybody else but different.

From a very early age, I believed I was being prepared for something. I couldn't yet understand nor even recognize my precise mission or task, but by seventh grade at Immaculate Heart, I was writing to seminaries in the Louisville area and around the country. The Jesuits, Franciscans, Dominicans, and Mary Knoll Orders. I even inquired among priests who cloistered themselves behind locked walls to pray and fathers who worked solely in the Louisville area as diocesan priests in parishes, hospitals, and schools. In the end, I settled on the Order of Priests that produced Fathers Sam and Mondini—my priests, mentors, and benefactors at Immaculate Heart of Mary. These were the men, where there had been no men of any weight, to take me to the edges of my ghetto fences to show me the world that existed beyond my meager existence.

I was made to believe that as a child of God, I was also a citizen of the world. I had great value, regardless of the messages I had been receiving from the other people around me. I knew my decision was making my mother proud. She also must have thought her boy would be a lot safer away in the seminary than in her house where a gun was going off, and pots and pans were tossed like missiles when she and James went to war. There might have been another reason for her wanting me out of the house and out of sight, but I wouldn't learn that news for many years to come.

The order of priests that I aspired to join was called the Verona Fathers, or the Sons of the Sacred Heart, or the Comboni Missionaries. These priests were dispatched to some of the world's most unpredictable and dangerous places. No one got to stay at home like the diocesan priests who were assigned to most of Louisville's Catholic churches.

Daniel Comboni founded the order and planted a stake in Africa, at about the time my great grandmother, the child of African slaves, was born on a Kentucky plantation.

Ma believed a Catholic school education and the discipline that came with it would give her boys a better chance at success in life. James insisted his children with Ma not go to religion school.

Leaving my mother did come with trepidation. In my mind, I had been looking after her all these years...in the Cotter homes. Even later after she married James, I was still her protector.

I also worried about my siblings, especially my younger brother David. I had made him my responsibility, taking up fights for him against our older brother Les in the house and neighborhood bullies on the outside.

Father Joe pointed the car north up Interstate 65 toward Cincinnati and Sacred Heart Seminary. We made small talk. It was just a two-hour drive, but it could just as easily have been ten. It didn't matter. I had all the time in the world.

Joe, a twenty-seven-year-old newly ordained priest from Milan, Italy, on his first assignment, was an official recruiter for the Verona Fathers in this country. After delivering his latest recruit, Joe would be on his way to Uganda for ten years.

Father Joe and I had first met earlier in the summer when he showed up at Immaculate Heart Parish to ask if I wanted to attend summer camp at Sacred Heart Seminary. Initially, it seemed like the first and maybe last offer I would ever get to leave home and see a place outside my own existence. I questioned the offer: Had I earned this? Why was I the only one going? Why hadn't my brothers and some of my classmates from school, like Charles London and Tony Weathers, been invited to come? Maybe it was grace, like a lot of other opportunities that would come my way. Instead of asking why me, maybe the question we poor kids should be asking is why not me?

I met some freshman classmates during those two weeks at summer camp. There would be only thirteen of us, and only one—John Fisher of Cincinnati—would stay the full thirteen years of study required to become a priest.

Over the decades that followed that summer, I found good reason to reach out to some of those old friends. When the sex-abuse scandal hit in 2002, I tracked down Father John Fisher and others, as a news reporter and former seminarian. Our lives had been forged by the experiences on the campus of Sacred Heart Seminary. I wanted to know if there had been anything nefarious that marred their seminary experiences? I was stunned to learn of two incidents that involved one of my best friends. It took him another ten years after our initial chat in 2002 to share the details. People should have been prosecuted.

I'm protecting his identity because he has not shared his story with church officials, law enforcement, or any other former classmates. My friend was a really small guy. He told me that two upperclassmen at Sacred Heart forcefully pinned him against a tree behind one of the buildings. One of them then unbuckled the boy's pants and despite his pleas for them to stop, one of his assailants inserted his hands into my friend's underwear and fondled him. He was warned not to tell anyone before he was allowed to go free. But there was a second and more violent incident in which a priest on staff sexually assaulted my friend while he was ill in the seminary infirmary.

What mother sends her fourteen-year-old son away to a place she has never even visited, with an adult she barely knows. Blind faith is the reason why, for my friend's parents and my mom. If Ma had the chance to send my siblings to a place to spare them the trappings of the negative influences that waited just outside our door step, she would have jumped at the chance.

Two of my brothers, Les and David, ended up like a lot of our friends from the projects—in prison. They started down that path of trouble at about the time I was away. What path was there for me had I stayed? I don't think I would have become just another young drug dealer. If I did turn to crime, I would have insisted on being the leader of the gang. Honestly, I later saw some of my talent and ambition in the teenage drug pushers that I reported on and got to know up close in D.C.

Ninth grade was way too soon to know for sure what I wanted to do for the rest of my life, but two years at Sacred Heart Seminary were transformative for this poor Black kid. I think it was there outside Cincinnati, Ohio, that I decided whatever I did, I wouldn't be a poor person and struggle like my mother and her grandmother.

Sacred Heart Seminary became a game changer for me. My reading, math, and language skills improved by leaps and bounds. I learned Latin, and by the third year I would be required to learn Greek! Why? I don't know.

I liked independence and understood the need for structure too. What teen doesn't need structure? But there was free time, time for walking with friends, hiking, swimming in my choice of two man-made lakes. I excelled in every sport but baseball. (Remember, as a kid I didn't have a dad to play baseball with.) Peace and quiet took on new meaning for me at Sacred Heart. Back in Louisville, whether in the projects or in a crowded house on Kaiser Court, there was never quiet and rarely any peace. I still need those things today. I felt, it turns out naively so, that every clergyman, teacher, counselor, and classmate cared for me and wanted only what was best for me.

They had to think, as I did, that I would make a good priest, if not a great one.

As I write this, I'm asking who in the Catholic church figured that high school seminaries were a good idea? It certainly wasn't cost-effective given the dropout rate.

I'm sure the clergy sex-abuse scandals brought an end to recruiting boys to the seminary.

Father Joe guided the car across the bridge that connects Covington, Kentucky, to Cincinnati. He then pointed the car east toward Mount Washington and Forestville. In about a half an hour, we pulled into the seminary's spacious grounds at 8108 Beechmont Avenue. Tall pine trees lined the long driveway and helped hide the main building from the road. On the left was a soccer and football field. Beyond that, a baseball diamond. The long driveway ended at a circle that surrounded a statue of the Virgin Mary. Behind the circle and mother of Jesus sat the main building, a two story, sand-colored simple structure of cinder block and brick with two wings at each end.

Nothing fancy but it would do. The place was several grades above the crowded house I had left on Kaiser Court and lightyears ahead of the Cotter Homes and my great-grandmother Millie's place in the back of Floyd Street. If all went well, after high school, college, novitiate and theology training, I would be ordained—Father Bruce! Committing myself to a life of obedience, chastity, and poverty. No sex, marriage, or kids.

Several cars arrived as Father Joe and I pulled up. Most of the boys were being dropped off by their mothers and fathers. I immediately felt self-conscious. My mother had never visited the seminary. How would she get there? Did she ever insist on seeing the place where they took her son? Probably didn't think she had the right.

The other students were nearly all White and looked well-scrubbed and rich, like Ricky Nelson, Ozzie and Harriet's son on TV. I knew from my experience in summer camp to report to the dorm. I recognized some of the boys I had previously met. David Thomas, a redheaded, freckle-faced freshman, was also from Louisville. He had a big smile and goofy walk that reminded me of a cowboy.

The inside entrance to Sacred Heart Seminary opened to a foyer that covered two floors. The stairs on either side led to the second floor chapel. We began and ended our days there. To the left, down the hall from the chapel, in the west wing, was the freshman dormitory. There weren't any cubicles, just open space. Each bed was positioned next to a metal locker for clothes and other personal items.

I took great pride in arranging all my new clothes and toiletries.

On social occasions, we would be putting on our black cassocks for services. I liked the fit and the flow and the thought of one day being allowed to add a collar to my garment after I became ordained.

Sacred Heart Seminary was a special place, but on so many levels it was just another elite college prep high with a handful of male students. There were sixty seminarians in the entire school. Some boys clearly had no desire of becoming clergy. They were here because parents didn't want them at home and needed someplace safe to stash them.

I was surprised to learn that some of my classmates had never known a Black person. But I didn't go into the seminary to teach a bunch of rich White boys what it was like to be Black.

"Do Black people get sunburn?"

"Can I touch your hair?"

Had I not been so suspicious or scared of them I might have realized these might have been sincere questions. My reaction could have been, "Yeah, we get sunburn and can die of skin cancer, just like you; and sure, you can touch my hair if I can touch yours." I had no idea what White hair felt like. It felt nothing like the chemically processed hair that the Black men in the neighborhood pretended was their own natural hair.

No one here knew how to cut my hair. One student, an upperclassman with a huge vocabulary, was in charge of the haircuts. "You belligerent waif," seemed to be one of his favorite expressions. Twenty-five cents was the going rate for a cut. For the White guys it was a basic cut. Get the hair off the collar. Out of the face. For me it was just cut, and whatever it looked like in the end, that's what I got. There were four other Blacks at Sacred Heart, including Tom and Willie. They had horrible cuts too. I dreaded going back home to Louisville's west end with the look but knew I could get a real cut from Danny, the neighborhood barber who had been cutting our hair in the basement of his home while dispensing dirty jokes and ignoring his wife's yelling from upstairs.

It never dawned on me that my time in the Seminary was costing somebody a lot of money—that nothing in this country is free, including my training for the priesthood.

Turns out, an elderly White couple from Wheeling, West Virginia, had agreed to foot my bill at Sacred Heart. How much did it cost to train a priest? What came first? The poor boy from Louisville who wanted to become a priest or the family that wanted to pay the way for a future priest? I never asked. I don't know if the matter was ever discussed with my mother.

Mr. and Mrs. Kline from Wheeling, West Virginia, not only paid my seminary tuition, they sent me an allowance, about twenty-five dollars every month with a religious card stuffed in an envelope.

I looked forward to the message and the cash. I was reminded by Father Mario, one of the priests at Sacred Heart, to write and thank them and report on how my studies were coming. This was easy enough, but when Mr. and Mrs. Kline made their first surprise visit to see me, it was an incredibly awkward experience for me. After a priest tracked me down, I walked the grounds with my benefactors, giving them the tour that I'm certain they had probably taken a few times before.

They said very little and I said even less.

"Bruce, how are you?"

"Fine."

"How's your mother?"

"She's fine too." Did they know my mother? The silence lasted for many steps. What was I supposed to say?

"Thanks for the money," I blurted out.

"Oh, that's okay."

I'm sure I eventually would have opened up to them. I wasn't a shy kid, but I wasn't used to strange people wanting to help me with no *quid pro quo* in mind.

I figured the four other Black seminarians were probably as poor as me and getting a free ride also. Probably a few of the White guys too.

I had thought for all the time I was there that Sacred Heart Seminary was every bit the sacred place, and a safe place. The peace and quiet were infectious. The chapel was always open for my quiet time to pray for the starving children in Africa, my mom and siblings back in Louisville. And for James, my stepdad, who just didn't get me, nor I him. Never knew what he was thinking about. Or what his dreams were…if older Black men were even allowed to dream back then.

There were pleasant surprises at Sacred Heart! One was that I was required to take a sex- education class. This was taught during our regular class schedule, and the old priest at the head of the room wasn't about to sugarcoat anything for a bunch of seminarians. He told us in graphic detail, and may have even used props to demonstrate, how a man impregnates a woman. I was shocked and incredibly curious at the same time. It was easily my favorite class.

Interestingly, if my classmates felt the same way, not one of them ever discussed that class outside that room.

Another surprise was that I learned to load and shoot a gun.

One day in the seminary during a break from classes, near the concession stand, but outside a basement door, I heard gunshots. In the back of the building, an old pipe-smoking priest, Father Ruby, was teaching some of the students how to aim and fire a long-barrel gun. I inquired as to how I could become part of the sport and was told all I had to do was pay for the ammunition. I at once paid the fee and proceeded to the basement and out the back door where the priest loaded the pistol in front of me. I can't remember the caliber. I took aim away from the building at a target that had been pinned to a tree. *Pow, pow*. I liked the sound and sense of invincibility that it gave me. I had been curious about guns ever since my stepfather fired a shot in a fight with my mother.

I never asked why we needed to know how to fire a weapon and nobody volunteered. Maybe it was because of the dangerous work that awaited us out there in the real world as missionaries amid hostile governments.

Being away from home at any young age can be difficult even for a poor kid. My imagination would kick in, and I would contrive a make-believe world all in my mind. I would reminisce about all those hugs from Ma that never really happened.

Her letters from home were bittersweet. She wrote maybe once or twice a month and always included five dollars in the envelope, which I knew she couldn't afford to part with. She always kept from me the complete story about what was going on back home. It was always "good news" in the letters. "Everyone's fine. I'm going okay." Why was it now okay after I was gone? I don't remember home being that okay. Was I the problem all along?

When my mother and stepfather James visited me at Sacred Heart Seminary, I both yearned for and dreaded their arrival because they were always late, by several hours, arriving well after the other families had in the morning. Most parents wanted to get as many hours in as possible with their sons, while my people merely wanted to get in and out. They never mingled with the other parents, Black or White. The family day programs, luncheons, and dinners were always winding down or over by the time they pulled onto the campus.

When I spotted the car coming up the drive, there was always another couple with them; a foursome on holiday. They would use the two-hour ride from Louisville as a road trip. You could smell the cigarettes and booze the moment my mother opened the car door. We hugged and I knew immediately that she had missed me and was grateful that James had brought her, even if they were embarrassingly late. I wondered: Had he planned it that way?

Looking back, I'm sure my family felt they didn't fit in and wouldn't be accepted by all those rich White people. The friends who came along for the road trip were there to help them feel comfortable.

It was good to see and feel my mother up close and look into her eyes for some clues as to how things were really going at home with her and my siblings. We talked by the car, then walked a bit. James and his friends never got out of the vehicle. I don't think we did more than shake hands. In less than two hours they were gone. No time to meet any of my friends. Didn't seem to want to stick around to talk to my teachers or mentors. But I didn't insist either. Was I a sellout? They had to get home.

Still, I was glad they came. Sometimes I even tried to convince myself that James, for short periods of time, from a distance, wasn't so bad…but I was sure he still resented me for some reason. What was it about me and not the rest of my brothers? Before they left for the return trip home, Ma would give me a few bucks and some clothes.

During my second year in the seminary, grandma Millie died but not before I was able to get home to see her one last time. The Rector of the seminary, Father Charles, provided me with a free Greyhound bus ticket for the trip home to say my final goodbyes. My great grandmother was diabetic and eventually lost both legs to the disease. I miss her still and see her brown, wrinkled face and white hair. She passed away a couple weeks after I returned to Cincinnati. She had gone home. I was glad for her because she had suffered so much for so long. To this day, I still talk to her during my tough times, which don't begin to compare to what she went through.

My second year at Sacred Heart Seminary, I returned from summer break with a heavy heart and confused mind. The very first summer back home had been perplexing and frustrating for me. I wanted to be a seminarian on break. Spend time at Immaculate Heart of Mary. Work with the good priests who had always been there for my mother, brothers, and me. But I was also drawn to those things that most fifteen-year-old boys crave: girls!

I noticed their shapes, their fresh smells, their smiles and laughs; my sexual feelings were at full throttle. I fell in love with Elaine Taylor during those summer months.

Her parents, Jim and Lois, had been friends with my mother and James for years. Jim worked for the Air Force as a civilian at Langley Air Force base in San Antonio, Texas. There were eight Taylor kids and eight of us.

Elaine and I were almost thrown together immediately: same age, same likes and dislikes. We were inseparable for the summer weeks her family was visiting relatives in Louisville. I knew I had compromised my values as a seminarian. But I had rationalized that I was a seminarian only in Cincinnati. When in Louisville, I was like any other teenager.

I returned to Sacred Heart somewhat reluctantly, hoping my vocation could be jumpstarted and hoping at the same time that I could gain some clarity as to what God wanted me to do. I could serve him as a layperson with a wife and children, but I wanted that higher calling. In hindsight, I really wanted it all: I wanted the life I had discovered in Cincinnati, but I wasn't able to do without a wife and children. How many more priests might there be if we could be married? It's not my call. Celibacy now scared me. I felt isolated. Could any of the other boys returning be feeling the same way? If they did, no one talked about it.

It wasn't the same anymore. As a freshman I had been holding my own in the classroom, but I struggled that second year. I prayed for it. I stressed out on it! It never occurred to me to talk to my advisor, a prefect, or even Father Joe about this. What would my mother say if I brought it up to her? Her adopted White parents, Frank and Catherine O'Callahan, had a son who was a priest. His name was Frank. We called him "Jack". He was a Jesuit and I felt my mother wanted a priest of her own in the family. I so much wanted to please her.

At night in the dormitory after the lights were out, I no longer dreamed about Africa and the people I would convert to Catholicism. Those images were replaced by visions of me and Elaine. With her in my arms. I became aroused. I was dreaming about sex. It's not a sin. It's beautiful with someone you love. I was even getting letters from Elaine. Giving her my address must have been a cry for help. Surely, they were scanning and reading our mail.

The prayers at chapel no longer brought comfort. I still wanted world peace, but peace of mind was also high on my wish list.

Father Charles and others were experts at spotting who wasn't cut out for the seminary and a pious existence. They moved quickly to weed out the boys with "too many earthly needs." Some seminarians were advised to take off some time and reassess. Give the world a try and if you make your way back here, okay. If not, that's okay too. You were mistaken, it wasn't the voice of God calling you to the priesthood.

I got the letter in the summer while at home in Louisville. It was addressed to me and not my mother. It was from Father Charles and it read very formally that I wasn't being invited back in the fall. I was hurt. Nobody wants this kind of decision made for them. But it was made for me and it was the correct decision.

⌒

It turns out that my not returning to seminary studies was more the norm than outlier. There were thirteen students in my freshman class. Only one of us, John Fisher, finished his nearly thirteen years of study.

Sacred Heart Seminary closed years ago. Vocations to the priesthood and the missionary brand were already declining around the world. I visited the seminary grounds twice in recent years. It was in between those visits that I learned the details of the abuse reaped on my best friend and former classmate who was forced to suddenly leave his studies to become a priest.

Sacred Heart Seminary turned out to be no fortress from sin and evil.

My seminary classmate and former best friend has no intention of going public with his story. He tried, with therapy, over the years to deal with the innocence that was taken from him by a priest who, as far as we know, was never investigated or punished for his crimes. My friend chooses to remain anonymous. He did give me permission to tell his story for my book. He identified his assailant as "Father Ruby," who is now dead.

In a lengthy telephone conversation that took place during the coronavirus pandemic, he relayed to me how at Sacred Heart Seminary he had become ill, possibly with the flu. One night while asleep in the infirmary, he was awakened by Father Ruby, the infirmary attendant. The priest was insisting on giving him a sponge bath. Before the seminarian could object or even speak, his pajamas were pulled down around his ankles. Father Ruby, the same priest who had taught me to fire a gun, began fondling his victim's penis. My friend was terrified, unable to move. This minor was being sexually assaulted in the middle of the night by his infirmary attendant—a priest! He became paralyzed with fear, unable to scream for help or beg his tormentor to stop. It gets worse! My friend says that during the assault, the priest confessed that other boys experienced an erection when he did the same thing to them. He was admitting there had been others. I could hear the anger in my friend's voice as he told the story. His anger was still there decades later. Father Ruby—he could hardly repeat the name. "He was a serial pedophile."

Without giving a reason, my friend left the seminary as soon as he could. Father Charles the Rector seemed stunned by his insisting that he leave immediately rather than wait till the end of the semester. He called his parents to say he was coming home. Nothing more. No details. He demanded that Seminary officials provide him a one-way ticket home, which they did. My friend says he remained a virgin for forty-five years after leaving the seminary. He wasn't able to have what most of us would consider a normal adult relationship with an intimate partner.

It would be four decades before he was able to overcome the shame and open up to his parents about why he abruptly left Sacred Heart Seminary and years after that before he was able to open up to his wife.

He gave me the awful story, with details, only after he learned that I was writing a memoir that included my experiences in the seminary. He knew that my professional coverage of the clergy sex scandal would be part of this former seminarian's book.

I had gone back to Cincinnati to visit the grounds of Sacred Heart Seminary as part of my healing with the church. It's a work in progress. I'm still angry and trying to find a place in my heart to forgive all that had been done to victims of clergy sex abuse.

I think my being a lifelong Catholic, a former seminarian, and a veteran reporter in Washington put me in a unique situation to cover the sex-abuse scandal. I must admit it was as much a personal disappointment as it was an incredibly big story. In hindsight, I was actually built for this.

When the Archbishop of the Washington Archdiocese, Theodore McCarrick, was elevated to a cardinal in a ceremony in Rome, I was dispatched to the Vatican to cover the story. Same for when his successor, Donald Wuerhl, was elevated to cardinal. When Francis was elected Pope, I was on the ground in Saint Peter's Square to declare on videotape that was broadcast back in Washington, "There is the white smoke, we have a new Pope!"

But I also pursued Boston Cardinal Bernard Law as he tried to rush into a cathedral in Rome to avoid my questions about his protecting pedophile clergy in his archdiocese.

I went through an emotional and confused state when my work forced me to interview my own pastor and friend at Saint Augustine Catholic Church in Washington, D.C. Monsignor Russel Dillard, a handsome African American priest, eventually was defrocked after a woman came forward by letter to Archbishop McCarrick to reveal that years ago, when she was a teen at Saint Anthony's Parish, Father Dillard, then in his early thirties, kissed and fondled her during a consensual relationship.

They both said in interviews or conversations with me there was no sexual intercourse. But she was a minor. Dillard was in his thirties. Staunch supporters insisted there had been no due process; church law doesn't afford its clergy the same protections as laypeople get. At the same time, the church wasn't requiring its bishops to report suspected criminal behavior to outside authorities. So all but a handful of clergy escaped arrest and prosecution. Dillard would appeal his firing. After twenty-four years as a priest, Dillard was tossed out of the church. There would be no pension, no health insurance, no means of support. He moved into his family's duplex in northeast D.C. He got a graduate degree in social work from Catholic University. A fellow Catholic and friend gave him a job that lasted only until the healthcare firm where he worked folded. Over lunch Russ Dillard told me that he still considered himself a priest and attended mass every day at the Shrine of the Immaculate Conception in Washington.

~

Who knew at the time that Washington's Cardinal McCarrick had his own secrets? The former archbishop had been a rock star in the church. So well connected that he tipped me off in 2010 that the college of cardinals was likely to elect the next pope, not from Europe, but from South America. He was right. Jorge Mario Bergoglio of Buenos Argentina was elected Pope; The first from outside Europe. I was among the many thousands who stood in Saint Peter's Square when Pope Francis stood on the balcony and asked us to pray for him.

Nine years later and Cardinal McCarrick was laicized. Fired, just like Russel Dillard. McCarrick became the first and only cardinal dismissed from the clergy for "sins against the Sixth Commandment with minors and with adults." Seminarians and young priests had charged that over the years McCarrick had used his authority to sexually molest them.

I wouldn't leave my church. Where would I go? I returned to mass at Saint Augustine's. A new pastor, Father Pat Smith, has put his stamp on the church. He's raised funds needed to keep the parish grade school open while scores of other church schools were folded, in no small part due to shrinking donations and payments awarded from settlements with victims of clergy sexual abuse.

I continue to know a lot of really good priests out there. They continue to do God's work.

In September of 2015, Pope Francis visited Washington, D.C. He was at the White House where I proudly watched the choir from my parish, Saint Augustine's, sing for the Pontiff. I anchored our TV coverage of Pope Francis at the National Shrine with a co-anchor, Father Avalino Gonzalez, pastor of Saint Gabriel's Church. Gonzalez entered the seminary as an adult and was ordained by Cardinal McCarrick, who proclaimed a new crop of priests would restore the status lost in the church because of the clergy sex scandal.

As of this writing, Gonzalez was proving to be a rising star in the church, assigned to the Vatican.

The Washington Archdiocese got a new leader. Wilton Cardinal Gregory was appointed Archbishop in April of 2019. We had met nearly twenty years earlier in Dallas, Texas. Gregory was president of the US Conference of Bishops. That group was under incredible pressure to produce the first "no-tolerance" policy to deal with clergy sex abuse.

Prior to traveling to Rome, where he was elevated to Cardinal, Gregory told me, "Bruce, I think we are in a better place than we were in 2002 in Dallas, but I think one of the things we have to acknowledge is it's an ongoing struggle to make sure children are always safe in the environment of the Catholic church."

Pope Francis elevated Archbishop Wilton Gregory to Cardinal in November of 2020. He thus became the first African American Cardinal in the United States. If not for the coronavirus pandemic, I would have been there as a working journalist and a grateful former seminarian.

CHAPTER 3

Life on Grand Avenue Court

MA HADN'T COUNTED ON ME returning home to Louisville from the seminary. There was literally no room for me.

She had left James Marbry during my last year at Sacred Heart Seminary. By 1966, my oldest brother, Les Junior, had left home to join the marines and was quickly shipped off to fight in Vietnam with his best friend who we only knew as "Price." They were too cool and had spent most of their high-school years dressing sharply and chasing females.

Ma had moved the rest of the family into a small home on Grand Avenue Court. It was a tiny house with a nice porch but barely furnished on the inside. It seemed she left our home with James on Kaiser court with only what she and my siblings could carry. Not one piece of furniture that was new or hardly used. It appeared as though we on our way back down after being up and out of the projects for several years. It's how it goes with us poor folk. We can get away but we rarely get away clean! One crisis, and we're back in deep waters!

I immediately proclaimed to no one but me that I would be staying at Grand Avenue Court only to finish high school; after that I'd be leaving again for parts unknown.

The front door opened to a small room with a sofa, chair, and floor lamp. A second room on the first floor served as a den with TV, pullout couch, and a separate single bed. There was an eat-in kitchen and three small bedrooms on the second floor. How she planned to fit eight siblings into that tiny space without a shoehorn is beyond me. This was the first house my mother could afford after working all those years—most of that time at two jobs. She still didn't have a car or know how to drive. But looking back, this house was a big accomplishment for a woman who had lived in an alley as a child.

Ed Faye, aunt Mary Louise's husband, co-signed for Ma's new home. I'm sure it was part of some poverty program. Uncle Faye was a social worker.

The twelve houses squeezed into Grand Avenue Court faced one another—six on each side of a sidewalk that ran down the middle of the court. These were single-family houses. They were so close together you could talk to the kids three or four houses away and not have to shout.

Several houses away on Grand Avenue, in the middle of the block, sat a small pink house. That's where Louisville's biggest star ever, the greatest fighter in the world, Muhammad Ali, had grown up. More on our hometown hero later.

⤴

It had never been my intention to return to the place of my birth. *Any place but here* had been my mantra. My home had been unstable and unsafe at times, the neighborhood too confining, the Louisville area too segregated for my tastes. Black people in the hood stuffed their anxieties until there was an eruption. We didn't fight every day, but when situations reached a boiling point, it was always against one another—oftentimes family. While away at the seminary I learned that contrary to what a lot of Black people around me felt, most White people don't wake up mornings thinking about Black folk. They had real estate agents who used redlining to keep us away from them—out of sight, out of mind. Some factory and plant workplaces were integrated because of the need for workers. But neighborhoods and neighborhood schools were not to be shared. Not on Grand Avenue or Grand Avenue Court, or in most other Louisville communities. The White majority could stuff their dislike or even racist views of Blacks until we tried to move in next door or call them on their unfair treatment.

In 1966 Shawnee High, on Market Street, not far from Shawnee Park and Fountain Ferry Park, was still mixed but changing rapidly when I enrolled to finish my last two years. Except for the athletic teams (I played football), Black and White students kept to themselves. The basketball team was led by guard Skip Reed and seven-foot center, Thomas Payne. They won the Kentucky State Triple A title. I don't recall any White players on the team. FYI, the team mascot was the politically incorrect "Indian." The coaches were White. Most but not all teachers were White, including the all-important shop teacher. Not everybody was going on to college. The shop teacher was there for the male students to stroke that interest in a trade skill or even the military.

I came home when the country and my hometown were heating up and it wasn't just the summer temperatures. Movements had been building on fault lines that included Vietnam, civil and human rights, the Cold War, and my generation flexing their muscles and determined to change the world.

That had been my goal all along—to help change the world. I should have been placed in an advanced college preparatory program, had somebody not determined that I was average and not able or willing to be challenged academically. I was never good at math, but I excelled at world history and could name every world capitol and every state capitol.

At Shawnee, one of my basic courses was a wood-shop class. Vocational classes seemed to be mandatory. I made a coffee table in shop class, and that table sat in my mother's living room for years after I left home. She was alone in her pride. I think I got a "C" in the class.

I didn't see interracial dating at Shawnee High, and I certainly couldn't imagine a Black teammate going home to meet the father of a White girlfriend. The segregation I left was still in place in Louisville. How could I expect changes just because I went to live and learn with White seminarians for a couple of years?

Racial change was beginning to happen in Louisville and Kentucky, although at a much slower pace and out of the national headlines that favored the racial strife of the deep south.

In my first year back home, Georgia Davis Powers became the first Black person elected to the Kentucky State Senate.

In 1967, Wilbur Hackett—a star running back and linebacker at rival Dupont Manuel High—became the first African American scholarship athlete at the University of Kentucky. I played the same position on the field for Shawnee High but failed miserably to pattern my game after Hackett's. Can anybody explain why it took his high school nearly twenty years to induct him into its hall of fame? It took UK more than fifty years to bring Hackett back to award him a college degree.

There was no class in high school that helped me know and understand the history and contributions that my people made to America. I don't recall any teacher talking about Kentucky's slave history and how Louisville had been an active slave transfer location that saw Africans shipped to all parts of the deep south from here.

I regret that extra curriculum reading and writing were no longer required once I left the seminary.

There was no way somebody of my family's few means could meet incredible Black leaders like Lyman Tefft Johnson. He was a scholar and teacher at my mother's alma mater of Central High School. His lawsuit opened the doors of the University of Kentucky to African American students in 1949. Too late for Mister Johnson, but armed with a master's degree from the University of Michigan, Johnson already had been teaching history for sixteen years at the segregated Central High. The civil rights leader also succeeded in getting Black teachers equal pay to Whites in the Jefferson County school system.

What poor Black people didn't get from the classroom and local White media, we were able to pick up in news, although not in real time, from the Black press.

The Louisville *Defender* newspaper or *Ebony* or *Jet* would be passed around and shared in the schools, homes, barber and beauty shops, work places…wherever Black people were found. Sometimes the magazine covers were worn off from the pages being turned so many times. It wasn't unheard of or unusual to find stories missing cause people would rip out their favorite passages before passing the rest of the publication on to the next reader.

Frank Stanley was publisher of the *Defender*. He drafted the legislation that led to the integration of Kentucky's public universities.

He did the same for the establishment of the Kentucky Human Rights Commission. Stanley was a staunch advocate for racial justice in employment, housing, education, and public places. He also insisted on integrated military units when a service career was seen as a viable path to the middle class for Black males.

In 1983, Frank Stanley was inducted into the University of Kentucky Journalism Hall of Fame. I followed him into the UK Journalism Hall of Fame in 2020, nearly forty years later.

It took a racial riot in 1968, my last year at Shawnee High School for the three local TV stations to put Black people on camera and as news reporters. This was such big news that the newspapers covered the hirings. A June 29 article read, "Three Louisville TV Stations Hire Negro Newsmen." WAVE-TV hired thirty-eight-year-old Jerry Tucker, who had been news director at the iconic Black WLOU-AM radio station, where I would later work as a disc jockey and news reader while in college. Britt Arrington was another hire. He was twenty-four, from Washington, D.C., and a graduate of the Historical Black Kentucky State College. (It later became a university.) Philip Buckman, a Central High School and University of Louisville grad, went to work for WHAS-TV.

Had I known I was going to become a journalist I might have studied harder at Shawnee High, but left to charter my own course, I eventually decided it was better to be accepted and liked than to be really smart.

The Sacred Heart Seminary experience was fading really quickly. I needed to catch up—make up for the two years away.

Like most teens, then and now, I wanted it all. I never had learned how to hand dance. On the football field, the coaches thought they had recognized the natural ability and some speed, but I was constantly playing catch up to teammates who had a two-year head start on getting drilled on the fundamentals of football.

As a high school male, a driver's license and then a car are a rite of passage. I learned to drive my Uncle Faye's car, got a part-time job, and then bought my own car, a 1959 Buick LeSabre that a friend rightfully labeled, "a war wagon." The car probably cost me several hundred dollars. The car was a four-door, blue-grey with a wide front grill and fish tails in the rear.

Today, young people on D.C. streets would describe it as a "Hooptie." The vehicle was often broken, a real mess that sometimes got me to where I needed to be. The power windows had no power, so I rigged them to stay up. Louisville summers were extra brutal when driving because the car had no air conditioning. The reverse gear eventually went out, forcing me to park my war wagon in places where I only needed to move forward. If another student parked in front of me outside school, I literally had to wait until the student arrived before I could pull out of my parking space.

I reluctantly drove my Buick to the high school prom because no one in my family, no one in my mother's social circle, had a better car. No one had money to help with a rental.

Having a car, albeit a clunker, brought instant popularity. Isn't that what we all want at that age? Status, security, and sex.

⤙

That Buick LaSabre could have sent me to jail. Poor, desperate people can make poor decisions they can't come back from if caught. There is no safety net for us.

I will never forget how it must have been grace. God's goodness kept me from getting caught and going to jail. I should have been arrested.

My car was parked in the alley off Grand Avenue Court with a dead battery. I had no money to buy a battery. I could no longer count on asking a neighbor for a charge to jumpstart my car because it would no longer hold a charge.

I needed to do something, or so I thought. So I planned out how to steal the battery from a neighbor's vehicle. This was someone I knew and liked. Someone who went to work every day and cared for his family. Their car had been parked in the driveway for days. I wasn't even sure the battery would work.

I had cased the location and mapped out a plan. I waited until dark, walked to the end of Grand Court to Grand Avenue, lifted the hood, used a wrench to loosen the battery cables, then lifted the battery from its harness. It was heavy. I sat the battery on the ground, quietly closed the hood, picked up the battery and, under cover of dearness, like the thief in the night that I had become, walked away back toward my home. After installing my neighbor's battery in my Buick, I turned the key and listened anxiously as my vehicle started up. The former seminarian is now a thief. There is no justification. My self-centered solace was that I needed that car battery more than he did.

Decades later I heard that same kind of irrational selfish excuse on camera from young people already confined in juvenile detention. I never told anyone about my crime, not even my siblings. I would have confessed to a priest at confession, but I had already stopped going to mass at Immaculate Heart of Mary. The church could no longer get me where I wanted to go. I had become a creature of my environment. Unsupervised, unaccountable. I don't know how my neighbor reacted when he discovered his property had been stolen. I can guess. I've been robbed before...had cars broken into, valuables stolen. In the jungle on any given day, the predator can become the prey.

At Shawnee High, I discovered that unmotivated, average students were never penalized by having to miss parties, sporting events, and being on stage for talent shows. I eventually settled for being just "okay" at everything in public high school. There was no one pushing me at home or in school to be all that I could be.

I was an outsider at Shawnee. I had but two years to get in where I could fit in. I could have been a nerd, dropping the southern accent, using instead some of the White skill set I learned in my seminary days. That would come in later when trying to land a job working in my first all-White TV newsroom in Cincinnati.

I wouldn't dumb down to get along, but I was willing to take some risks! I formed a singing group and entered the Shawnee High student talent show. Big mistake. I couldn't sing; neither could our lead singer, Skip, who thought he sounded like David Ruffin of the legendary Motown group, the Temptations.

I forget the name we chose, but I went out on stage with Skip and two female classmates. We were going to sing a number by The O'Jays: "I'll Be Sweeter Tomorrow." The females and I sang backup. Skip sang with passion but totally flat and off-key. He was terrible, and I was just as bad. I resorted to lip syncing. The females carried me. Skip thought if he sang louder, the result would improve. He couldn't have been more wrong!

The doo-wop guys came on stage next with their starched shirts and pressed jeans that had been rolled up to display their matching red socks inside their polished wing-tipped dress shoes. And could they blow! They sang a classic tune by the Tymes "So Much in Love." Their look and tight harmonies had the girls screaming. A whole slew of females was waiting for them after the talent show with hugs and kisses. These guys lived in the Beecher Terrace projects. Singing and chasing girls was their biggest sport.

I learned to dance, a little. Couldn't hand dance, which was the signature of being cool for the guys. Slow dancing was a must and really the one dance I couldn't pass up if Aretha or Smokey tunes were playing at a party.

By the end of my senior year in 1968 the country was ablaze. In Watts, Detroit, Newark, and Louisville, we were in the streets. The war in Vietnam had already claimed the neighborhood's older males, Black and White. The draft was an equal-opportunity employer. My brother Les and his friend Price joined the Marines. Both survived their three years but came back changed. They didn't owe the country anything, and now the country certainly owed them. Black veterans weren't scorned because few had proclaimed loyalty to the flag as they were being sworn into the army. Louisville and the rest of Kentucky had sent more than their share of young men to fight in Southeast Asia in a war none of them understood. Fort Knox Army base was just outside the city, and public schools made sure we all took part in class trips to the massive training base to stoke the fire of patriotism.

That worked with a good portion of young men, especially those with no plans for college or no plans at all after Shawnee High. I recall a couple of White guys on my offensive line in football saying they couldn't wait to volunteer. They looked forward to some action.

As for my peers, we couldn't wait to get to the streets. The civil rights movement of the 1960s was coming to an end. There had been voices like A.D. Williams King, pastor of Zion Baptist Church, and Reverend Martin Luther King, Jr. Back in 1965, while I was away in the seminary, Dr. King had come to the state capitol in Frankfort to speak to thousands protesting the state's blatant segregation policies in schools, housing, and the workplace.

The year before he was assassinated in Memphis, Dr. King had come to Louisville to lead an open housing march in the city's south end. The march threatened to disrupt the city's famous Derby Day at Churchill Downs.

When Dr. King died in 1968, there was no convincing my friends and family that his murder wasn't part of a White conspiracy to silence our Black hero who had become too loud, too important. We certainly didn't believe the FBI conclusion that James Earl Ray was the lone conspirator, given how the bureau had followed and recorded Dr. King.

But the class of 1968 had already pushed the clergy and the civil rights movement to the side. Too old, too much turn-the-other-cheek for us. We wanted confrontation.

The Black Panthers and the Black Muslims reflected our anger. A classmate—his name was Carl—showed up in the hallways in a black leather jacket, a black tam hat cocked to the side of his head, and black motorcycle boots. He was a Panther, and that surprised me because he had been a quiet one at school. Carl was signing up students to march downtown against restaurants and hotels, the police and President Lyndon Johnson's escalation of the fighting in Vietnam. Students boarded a huge truck that had been parked out front on Market Street. It would soon be packed. I was going to the march, but I was too smart to put my signature on paper.

By May, parts of Louisville's west end had erupted with fires and looting. Places had been tinder boxes even before Doctor King's murder. Tensions between police and Black men had been at the tipping point for months.

Once, a White Louisville police officer was reinstated after beating a Black man. You could sometimes see and hear the reaction if you lived in the city's west end neighborhoods.

Our house on Grand Avenue Court was in a neighborhood in the middle of the violence. We were often close enough to walk to the action in Louisville's segregated west end. Police had to come to us. If we weren't in the action or witnessing it, we certainly could hear the commotion and smell the smoke. Sirens wailing. Tires screeching and inaudible commands from police to crowds of mostly young Black males who were under no particular command with no obvious plan other than fuck with police.

In but one instance, three hundred to four hundred people had gathered to protest the arrest of two Black men by White police officers. Cops had stopped a car because they said it fit the description of a vehicle used in a burglary. The driver of the vehicle was Charles Thomas, a schoolteacher. A second man, Manfred Reid, witnessed his confrontation with police. Both men eventually were arrested. As the rally was ending, there was a scuffle between people who had attended the rally and police, who had been at 28th and Greenwood monitoring the activity.

An even bigger incident turned into a riot that lasted for days in the west end. Nearly two thousand National Guardsmen were ordered to town. At the corner of 32nd Street and Hale Street. I saw crowds smashing the windows of the corner liquor store—going inside to help themselves and passing cases of liquor to their friends, who waited outside on the other side of the broken windows. The guard never moved. I stood watching, with one eye on the guard and the other on the alley to make sure nothing blocked our escape route back to our house, which was only a hundred yards away, no further than a football field.

There was a dress shop on the corner. Without warning, my next door neighbor and good friend, Chucky, smashed a window with a brick and ran inside the store with a dozen other people. I didn't recognize anybody else as a friend or neighbor. Where did these people come from? I stood my ground on the corner. Refusing Chucky's invite as he waved me forward to join him. He was totally into this! I had never been inside that store. Nothing in there or in the nearby liquor store that I wanted or needed. In a flash, a burst of speed, Chucky emerged with a roar and both arms full of dresses, that he would later discard as we ran back home through the alley. The owner of that dress shop probably lived in the neighborhood, before moving to the suburbs. He never returned to reopen his store. Same for the owners of the other businesses that were burned and looted.

At the time, I felt there was no rhyme or reason for what I witnessed at 32nd and Hale Streets. If it was part of a protest, what was the point? If these were the voices of the voiceless, as I've heard advocates explain, I question how many of the rioters benefitted from the social or economic changes that did come our way after the 1968 riots.

Two people were killed in Louisville's riots. 472 people were arrested. The burned-out businesses stayed that way for years. Some west end communities are still waiting on change.

It would be fifty two more years before my hometown erupted in this way again. This time, the war was against Louisville police and the overpolicing in the city's Black and Brown communities. This overpolicing included petty arrests for drug possession and dropout squads that would pounce on a crowd of Black youth based on a hunch or suspicion. Police shooting unarmed Black people already had given birth to the Black Lives Matter movement, and the police slaying of twenty-six-year-old Breonna Taylor brought the national movement to Louisville—Derby town, USA.

I would have gone to Louisville to cover the story if not for the Covid-19 pandemic and my being sent home to anchor two newscasts live every week day from my dining room table. I would not have trusted local media and certainly not national media to get all angles of the story right.

This was my home. Coincidentally, Breonna Taylor and I also share the same birthday; June 5. She won't see the many years she had coming until Louisville raided her apartment on March 13, 2020.

Police were serving a no-knock search warrant that I suspected almost immediately never should have been issued. No drugs or weapons were found. No one named in the warrant was arrested. Her startled boyfriend, Kenneth Walker, fired a single round, wounding one of the cops. He claimed he thought intruders were breaking into the apartment. An attempted murder charge against Walker was dropped. Louisville police had responded instantly with a barrage of thirty-two shots, killing Breonna.

No officer was charged in Breonna's slaying. Two of the cops were fired. A tragedy is what Kentucky State's Attorney General, Daniel Cameron, called it. Cameron, an African American, the first to be elected statewide, said he didn't have the evidence to bring charges in the slaying. A couple of grand jurors insisted they were never asked to consider charges against the officers for the slaying.

The state's attorney accused outsiders of meddling in Louisville and Kentucky affairs. Trying to stir the pot, he might have suggested. I disagree!

I offered my take on the matter in a commentary on WUSA9 (CBS) broadcast. It was this: the world outside Kentucky might not have known about Breonna's killing had it not been for the video of George Floyd's killing by Minneapolis cop, Derek Chauvin, who knelt on Floyd's neck for over nine minutes. Breonna Taylor was slain two months BEFORE George Floyd, and the attention his case received garnered belated attention for Taylor's case as well. The state's attorney accused outsiders of meddling in Louisville's local affairs, but I don't trust Louisville to bring justice in the death of Breonna Taylor. I will forever remember Breonna on our shared birthday.

"Something will always bring you back home if nothing but death in the family!" That expression was shared with me while on assignment by an old pig farmer in Rocky Mount, North Carolina.

When Muhammad Ali died, it was a death in the family!

On June 10, 2016, I was called to return home to cover the send-off Louisville gave to my hero, the greatest boxer, and world renown humanitarian—the city's most famous son, Muhammad Ali!

My only interview with Ali was years before, when he toured Washington, D.C.'s old children's hospital. I was assigned the story and when I got the chance, I whispered that I too was from Louisville and lived close to his home on Grand Avenue. The world's greatest boxer then threw a fake punch at my chin. I intentionally didn't duck, hoping he would connect. I needed more time. I wanted an exclusive interview. Can we talk about Chickasaw Park?

He wouldn't know me, but we go way back to the Park. He was Cassius Clay to us in 1958. He was eighteen and I was eight. Louisville legend says the spot in Chickasaw Park where we would jump into the Ohio River for kicks, is the very same location where Ali tossed his Olympic Gold Medal into the river. He was reportedly upset because a downtown restaurant had refused to serve him. The story likely is untrue but that hasn't stopped us from repeating it.

Muhammad Ali's mother was Odessa Grady Clay, a stay-at-home mom. His father was Marcellus Clay, a commercial sign painter. Some of his best work still can be found in church windows in Louisville. He named his son "Cassius" after a famous abolitionist, a former slave who is featured on a statue, chains broken, kneeling at the feet of President Abraham Lincoln. I never liked the statue in Lincoln Park, not far from the US Capitol. Why couldn't the freed Negro be standing up in the sculpture?

As kids growing up in Louisville's west end, we huddled around the radio before we could watch every Ali fight on TV. He was a product of Central High, and word on the street was that he barely graduated high school—that he clowned around too much. But Cassius Clay and then Muhammad Ali came along when we were begging for more younger Black heroes. Some man to stand up to any man. Someone who would stand up for us.

After beating Liston, Patterson, and the others, Ali always mentioned his hometown of Louisville in his post-fight interviews. When talking to the guru of sports reporting, Howard Cosell, regardless of where they were in the world, Ali gave a shoutout to his hometown. I always thought he was talking directly to me. His spirit and confidence encouraged me to persevere, seek my destiny, and not settle for other people's expectations of me.

At the funeral, I got interviews and photos on my cell with boxing heavyweight champions Riddick Bowe and Evander Holyfield but missed Mike Tyson and Lennox Lewis. They all came to pay homage to the greatest.

Ali had planned his own funeral, including the speakers: President Clinton, Bryant Gumble, and Billy Crystal. And Louisville was strutting its best stuff for the send-off of its favorite son. The eighty-million-dollar Muhammad Ali Museum and Cultural Center had become Louisville's biggest tourist attraction. Local authorities voted to rename the local airport after Muhammad Ali.

The diversity that arrived in my hometown for the homegoing was stunning. Muslim, American, and Jewish leaders brought their children to witness the send-off. Rizwan Jaka, my friend and noted figure in the Washington area Muslim community, had come with his sons. We did on-camera interviews that I fed back to my station, WUSA9-TV (CBS).

An added high point of my visit was returning to my old neighborhood, which was also Ali's neighborhood. My old home on Grand Avenue Court was no longer standing. Time had not been kind to the Court although several homes on nearby Grand Avenue had been recently renovated as though anticipating the crowds for this incredible sendoff. Muhammad Ali's pink house on Grand avenue had been turned into a museum, with a crowd flowing in throughout the day.

Lawrence and Violet Montgomery used to live next-door to Ali's house. We played basketball in the alley behind their home. The city had bought the Montgomery home and made it part of the Ali Museum. I spotted the Montgomerys across the street on the front porch of their new house as they surveyed all the international visitors showing up to see Ali's childhood home.

Reporters were lined up to ask the couple, now in their mid-eighties, what Ali had been like through all the years. Cassius Clay and his brother Rudy actually babysat the Montgomery children. I introduced myself, knowing they wouldn't remember me, but they remembered us kids shooting hoops in their backyard with their son who now lived out of town. I was moved to the front of the line to interview them on camera while a few network crews were told to wait.

Ali had been drafted during Vietnam but refused to report at the selective-service office, citing his Muslim religion. In June of 1967, when it was time for Ali to step forward with thirty others to take the oath for induction, Muhammad Ali remained motionless.

He paid the ultimate price. Boxing officials stripped him of his heavyweight title for three and a half years. He was eventually indicted, convicted, and sentenced to five years in prison.

Cheri Bryant, a high school friend and Metro councilwoman, helped connect me to residents to interview, including men who had been drafted and forced to serve in Vietnam. We met on a picnic table at Chickasaw Park. "I admired him for standing up and not going," said one of the veterans. In 1971, The U.S. Supreme Court unanimously overturned Ali's conviction.

Louisville, with its southern military leanings, didn't like Muhammad Ali back in the day. Probably hated him. Black people like my mother loved him and feared for his life. But she didn't just fear Whites who wrapped themselves in the American flag, she feared his new religion, too. "Black people are supposed to be Southern Baptist." That from a Catholic convert. Louisville's Black people were entrenched in the Southern Baptist tradition and knew few members of the "Black" Muslims, followers of Elijah Mohammed. They steered clear when the Muslims Street corner preaching started blaming White people for the plight of the poor Negro.

On the day of the funeral, cameraman Brooks Meriwether and I positioned ourselves along Muhammad Ali Boulevard, about where the west end begins and downtown Louisville ends. I wanted to snuggle with some of Louisville's public-housing residents for this moment. The kind of people I grew up with. This was going to be special when the procession paraded by carrying Muhammad Ali one last time through his hometown, the west end neighborhoods, where we hitched our dreams to his rocket ship as he ascended into the earth's orbit.

I easily spent a couple of hours talking to folk, introducing myself and letting them know that I was a Louisville native and came home only to help give Muhammad Ali the send-off he deserved. I wouldn't trust anybody else on staff to tell this story. My newfound friends appreciated that I had lived in the Cotter Homes projects. They knew the struggle to get from there to here. Ali knew too. He once helped pay law school expenses for a classmate and friend, Jan Waddell, who was also Ali's first cousin. Jan told me he didn't ask for help, but Ali saw him once in a shirt and tie and said, "You look like a lawyer." He then sent him $2,500 each year. Jan says he suggested the amount. He could have asked for more.

When Muhammad Ali's coffin drove by, the street erupted. Flower petals were tossed at the hearse. People flooded into the streets. Actor Will Smith, who played Ali in a movie, was in the procession. He rolled down a window to wave and that sent the people into hysteria. And then it was over. The procession continued down the street to Grand Avenue and other parts of Louisville's west end where people were waiting to bid farewell to the champ, Muhammad Ali.

CHAPTER 4

What's Happening, Brother? My College Years

I MAY HAVE TRIED TO kill myself while in college. I'm not sure.

Flashing red lights from twenty police cruisers were bouncing off the darkness, the townhouses, and front yards. There was no room to get to the parking space in front of our townhouse. This was the Kentucky State Police and they had arrived quickly and unannounced. Their cars stopped in every direction, motors running, doors swung open.

I was a third-year student at Kentucky State—a historically Black college (HBCU) that later became Kentucky State University. It was after midnight, a Saturday, and I was returning from a part-time gig as DJ at WFKY radio in downtown Frankfort. My roommates and fraternity brothers would be throwing another loud party (is there any other kind?) with lots of weed, brew, and fine young ladies.

I was driving my prized 1966 bright-yellow Dodge Dart, with wide black tires, each with a red stripe and shiny silver rims. I pulled over to the side while I surveyed what was in front of me and weighed whether I should get out of there. No young Black guy goes up to lots of cops to inquire, "What's going on, officer?" Only curious White people do that. Too late! A tall muscular Black trooper approached my car. He made me feel only slightly less nervous. "You live here?"

"Yes," I replied, "That's my townhouse over there."

"Hey! You sound like that guy on the radio." *Cool!* I thought. *He recognized the voice.* I had a small following in town among Frankfort's Black residents. But I was really popular on campus, where it counted most among my peers. I was the only Black disc jockey at WFKY and I played R&B for four hours on Saturday and Sunday nights. My classmates at KSU would bring me albums of their favorite artists from back home. It might be Chicago crooner Walter Jackson's "Welcome Home" or anything out of Detroit. The radio gig led to my sometimes serving as announcer at KSU basketball games.

The state police officer waved me into the parking lot and yelled out to other police at the door, "He lives there, and he's the guy on the radio." I'm thinking, *I hope this helps me and everybody on the inside.*

I sensed people were about to be arrested. Was this about drugs, guns, or something else? I prayed that I wouldn't enter the house and find any of my classmates hurt. Wouldn't surprise me if one of my roommates, Clint, had a gun. He had transferred to the school just this semester from Indiana State University. He never explained why.

Was he hustling selling weed?

Inside the townhouse I recognized everybody: it was a Who's Who list! The president of the student government; our homecoming queen, who would go on to become a medical doctor; a couple of athletes out past curfew; fraternity brothers and more. Maybe twenty-five people! They were sitting on the sofa, on the floor, all of them in police custody. Meanwhile state police hardly noticed me as I went to the kitchen and then to the three bedrooms upstairs. Cabinets were being searched, closets were emptied, and everything was left on the floor and counters. This was a drug bust! Does this sort of thing happen to White students in Lexington, Kentucky, at UK?

They called for wagons. The men were cuffed and led into the vehicles for transport. The women were placed into the back of the remaining police cruisers. Their hands remained free. Off they went to Kentucky state police lockup. I watched it all while giving each of my school mates a look that reassured them, I would do what's needed to get them out of this. I was proud that no one appeared afraid. Many of us had been in battle with police back in our hometowns just this past summer. Getting arrested, while not something one hoped for, was certainly something to expect considering the times of upheaval. It wouldn't be the first encounter with Kentucky state police.

The dean of students and I were back at the jail within an hour. The women were released that night. The males, the next morning. My two roommates were held a couple days. One of them begged me, "Whatever you do, don't call my father." Charges were eventually dropped. I never bothered to ask what led Kentucky state police to our townhouse that night.

You learn quickly when attending college in small southern towns that there is bad history between police and Black students. It escalated in the early 1960s with the freedom riders. The Student Nonviolent Coordinating Committee put students like John Lewis, Julian Bond, and Joyce and Dorie Ladner on buses, and sent them at great risk to sit in at Whites-only lunch counters or to register Black people to vote.

Frankfort, Kentucky, should have been one of their stops. Its Jim Crow history is especially violent even when compared with the deep south. Local students attending Kentucky State warned us about their hometown and suggested we not venture too far from campus.

The capital city is only fifty-three miles from Louisville, but there was nothing in my growing up in the all-Black west end neighborhoods to compare.

Frankfort was predominantly White, conservative, and surrounded by farms and rural communities. It sits along the Kentucky River in the north central part of the state. Most websites say it's among the safest towns or cities in Kentucky.

Students at Kentucky State came from some of those small places, but in the late 1960s it was the young men and women from Newark, Detroit, New York, Gary, and Chicago and other urban areas who set the tone and mapped our direction. We are the descendants of slaves. We are the children of your servants and field laborers, but we will fight you and die rather than accept what has been the status quo.

Frankfort was considered "country," a slang that Northerners had pinned on the town we found that seemed to cling to its Jim Crow legacy.

In the 1950s, Frankfort's Black children could attend one school, Mayo Underwood, from first grade through high school. Blacks were not allowed to try on clothing until the evening hours at the main department store, J.J. Newberry's. They were not allowed in restaurants alongside Whites.

In the 1960s, Dr. Martin Luther King, Jr., Muhammad Ali, and other civil rights activists stood on the steps of the state capital building to address the racial disparities.

By the end of the 1960s, when my classmates and I arrived on the scene, older Black people born and raised here, including my first set of in-laws, still addressed White people as Mister and Miss while White people called them by their first names. There were no Black-owned businesses to speak of. Most Frankfort parents were urging their children, including my college girlfriend and first wife and her two sisters and brother, to leave town upon graduation.

More recently, the area African American leaders have gathered to remember what their ancestors were put through.

Here's but one example. In August of 2019 Black community leaders and Black-elected officials gathered in the state capitol to remember two Black men, Marshall Boston and John Maxey Week, who were lynched by mobs who stormed the county jail and dragged them to nearby bridges over the river, where they were hanged. Boston had been accused of raping a White woman in 1894. The alleged victim identified him. He was arrested, jailed, then pulled from a cell by a White mob who met no resistance from lawmen. Marshall was lynched without a trial.

John Maxey was accused of shooting a White circus worker. He was hanged in 1909.

Kentucky has a history of lynchings. According to the Equal Justice Initiative, a nonprofit based in Montgomery, Alabama, at least 169 lynchings occurred in Kentucky between 1880 and 1950. Representatives in the state legislature, Derrick Graham of Frankfort and Joe Graves of Versailles, spoke at that service in 2019. Students from Kentucky State University were in attendance on stage and in the audience.

There was no better time to be leaving home and finding oneself on a college campus than the late 1960s and early 1970s. James Brown was ordering us to "Say it loud. I'm Black and I'm Proud."

Edwin Starr was asking Black and White students "War, what is it good for?" and later Marvin Gaye gave us our own national anthem when he begged the question, "What's Going On?"

"What's happening, Brother?" It was another way of saying; I care for you and I will be there for you. I had never heard that commitment from another Black man. Not from a father, step father, older brother. No one!

Langston Hughes and Nikki Giovanni, among others, became must-reads. What had been left out about this country's founding and the role of slavery was put back in.

I learned the role of the Catholic church as slave ships left Africa heading for the Americas, with their human cargo who would toil the fields for slave masters who attended mass and received the sacraments.

I discovered that while I was away for two years, safe and studying to become a priest, Black people in my hometown and elsewhere in America were catching hell.

One story that I had totally missed involved the disappearance of a young Black woman in Louisville, a story that left me stunned and asking where the hell was I when this happened? In the seminary, of course.

Her name was Alberta Odell Jones, and she was killed in Louisville in August of 1965. She was only thirty-four years old, a graduate of Louisville Municipal College and Howard University Law School in Washington. Ms. Jones was active in the civil rights movement, one of the first African American women to pass the Kentucky bar; she was the first African American woman to become a prosecutor for Jefferson County, Kentucky.

Alberta Jones' death was first attributed to drowning. Her body was pulled from the Ohio River, but a subsequent investigation turned up her car several blocks away with blood in it. An autopsy determined that she had been beaten before being thrown into the water. No arrest was ever made. Her sister Flora Shanklin, told the *Courier Journal* newspaper, "Because things were still so segregated in Louisville, then, I believe, if she had been a White prosecutor, they would have turned over heaven and hell to solve this. But she was black. They didn't do anything about it."

I was especially curious because I knew Ms. Jones had received threats from men she had prosecuted for nonpayment of child support. I'm wondering if the media pursued this case and insisted on answers, or was Alberta Jones' slaying treated just like my stepfather's murder and countless others—just another Negro life, lost?

꒰

When I first arrived at Kentucky State, I made promises to myself. I was going to graduate and I wasn't going to end up poor. I was going to bring some pride to my mother and great-grandmother.

I had classmates who knew they would become high school teachers. Fifteen grand a year would be enough, they said. Work twenty years, then retire. Not me! I wanted the kind of work and income that translated to economic freedom. Live where I want. Say what I want and be taken seriously about more than just the Black point of view.

It would be years later when Harry Belafonte, the singer, movie producer and star, civil and human rights activist told me, "You need four million dollars." He said as an entertainer he hadn't been able to get lucrative work in the U.S. because of his political stances. So he had had to leave the country to perform and earn that kind of money. Harry Belafonte told me that he netted four million dollars that he invested and could now live off the interest. That was over thirty-five years ago.

When not thinking about our futures, we spent all our time on campus fearing the Vietnam War. Getting drafted was an obsession for most of us.

The North Vietnamese had launched the Tet Offensive. President Johnson responded with a demand for more young men to go to Southeast Asia. We thought we'd get exemptions because we were enrolled in college, but some guys at Kentucky State University were drafted right off campus. A couple served their two years then came back to school on the GI Bill. It seemed like a good deal, but at what price? Some of my high school and college classmates died in battle.

A few came back addicted to the drugs that were easily attainable and highly addictive in Southeast Asia.

Every one of us was eighteen or older and afraid of Nam. And we were angry, as young Black men, at being ordered to go fight against a people we didn't know who had done no harm to us. No, our battles were against systemic racism here at home and against the apathy among our own people to do something about it.

The Vietnam draft lottery, the first since 1942, was held in December of 1969. I was nineteen years old. After the numbers were pulled, every male on campus took that sentenced-to- die "dead-man walking" stroll through the student union to discuss the number he had been given by the selective service commission. We complained to one another that well-connected White boys our ages were not getting drafted. Their dads were getting them exemptions. Doctors were finding ailments rendering the rich unfit to serve.

I knew poor White boys back home also were being drafted or volunteering to go to war. The group Creedence Clearwater Revival penned their plight in the classic anthem, "Fortunate Son."

Turns out I got lucky. My draft number was really high. They didn't get to me.

Years later as a journalist in Washington for WUSA9, the CBS affiliate in Washington, D.C., I covered the construction of the Memorial to Vietnam Veterans. Like the war, there was controversy from beginning to end of the project—the funding, the design! Today The Wall remains the most impressive war memorial on the Washington Mall. Bring tissues when you visit. The names of more than fifty-eight thousand casualties are engraved there. The Vietnam Memorial remains one of the most visited monuments in the Nation's Capital.

I escaped going to Vietnam, but I remained curious as to how the war affected other men my age who did get drafted or volunteered.

In 1988, I convinced news management to let me take a TV crew to Southeast Asia to report on expatriates from the war who stayed on, refusing to return to the states. Producer Jody Small and cameraman Kline Mengle and I found Vietnam veterans living in Bangkok, Thailand, who seemed to be locked in time, from 1968 to 1972. They lived off their service pensions. Some had Thai girlfriends or wives half their ages. They gathered at a place called the cowboy bar with a juke box that spilled out music from another era.

How to pay for college was a source of constant stress for me. The Kline family from West Virginia had paid my tuition when I was in the seminary studying to become a priest, but there would be no free rides from this point on. My mother had no money for me. She had small children from her second marriage to James Marbry still at home.

I would take out a government-backed student loan but only the minimum. Just enough to cover my books and tuition. I would find part-time work to pay for food and lodging. It was a plan, albeit not a practical one. A number of my classmates took as much money as the government would allow. One freshman joked, "If I graduate, I'll pay it back; if I don't, I won't."

Not all my new classmates were poor and from single-parent homes. Some of the young men and women came from proud college traditions. Their mothers and fathers had gone to Kentucky State before White universities opened their campuses to Blacks. A degree from a historical Black institution, such as Howard University in Washington, Fisk University in Nashville, or Morehouse in Atlanta, Georgia, gave one instant status upon graduation, if only in the Black community, till one proved his or her worth when given opportunities in White institutions.

Lyndon Johnson had his faults, but passage of the Voting Rights Act and Civil Rights Act were game changers for Black folk.

One of my roommates, Larry Rideaux, was from Chicago's south side. He said he applied at Illinois' big White universities and was rejected. Kentucky State was his mom's idea. "It proved to be perfect for me," he said. "Small enough for the nurturing I needed and yet supportive enough to allow me to succeed at everything I tried."

There was also an upper classman known as "Big Juan" from Indianapolis, a member of the football team who took seven years to graduate. Juan later became a preacher in his hometown of Indianapolis.

The basketball Thoroughbreds were our pride and joy. Coached by Lucious Mitchell, a graduate of Jackson State in Mississippi, the squad included Mike Bernard, Jerome Davis, and Vincent Williams, but the big stars were Travis "Machine" Grant, a six-foot-nine power forward and seven-foot Elmore "Big E" Smith. I sat in the stands inside Exum gym one night as Travis scored a whopping seventy-five points against a visiting team. He ended his college career as the all-time leading scorer at any level ever and eventually was a first-round pick of the Los Angeles Lakers. Doctor J, Julius Irving, paid tribute to Machine's scoring ability at a legendary player's luncheon. Travis finished his career in the ABA. "E" was also a number-one draft pick, going to the Cleveland Cavaliers.

Some of us had hoped that talk of a scrimmage with the powerful University of Kentucky and coach Adolph Rupp would materialize. It would mean a chance to see my Shawnee high school classmate, seven-foot Thomas Payne again. He was on scholarship at U of K, the first Black player recruited by Rupp. The showdown with the big school up the road in Lexington, Kentucky, never materialized. Why would it? They had everything to lose and we "the little school that could" had absolutely nothing to lose.

The small liberal arts school had roughly 2,500 students. By day, we were a majority Black campus. For the first time in our young lives, we were in the majority. We didn't have to check our conversation, our behavior, where our eyes were going. The White students attending Kentucky State lived in the town or the surrounding Franklin County. They were mostly part-time students, attending classes at night while working for the state government during the day. It was really two separate colleges.

Dr. Winona Fletcher was a favorite. She single-handedly ran the school's
theatre and drama department. We performed the classic musical *Simply Heavenly* by Langston Hughes to rave reviews, although none of us were trained singers.

Dr. Henry Cheaney was easily the most popular history and political science professor—hard but fair and one of the best storytellers to ever set foot in a lecture hall. During his forty-six-year tenure, he wore every hat: debate coach, boxing coach, publicity director, and chaplain. I never missed a class. Cheaney not only was brilliant, but he also was entertaining, even funny, at times, and he demanded that his students be well-read and able to discuss researched matters, whether it was the Cuban missile crisis, the White westward movement and the Native American Trail of Tears, or the history of slavery in Kentucky.

It was Cheaney who told me that my hero, Cassius Clay, was named after a Kentucky Abolitionist, which helped explain his own courageous social stances.

On many levels I thrived at Kentucky State. I pledged a fraternity, Kappa Alpha Psi, where I made lasting friendships with the late Dwight Carter, Bernie Grimes, and Bobby Calbert, the three men who pledged alongside me as the "Fantastic Four." Together, over one summer between Kentucky State's campus and the University of Louisville, we were put through some serious challenges before we were allowed to cross the burning sands for our secret initiation. Today, I am a life member of the fraternity.

At times I thought it odd that we needed a Black Student Union on a predominantly Black campus, but it was in this group that I discovered W.E.B. Dubois, Langston Hughes, Countee Cullen, Nikki Giovanni, and Amiri Baraka, among others. We met for poetry readings and discussions about the Black Diaspora. We braided our hair by night so our afros could reach for the sky by day. Dashikis, jeans, and platform shoes were the preferred uniform. Our music was Funkadelic's "Free Your Mind…and Your Ass Will Follow."

The musical talent on that small campus could fill an *American Idol* broadcast for an entire year. You couldn't fake talent either, not when Dennis Rowland of Detroit was going to be headlining the annual talent show. My fellow Kappa brother had a voice that could stop the most gorgeous woman in her tracks.

After graduating, Rowland toured with the legendary Count Basie Orchestra. Janice Carter, my classmate from Shawnee High, was another big talent at Kentucky State. She left school for a time to join a successful R&B group founded by Motown legend Harvey Fuqua. Janice sang with the "New Birth" before returning to school and earning her degree on time with our class.

On the outside I may have appeared to be thriving at Kentucky State. Truth is, I was broke and often hungry. Free meals at my girl-friend Madge Williams' parents' home saved me. But I was barely holding on with part-time jobs on a full-time college schedule.

During my junior year I became homeless. I didn't want to accept another student loan that I couldn't pay back. I felt I could string enough dough together to pay my tuition if I didn't purchase a meal plan.

One of my part-time jobs had been cleaning an off-campus government office building a few nights a week. I kept the place spotless—buffed the floors, emptied the trash, and washed the windows.

Mike, Clint, and I had been kicked out of the townhouse because I could no longer come up with my third of the rent. My take-home pay from the radio station and the cleaning job was not enough.

Dean Williams had an empty bed on campus if I could come by late at night after the dorm had closed. I'd shower and leave by morning.

At one point, another frat brother, Ronnie Whiteside, told me they were hiring at his full-time job down at the state mental hospital. I applied and was hired and immediately assigned to the midnight to eight-in-the-morning shift.

All I had to do was watch a roomful of the sometimes violent, most severely mentally handicapped men in the facility. My first night on the job, I had help. My second night I was on my own. None of the patients could communicate except for grunts and moans. One of the scariest men never went to sleep. As soon as the lights were out, he leaped out of his bed and patrolled the room, sometimes climbed into bed for sex with another resident, or he stood over me, scaring me half to death as I yelled profanities to get him to back off and get back to bed.

I once saw him snatch a lit cigarette out of a staffer's mouth and swallow it—flames and all! For days, I was afraid of what could happen to me should all of the patients rebel. They wouldn't find my body until breakfast time when the door was unlocked on the ward. Ron Whiteside had promised I could sleep on this job. He lied. I never did.

It was after breakfast that I should have been reporting for my first classes back on campus. I was often late or a no show. Tired and unprepared, I crashed in my car or a frat brother's dorm, or off campus at Madge's home. We had met in a freshman general-assembly class. By the beginning of our sophomore year, we were dating. Madge lived just off campus. Her parents, Clarence and Evelyn, worked in downtown Frankfort at the state capitol building. Clarence worked a second job as bartender and waiter at parties thrown by local judges and other top officials. I could not have lasted the three years at K State without their inviting me into their family. Madge was the oldest of four children and a Home Economics major on course to graduate in four years. Her plan was to become a high school teacher. She would follow her aunts and uncles who earned degrees from Kentucky State and then fled Frankfort soon afterward. Our plan was to get married, but I had no idea when or how that could happen. It wasn't all that unusual at the time, but no young man or woman should consider marriage immediately before or after college.

My grades were tanking. I withdrew from a class or two rather than get a failing grade. I was stressed, and graduation from college in a year seemed like a pipe dream.

As if this weren't enough, I got fired from my radio gig. It was my fault, and it should have happened months earlier. Despite warnings from the general manager, I stayed on the air long after the station's required sign-off time. This was no small matter. The Federal Communications Commission could have taken away WFKY's license.

I had all these records from classmates that I had borrowed on the condition that I play them. New Jersey wanted to hear the "Moments." Memphis wanted the Barkays and Otis Redding. Detroit students wanted "Runaway Child" by the Temptations, and everyone wanted the entire "What's Going On" album by Marvin Gaye. I stayed on the air in order to get all of the student requests in before signing off. It's no excuse. The Radio General Manager told me he really liked me and felt I had a future as a disc jockey. I collected my little check, thanked him for the opportunity, and left.

I thought I could make up some of the classes in summer school, though I wasn't looking forward to more classes. Stressed, tired, and depressed, if I didn't turn this thing around, I was heading toward academic probation. I figured I would have to carry twenty hours in the fall to get back on track.

I don't remember the exact date, but I was in between part-time jobs when I took a walk across campus into the night. It was outside the student union that I stumbled upon another summer-school student. This guy was well dressed and always had lots of women from the campus and the town. He was the campus dope dealer, just back from Nam. Word was he had police on his payroll, and that's why he was never busted like my roommates were.

I bought a half tab of mescaline from him that night. To this day I'm not sure why I tried LSD that night. I smoked weed and drank cheap wine and malt liquor, but I didn't do hard drugs.

Several classmates had been strung out on the hard stuff way back during freshman orientation week when they crashed their Volkswagen Beetle into a pole in front of campus. Everybody died.

Was I trying to kill myself? To this day, I'm not sure. Was it a cry for help? Maybe! I had never done hard drugs before. Too scared… too much at stake.

But I was in serious debt by the time that LSD tab hit my mouth. My credit had already been ruined by the several gasoline credit cards—Esso, Sunoco—that had arrived unsolicited in my mailbox. Was I the only student who filled out the applications? Why did they keep approving me for those cards? I never ever paid a bill, and yet they kept coming.

That summer night following my junior year, I was alone. Never really liked being alone, a by-product perhaps of being from a large family where there were always lots of people and noise. Laughter, an argument, or a TV going, somebody opening and closing a refrigerator, somebody always coming or going—though I didn't miss the cursing and violence.

The danger and bizarreness began almost immediately after swallowing the LSD. Rather than staying inside my room undetected and at least experience the ride without endangering myself or anyone else, I decided to climb into my car and drive. This was long before global- positioning systems, and I had no idea where I wanted to go, so my car took its own path. My car decided to take me home to Louisville. When sober, it's a ninety-minute drive.

I didn't go to the main highway; the fastest route is surely the most dangerous, with state police lurking and other speeders waiting to be tested. No, the car headed for the two-lane back road at sixty-five miles per hour.

If we crashed, I wouldn't feel a thing. Much like that carful of upperclassmen who crashed their green Volkswagen Beetle into a telephone pole in front of the VFW hall on East Main Street during my first week on campus. Russel Pearman and Stewart Shelton were juniors and were within a year of graduating and making their families proud. And then suddenly they were both pinned inside the vehicle, which had become mangled like a sardine can. Their bodies had to be pulled out in pieces. We had no reason to believe the cause of the crash was anything but drugs. There were no state police in pursuit. No blown tire. They couldn't have seen the crash coming.

Like me, on an LSD trip, they had to have felt no pain…just euphoria until they got to whatever is waiting on the other side of life. My body was there, but my mind was someplace else. My car, the bright yellow Dodge Dart, was heading West. Couldn't begin to tell you my top speed or how long the trip would take. I wasn't really there. The car had made the trip countless times. It would now find its way again. The drug took over my brain. Like today's high-definition TV, I saw the brightest colors—orange and blue. The road began to move under my wheels like a wave at sea. The streetlights now took the shape of brilliant paint spilling on a canvas. The road was swaying like a blanket being slowly shaken out. I was conscious, but barely, and certainly not afraid.

Somehow the car found its way home. I pulled up in front of my mother's house. She now lived on Hale Street in Louisville's west end. It must have been two or three in the morning. I was still alive although barely. Couldn't get out of the car—didn't know why I would even want to.

Don't know how long I sat there, but eventually the car started up again. Maybe I never turned the motor off. Now I was heading back to Kentucky State. The same road, opposite direction. Same spectacular bright lights and color show that I experienced before. I should have been killed on the road that night; a smaller price to pay would have been a state trooper pulling me over and locking up my young Black ass.

I appreciate how close I had come to killing myself back then. I look back and know God was watching over me and guiding the car.

I pulled into the parking lot of the men's dorm back in Frankfort and got out of the car, limped into the building, and stumbled into the community restroom to look for a mirror.

The pupils of my eyes were the size of saucers! I eventually climbed into bed, where I lay on my back, eyes open, for the remainder of the night. It may have been hours later when I heard students outside my door heading for breakfast. Maybe some food would help.

The cafeteria workers might let me by with no meal ticket, but I first needed a sip of water.

Big mistake. Absolute worst thing to do. My LSD trip started all over again. The room was spinning—got to keep one foot on the floor—*Please! Somebody…just shoot me!*

I dropped out of Kentucky State before the start of my senior year.

CHAPTER 5

Lights, Cameras, Finding My Purpose!

IN 1973, TWO GUNMEN SURPRISED an armed guard as he made his security rounds outside the Taft Museum of Art in downtown Cincinnati. After forcing their hostage back inside, they tied him up, and then stole two Rembrandt paintings valued at more than two million dollars.

At the time, I was a rookie reporter with Channel 9, WCPO-TV, the CBS station. The legendary local journalist, Al Schottelkotte, was our anchorman and news director. He was also a vice president of News Scripps Howard company. Translation, Al did what he wanted to do, including taking a small risk to hire me, a college dropout, in 1972.

I can't tell you what made me apply to work there. I'm not even sure there was a job opening. After leaving Kentucky State University, I had to return home to work briefly for WLOU radio. This was after first following a friend to Cincinnati, where I managed to get fired from a radio gig at WCIN. I just wasn't good enough.

Before returning to my hometown, I had stopped by the TV station and filled out an application. Months later, Schottelkotte called, and I was off again. I reminded my mother that Louisville was just a place that I was from, not where I wanted to be. Ma wanted me to stay in Louisville. She reminded me that I was supposed to be getting married to Madge.

I had been earning $100 per week at WLOU. Going back to the Queen City got me bumped up to maybe $7,500 per year.

I don't recall the job description, but I was given a seat at the news-assignment desk where all the police scanners were clambering away. I don't think I would have even been noticed had I not been the only Black employee in the entire newsroom. Two women were hired about the same time. They were the first also. Four years after Louisville stations started hiring Black journalists because of the riots, and Schottelkotte was bringing in his affirmative action team.

I could not have landed at a better place to start my career in journalism. It was never easy. Nothing was given to me, and I was allowed to make mistakes—fortunately for me, none were fatal.

The major theft of a Rembrandt painting was my first taste of the power of TV news. I was hooked from the start.

Schottelkotte was a maestro when directing reporters, cameramen, and writers in the WCPO-TV newsroom. I witnessed what might have been his best performance shortly after arriving to start work as a newsroom assistant.

Some local crooks had pulled off the biggest caper of their lives—a theft well above their skill set. They stole a couple of Rembrandt paintings!

The FBI and every available Cincinnati cop were looking for the stolen Rembrandts. Only the best art thieves would know how to quickly fence the paintings. In fact, a buyer already should have been waiting to acquire and hide them. But this was a local theft. The two bunglers passed up a pair of multimillion-dollar paintings for two lesser ones, *Man Leaning on a Sill* and *Portrait of an Elderly*

Woman, valued at just over $300,000. They would later explain they thought the two larger paintings were more valuable.

The first painting was turned in, not to police, but to Al Schottelkotte at a local bar. We didn't have live microwave or satellite trucks then. Al called the museum and confirmed he had one of the paintings but insisted that museum authorities and Cincinnati police meet him back at WCPO studios. Viewers tuned in at 11 PM. I watched with the rest of the news team on monitors or in the studio as Al Schottelkotte broke the story. He opened the broadcast with, "I've been in news thirty years now and have had some rather strange and unexpected things happen, and possibly the most unexpected of all took place tonight." Police and the FBI had been forced to stand by in an adjoining room until after Al Schottelkotte told his story. Three men from nearby Loveland, Ohio, eventually were arrested for the thefts. All but twenty-four dollars of the ransom paid was recovered. That money was spent on fast food.

Working for Schottelkotte was this rookie reporter's Christmas. I got everything I wanted and needed in that four-year experience; no postgraduate journalism school could compare.

On so many fronts, this was going to be tough. There was so much to learn, and I felt I was starting so far behind the White males who appeared so confident, so well prepared. They belonged. I would have to make a path for myself and whomever came behind me. I was determined to not only survive the deep waters, but to thrive.

As I would later say to my good friend Gayle King of CBS News, who called me while covering her first homicide in her first job as a street reporter in Kansas City. "Time to grow up, Gayle!" I had learned that you can't talk a journalist into how to do this job. You have to start by doing the job.

I was practically broke when I arrived. In fact, I had never recalled not being broke since my time growing up in Louisville. In Cincinnati, there was no family, no borrowed funds, no plan of where to live from the beginning. The TV station had not offered to pay any moving expenses, and I didn't know that I could even bring it up. There were a couple of nights in a hotel. Then I bunked with some Kappa Alpha Psi fraternity brothers at the University of Cincinnati. With my first two week's pay, I was able to settle into an efficiency apartment on Montgomery Avenue in a town called Norwood, just outside the city.

Everyone was polite, offering to help if needed. But how could I not notice there were no Black camera people, editors, writers, managers, reporters, anchors? Any job that I learned to do well or badly, I would be the first Black person in that job. Pressure from day one!

It wasn't much different at the competing stations. Only Channel 12, the ABC station at the time, had a Black reporter on air, and that was Ben Johnson. We would wave and glance at each other on the streets in those rare incidents where we ended up at the same assignment. There was never a lengthy conversation. We never exchanged phone numbers or promised to meet for lunch one day and exchange notes on how it was going. I'm guessing that we were both just trying to survive in our own respective newsrooms and felt the other couldn't help. Besides, we were competitors trying to get the same story.

I would learn that there are few real lasting friends in this business. This never seemed to change when I moved on from Cincinnati. There is fierce competition among reporters; constant pressure on producers to put forth the best broadcasts, get the highest ratings and the most pay.

Inside WCPO, I hadn't felt this isolated since my first days at camp at Sacred Heart Seminary. Mentoring is an option not a requirement. Not every veteran journalist is interested in helping advancing the careers of newcomers who may be coming for their jobs and bigger salaries.

I figured out early at the TV station that I would need to recall everything about White people that I had learned from my seminary days. Drop the Louisville drawl again when speaking! Pick up speed in my conversations. Less is better in newsroom conversations. The staff is far more experienced and informed. Don't try to impress them with what "little" you really know.

I looked at my hiring as an opportunity. A chance in a lifetime. I realized that no other Black person from my family, from my community, had ever gotten this chance before. It was a realization that would hover over me for years as a blessing, a source of motivation and a sense of immense guilt. I would often look to the sky after I came into television news and ask, "Why me, God?"

Soon after I arrived, Tay Baker, the coach of the University of Cincinnati basketball team, was fired. It was big news. Schottelkotte wanted to lead the 11 PM broadcast with the story. We had no contact until I called the campus and learned from my fraternity brothers that a number of the star players were African American and they could produce them, including Derrick Dickey, the star player, to talk with me. I let Schottelkotte know as he sat in the middle of the newsroom. He said, "Go, go!" He assigned veteran cameraman Greg Hahn to go with me. It was my first television interview. I didn't walk out of work that night. I soared.

Not long after that, Schottelkotte got a tip that Cincinnati was about to get a new Catholic archbishop. He wanted the exclusive. I called the seminary. They remembered me and were glad I was working and doing well. "We hear it's Joseph Bernadine out of Chicago." I told Schottelkotte, making sure I sounded authoritative and projected, so everyone else could hear. Al made a call to get a second confirmation. We led with the new archbishop story that night.

I was getting confident. Couldn't believe they paid us for this.

The exclusives mounted over the years. A police chief is accused of accepting kickbacks from officers he assigned to lucrative off-duty security work.

A vice mayor is forced to resign after padding his office payroll and then taking kickbacks.

The young daughter of the channel 12 news director is kidnapped. We scooped the rival station on when, where, and how she was rescued.

In April of 1974, we trounced the competition in covering the tornado-ravaged Saylor Park community along the Ohio River. Al Schottelkotte led the charge, putting on hold the mourning for his father, who had passed away.

I would learn the work could be hard on family and a marriage.

A big part of my job was monitoring the police-fire scanners that sat on the assignment desk/my desk. I became proficient at sorting out the news from the noise on the scanners. I never missed a breaking news story.

Eventually I built a solid rolodex of police, fire, political, and community contacts who would tip me off to breaking stories. Contacts were everything.

Al felt one needed at least five years' apprenticeship before being considered a veteran reporter. This, from a man who started reporting at about the same time he was old enough to get a driver's license.

A high school dropout, Al Schottelkotte got his start at age sixteen as a copy boy for *The Cincinnati Enquirer*. Only White males need apply for those jobs—writing obituaries or scanning overnight police-incident reports. Schottelkotte was writing his own column before most reporters.

It was in 1959 when I was still in grade school, that WCPO general manager, Mort Waters, convinced a thirty-three-year-old Schottelkotte to make the jump to TV.

In the beginning, there was Al as news director, anchor, and chief reporter. Allan White was editor and general staff reporter, and Frank Jones was chief photographer. Jack Fogarty was also part of the team. They were all still there when I arrived as the team's youngest recruit. When the old timers argued, it was like watching a family dispute. You knew one always had the other's back.

The Al Schottelkottee 6 o'clock and 11 o'clock newscasts were number one for four decades, including my four years under his tutelage. Over half the viewers tuned to TV news in Cincinnati were watching us every night. We were giving CBS Evening News legend Walter Cronkite the biggest lead in audiences of any local station in the country. Of course, the CBS network was on a programming role of its own in the early seventies with shows like *All in the Family*, *The Mary Tyler Moore Show*, and *Sonny and Cher*.

I learned on day one that after great ratings, nothing made Al more happy than hearing "I've got an exclusive story for tonight."

Reporters who developed their own contacts who provided them with exclusive news tips were at the top of the food chain.

Al wanted go-getters. That meant me! I was willing to work all hours and stay long after the competition had gone. I was always curious about everything and everybody…a fresh, young sponge looking to soak up everything.

I especially liked getting old people to share their stories or information. It meant affirmation for me. Acceptance! I protected sources and never lied to get a good story.

I couldn't type when I first started working. I was head down, hunting for and pecking the keys. Schottelkotte decided to help. After each 11 PM newscast we would square off in the newsroom for a one-minute typing contest that required we use every key. I never won but did get faster. I still look at the keys and use my own select fingers. I continue to practice the words:

"Now is the time for all good men to come to the aid of their country." It was Al's way of teaching me how to get up to speed and familiarize myself with every key on the manual typewriter.

If there was an after-hours social component to the newsroom, I was never included. I was never invited to Schottelkotte's home. Never met his wife or his dozen kids. If WCPO-TV had an annual Christmas party or summer barbeque, I never got my invitation.

I did pick up a few bad habits from the veteran journalists; cigarettes was one.

At night in the newsroom, it seemed as though smoke was billowing from every available ashtray, although I never saw Al lighting up.

We sometimes drank a lot too, another rite of passage for young journalists back in the day. Weed was illegal and didn't carry the same status as it did back on campus.

Booze and cigarettes provided the status, the acceptance, that I was seeking. It was as much about looking the part of a hard-charging journalist. Wasn't it comedian Chris Rock who said, "When you meet me you meet my representative; the person I want you to think I am"?

Stouffer's Hotel, a block away, became a popular watering hole. I first stopped in for lunch, spotted Jon Brickson, the backup sportscaster, and soon became a regular.

I worked six days a week, including Sunday nights, which meant the job of coming up with a solid exclusive newscast was mostly mine. One of my big scoops involved the city's vice mayor, Bill Chenault. I learned from sources how the politician was padding his payroll, adding funds to a female staffer's pay—taxpayer dollars that would be kicked back to Chenault, who had been through a bitter divorce. He eventually lost his job. The story was too big to trust to my regular Sunday reporter, so I would leave the assignment desk, meet with a source, and film several locations and a stand-up, with me talking on camera, to make sure I was included in Al's story that night.

I also had stories blow up in my face. For instance, there was a Black community activist, who would call me often to complain about police, drugs, and crime in the ghetto. He recruited some Blacks to patrol the neighborhood. They were vigilantes, taking the law into their own hands because Cincinnati's police could not be trusted. He was right on that.

One weekend, I picked up on a serious incident over the police scanner. There was a drug bust and a confrontation going down. A police officer was calling for assistance in the very area where the vigilantes would be patrolling.

I rushed to the scene with a cameraman. Police had put the community leader James and two of his followers in cuffs and sat them inside two cruisers. One cop, apparently a sergeant in charge, was talking to a White guy who had bruises and some blood on his face. My take is that he wasn't a drug dealer but a junkie in the neighborhood looking to get a fix when he was jumped by the vigilante group.

The sergeant is giving the White guy his script for our camera: "You say they beat you, then put the drugs into your pockets?" The sergeant was putting words into the junkie's mouth.

"Yea, that's what happened."

"Take them downtown." The community leader and his followers were being arrested for taking the law into their own hands.

In my prior conversations with him, I may have even encouraged him to be aggressive against the outside drug dealers. We both knew that Black people were not bringing drugs into the country. But it was just as clear that Blacks were running the street-level sales once the drugs arrived in the community. There were no clean hands.

This incident taught me when to keep my personal opinions to myself. And never offer advice to others about how to fix their problems. It's one of those situations where I could have used a mentor who looked like me. When am I to be just a reporter and when should I also be an African American who wants to better his community and empower his people. The answers would come later!

There was a feeling among Blacks in Cincinnati that the media and law enforcement and the judges were all on the same team. From much of what I observed, the assumption was often correct. Our crime stories always began with the official police position. "Police say or police responded, or police confirm!" Stories ended with a reassurance to the public, "Police are investigating!" Some stories were written directly from the Cincinnati police press release.

We felt obliged when police or judges did us a favor. For example, in Cincinnati and the Hamilton County courthouse, cameras were not allowed inside during court sessions. However, the sheriff's office and judges had arrangements with us reporters: deputies would walk the suspects down the hallway to the courtroom on our cue, allowing us to get our film or video as the accused passed by.

There was more than one occasion when we were late and missed the original walk. The deputies who liked being on camera—and dressed to impress—went into the courtroom, cuffed the suspect again, and walked him into the hallway, back to the beginning of the walk, for a repeat.

"Got what you need?"

"Yep, Thanks a lot."

That incident with the drug arrest was the one time I really considered quitting and maybe trying again to be a disc jockey.

The second time when I went as far as drafting a resignation letter in my head, was when I was reminded that maybe I didn't belong in the newsroom.

I can still remember Al White's words today.

"I don't think you'll ever be a good writer, Bruce." Even now, after over forty years in the business, I will never forget the sound of those words from Allan White. He was one of Al Schottelkotte's longtime and most trusted employees. His words carried a lot of influence with the staff and me.

Allan's desk was next to mine at the front of the newsroom. A door to the back of the room led to a big water tank about the size of an aquarium where Frank Jones processed our film for editing. If the film did not come out dry, Frank knew how to string it along the hallway walls with tape.

In the middle of the newsroom—much like a newspaper city room—sat Schottelkotte.

There must have been ten typewriters and chairs that circled him. It was more like a horseshoe with Al in the center. Everyone tossed their news copy written with carbon paper into a basket that was eventually scooped up and edited by Al. The first draft was rarely accepted. If he liked your story, there would be a comment that was eagerly scooped up by the reporter or writer who took Al's approval as an invite to make small talk with "the man."

Early on I was too scared to submit my copy to the basket for Al Schottelkotte's Scrutiny, and with good reason. I had never taken a writing course. I was learning on the fly, surrounded by a lot of accomplished journalists.

While English was always a good subject for me, this was a different level. These guys could turn a phrase. They had a deep understanding of the issues. Their command of the language was flawless. Mine was merely okay, for a Black guy. I was having to learn the definition of words that never came up at Kentucky State or Shawnee High and certainly not in my home.

I learned a lot in the newsroom about how little I had learned up until joining the staff. Words that I crossed while reading, I now had to pronounce. Words I thought I could pronounce turned out to be different when coming off the lips of these White people.

Allan White had been bothered by my attempts at news writing for a while it seemed. "Some of us are writers, but this isn't.... You can't write news copy for air. This isn't acceptable." Damn! This hurts! Everyone in the newsroom could hear as the editor, the chief writer, cuts me down to size! A lump began to form in my throat. My chest hurt. Here it came again! I recognized the feeling. It was a rejection. Like when I was put out of the seminary. Or when I lost my starting job in high school football. Or when my stepfather James was on my case.

But which Bruce was Al White about to be introduced to? Would I bite my lip and summon some humility? Would I dial up the militant—the proud Black man from the street who'd been dormant since the last time I checked? Would I reach inside for the hurt child and unleash a series of profanities on this old White man?

I thought, *Allan, you might want to talk with my childhood nemesis Donald Brown or my older brother Les, who know what it's like to be stood up to by me, before you try talking to me this way.*

In the end, I probably saved my job by doing and saying nothing. I don't know what guided me to keep my silence. It certainly wasn't my nature. A simple "Fuck you, Al" would no doubt have made me feel better, if only for the moment. That might have been my mother's response, but the vernacular of my old neighborhood wouldn't help me here. On the contrary. "Another angry young Black man bites the dust." I needed to buy myself some time. And I needed a bigger vocabulary.

I took my copy from Allan White, placed it into my typewriter, and quietly started to rewrite. I left work that night as the 11 PM newscast started, not sure I could come back the next day.

Should I call Ma that night? She couldn't help me. I never knew her to stand up to White people outside the house. How would the dad that I never had have reacted to Allan's harsh words? I had nobody to talk to. I needed a mentor. An older Black TV reporter. There was no one. Just me! I prayed.

First, I had to be honest with myself. Allan White's words ripped through me like a dull knife. Was he trying to hurt me or kill my career? Was it the kind of test that every good journalist must pass at some point? Was he implying that I couldn't write then and now or that I could never learn to write?

Did the senior news editor feel these jobs should still be reserved for White men only? I should have asked him…right there on the spot. Pin him down like he did me!

Instead, I said nothing. That was the correct response. A "thank you" would have been even better, but I didn't have enough maturity for that. My spirituality was also waning. Hadn't been to Mass in weeks. I had no regular parish.

Allan White was right about this much. I was no wordsmith. My copy wasn't acceptable back then. If I wanted to make it in this business, I had a lot of work to do.

From that point on, none of my copy was submitted unless I had completed three or four drafts. Nothing quick and dirty. I got a dictionary and thesaurus. After work, at night, I went through the newsroom trash and collected other reporters' polished copy that had been approved by Schottelkotte for air.

After a couple weeks' practice, I gathered the confidence to bypass Allen White and throw my copy into the basket for Schottelkotte to proof. One story he politely tossed back at me with a critique, just like he did for all the other writers. It was when that first story sailed through that a big smile appeared on my face that I couldn't contain. Watch out world. Here I come!

Allan White and I forged a good relationship over time. There was the generational gap for certain, but years later, after I had moved onto WUSA-TV in Washington, Allan White came to visit. He brought his grandson to meet me. Maybe I had taught Allan a thing or two.

⌁

There was still some unfinished business back home. I had become engaged to Madge, who was graduating from Kentucky State with the rest of my class in June of '72.

I wasn't ready, but decisions had to be made. Madge had warned me. There was no way she was remaining in Frankfort. Her parents were in agreement.

We married a few weeks after her graduation in Frankfort Kentucky her hometown. It was a Baptist wedding in the family church. An easy decision after the Catholic priest had insisted Madge would have to convert to my Catholic religion.

There was a funny incident on what was otherwise a nice June wedding day. My best man, James Alexander, a popular Cincinnati radio disc jockey, got lost on the way to Frankfort, Kentucky. He showed up at the church after the ceremony was over. The black tuxedo that I had rented for him, based on the sizes he gave me, was way too small. The manner in which he was holding it on the hanger made it look like the tux had been rented from a children's store. My mother had been determined this wedding was going to happen. She ordered my younger brother David to step in as my best man.

After the reception, that night Madge and I packed up our wedding gifts and the much appreciated several hundred dollar cash donations and drove back to Cincinnati and my studio apartment. My new wife would look for work as a school teacher. I would go in on Monday and ask Al Schottelkotte for a much-needed raise. I recall his upping my salary by about fifteen hundred dollars.

There was another issue. I hadn't finished college. I owed it to my mother, and it was a promise I had made to myself. I would be the first in the family to do so.

I enrolled in a new school across the Ohio River from Cincinnati in Highland Heights, Kentucky. At the time, Northern Kentucky University was in its infancy, a small commuter school that fit my needs for a couple of reasons. First, my credits from three years at Kentucky State could be transferred there. Secondly, I would be eager, like all the other students who were working full-time jobs. There were no dorms or students living on campus. This would be all business. I already had the job. I wanted the college-degree papers that a lot of others had to go with it. I wasn't going to waste time. I would enroll as a full-time student.

Al Schottelkotte fully supported my going back to school. He adjusted my work schedule. I got two days off during the week when I had a full class load. No need to get a Journalism or English degree. I was already working under the best in the business. I would earn a degree in Political Science.

The professors were tough but fair. They knew I was on TV, but I wasn't given any special consideration. I included a summer session to get in all the needed credits. I was a better student at Northern Kentucky because I wasn't broke and hungry, and I wasn't chasing me.

The strain on the marriage was there from the beginning. With school, study, and work, I was never home. There were always money issues. Madge was bored and unable to find work right away. An efficiency apartment had become a closet built for two. Neither of us had friends to break the monotony.

The best part of the early marriage was that our families were close enough in Frankfurt and Louisville that we could go home often. And Madge's two aunts lived not far in Dayton, Ohio.

When I graduated from Northern Kentucky University, our families came up for the commencement. My mother could hardly contain herself. She and several of my siblings, nieces, and nephews would be following my course.

The commencement exercise was held outside on a sunny day and we sat in folding chairs surrounded by a handful of buildings that eventually would be replaced by dozens more when Northern grew into a student body of nearly fifteen thousand students, while becoming the single-largest employer in Northern Kentucky.

I hadn't realized how proud Al Schottelkotte was of my college graduation. He dispatched a cameraman to Northern Kentucky to cover the event.

I wanted more and was awarded a full scholarship for graduate school at the University of Cincinnati to study for an MPA, a Master's in Public Affairs.

Al increased my pay a couple more times, to maybe eleven or twelve thousand per year. Madge got a job teaching at Woodward High School. It was enough for us to move up to a one- bedroom apartment in the Clifton area, not far from the University of Cincinnati. I would continue the torrid pace of working full time while attending graduate classes full time. On the very first day of an organizational theory class, the professor, a doctor Padgett, warned us, "if you are trying to work full time while attending my class, forget it." "It can't be done." That was the reception I got in but one class. A number of us formed a study group. We made it through.

At the same time, I was doing well at work. I was made anchor of the five-minute local newsbreak during the CBS morning news. This required my being at work at about five in the morning. I had to write the script, pull my own slides for air ,which were combined with overnight film to make for a tight, neat presentation.

Sitting in front of a live camera isn't natural for most people. It took lots of getting used to for me.

Viewers who are up at that time of day develop a kinship with the TV talent. If I blew a word, which I did every other day, my viewers would call or even write with the correction. I'm certain there were harsh letters, but they never came to me and no one brought them to my attention.

At the advice of a viewer, I took speech and voice lessons. I practiced my on-air delivery in front of a mirror at home.

Street reporter is where I would make my mark as a broadcast journalist. It's where I was always the most comfortable...in the fray, up close to the people. At my side from the beginning at WCPO-TV was Greg Hahn, a tough, blond-hair, blue-eyed, and blue-collar guy who described himself as "your typical redneck." Greg and his wife lived in a mobile home with their two small children in northern Kentucky.

He resented the college-educated staffers. I think he was a racist who made an exception for me. We both spent a lot of time proving ourselves, exchanging insults, and defending who had overcome the most obstacles to arrive at our places in time. Greg would have loved Donald Trump.

One of Greg's lines to end the banter was "at least I'm not colored," to which I would respond, "You couldn't handle being colored."

We were a great news team! Fearless, adventurous, and willing to do "whatever it took" to get the story and beat the competition. Greg never would have left me in a bind in some of the tough White neighborhoods. I always had his back in the rough Black communities.

We traveled in a Ford Mustang Fastback with the WCPO-TV logos taped all over it. Greg was a hot dog and loved to speed. He would have been a natural on *The Dukes of Hazzard*.

We often sped up and down a stretch of Reading Road that belonged to the street prostitutes. They were out there every night, year-round. One night, long after our late news and most people had come in from the streets, a Black prostitute was attacked and beaten.

I learned that it wasn't just a regular John who committed the crime. Word on the street was that a cop had been her date, and if

I wanted more information, I could find it downtown on Central Avenue at a bar and restaurant that also served as cover to a more sophisticated prostitution operation.

I went there alone one night, after work.

A White woman behind the bar owned the place along with her husband, an older Black man. They poured me a drink on the house and allowed me to ask a few questions.

It was a neat, clean place. Quiet, but dark. At the bar sat three women. Prostitutes, no doubt, but not like the ladies on Reading Road. A lot of the hookers on the streets were into drugs. Maybe even heroin. That didn't appear to be the case here.

I wanted information on the cop and the Reading Road hooker. This was the place where both people were known. The owners introduced me to the ladies working with her and encouraged each to share with me what they could.

The ladies here were upset about the assault and were willing to talk to me if I kept their names out of the story. Of course! I didn't need their real names or the names they used while working upstairs. They did give up the birth name and the street name of the prostitute who was attacked. From their police sources, who I suspected might also be their clients, the ladies gave me a name of the alleged assailant, a cop who had been placed on leave pending an internal investigation.

I had another exclusive. We got a story on the air the following night. I don't recall the police investigation concluding with a resolution. The lesson for me was a good reporter has to go where the people are to get the story. Sitting at a desk with police and fire radios is necessary but nothing beat meeting people face to face and letting them know I could be trusted with their stories. Sometimes jobs and lives were at stake.

I would make mistakes early and later as a broadcast journalist. One of my screw-ups involved a visit to Cincinnati by famed musician Billy Preston. You know, the "Nothing from Nothing" songwriter. Preston is often described as the fifth Beatle because of his many performances on the Fab Four's songs. However, the man who arrived in Cincinnati one weekend claiming to be Billy Preston...was no Billy Preston! He was an imposter! I should have known better, maybe found a picture of the real Billy—but there was no Internet then. No Google to download an image in seconds. He looked like Billy Preston, and I guess I was as gullible as everybody else.

I interviewed the guy. Even put him on TV. No one called in to dispute our presentation. In fact, a state senator who represented Cincinnati's inner-city neighborhoods stopped by and insisted that our "Billy Preston" accompany him and the wife and kids to church on Sunday. The imposter did, but once there refused all requests that he play piano and join the choir in a song, saying it would violate his contract.

Before he left town, "Billy Preston" asked to borrow my car. I at least had the good sense or suspicion to say "no." After the imposter had left town, I did come up with a picture. The guy looked nothing like the real Billy Preston! I let colleagues know. No one seemed interested in a follow-up story to say we had all been duped. That would include me. I would soon be leaving.

After four years of working for Al Schottelkotte—eleven months before completing his five-year tutelage program—I was offered a job in Washington, D.C.

Al wasn't happy, but he must have known he wouldn't be able to keep me. There was too much at stake for me and Madge, now that we had a daughter, Kurshanna, who was eighteen months old.

I had worked hard to earn undergrad and graduate degrees. I was considering law school if this broadcast journalism career fizzled. Turns out broadcast journalism needed me as much as I needed it. There were not a lot of people who looked like me on local and national TV.

I was a work in progress, still needing an on-air finishing school, but I was already a damn good reporter in search of a bigger market and bigger pay checks. I was heading to the nation's capital, Washington D.C., to WTOP-TV, the CBS station that eventually would become WUSA9. They didn't pursue me. I wrote letters, secretly sent out audition tapes, made countless phone calls, and practically begged for the opportunity.

Al and I would remain lifelong friends. I looked forward to his visits to Washington, D.C., which were at least once a year. I'm sure from time to time he would share stories about me and his role in hiring and training me. He deserved all the credit.

I was going to miss the news team, NKU, UC, and of course the Cincinnati Reds baseball team. I covered the Big Red Machine from 1970 to 1974 and can still name the starting lineups that included Joe Morgan, my all-time favorite player.

Al Schottelkotte died on Christmas Day, 1996. At his funeral Mass at Saint Martin of Tours, where he had served as an altar boy, the Reverend Francis Niehaus said he was for millions of people the reason to stay up late. The priest then ended his eulogy with Al's signature signoff, "That's it for now. So, until tomorrow, may it all be good news to you."

CHAPTER 6

Coming to Chocolate City, Washington, D.C.

I CAME TO WASHINGTON, D.C., on the Ides of March. That had been a really bad day for Julius Caesar, but March 15 of 1976 would prove to be one of the most important days of my career. The pay was fifteen thousand dollars, fifteen hundred dollars more than I was making when I left WCPO-TV in Cincinnati. I would have come for free! This job and this city were that important to me. I would still be here more than four decades later with twenty-two Emmy awards, enshrinement in a few journalism halls of fame, proclamations from mayors, resolutions from city councils, an honorary doctorate, and more civic and community service awards than I could mention, in addition to many incredible and sometimes dangerous reporting assignments in D.C. and major cities all over the world. By the time I retired at the end of 2020, my image would be added to the historic Wall of Fame on the wall outside of the iconic Ben's Chili Bowl restaurant on D.C.'s U Street.

At age twenty-five, I had just been hired by Jim Snyder, the news Godfather! He wasn't just the news director at WTOP, the CBS TV station in D.C.; Snyder was vice president for broadcast news for all the Post–Newsweek broadcast stations. Every news operation under his control was number one, and why wouldn't they be? The Post–Newsweek company was home to the *Washington Post*, home to legendary reporters Carl Bernstein and Bob Woodward. The Watergate legends were revered in every way that I hoped to one day be as a journalist.

⤙

I was hired to become one of the final pieces to an all-star news team that was already dominating local news. In a short time, I would become a perfect fit for what Jim Snyder was building, an all-star "One and Only" team, a legacy.

Max Robinson was the anchorman, a baritone—six foot plus, tan, handsome, and Black, with the smarts and confidence any reporter would envy. Max took me under his wing for those first two years and protected me from D.C.'s upper crust of African American business leaders who didn't take well to newcomers of any color. I recall he once took a call from a local D.C. figure who was complaining about a tough news story I had done about him. Max brought the concern to me but added that he told the influential figure, "If you guys weren't fucking up, Bruce wouldn't have that story to cover!"

One night, at his invitation, I joined him for drinks to celebrate his birthday at a bar near the station. Drunk out of our minds, we stumbled back to the station where Max was scheduled to anchor the eleven o'clock news. I watched him disappear into his office and close the door. I was off work but stuck around to see how the evening would unfold. When the red light went on above the camera, Max said, "Good evening, I'm Max Robinson." He didn't stumble or miss a beat. I was impressed.

Max could play the role of a TV star very well. He lived a couple miles from the TV station but insisted a car and driver be sent to pick him up in bad weather. And he refused to read retractions on the air. He felt if a reporter made a mistake, the anchor—namely Max—shouldn't have to apologize. Reporter Pat Collins once remarked, "Pay me what you pay Max and I'll do nothing but retractions on air."

Gordon Peterson was the other half of the most dominant anchor team in Washington. Great newsman, who seemed to stay out of Jim Snyder's journalism doghouse. Gordon seemed just as comfortable in the field pursuing a good story or interview as on the anchor desk. Someone once told me that watching Peterson, you were convinced he was really listening to the people he was interviewing and not just waiting his turn with his next question.

Eventually sports anchor Glenn Brenner, funny, quick, and the glue on set, rounded out the team. Glenn arrived less than a year after me and we grew close. At one point, the six-foot-five-inch former pro baseball prospect asked me, "Is this all there is?" This after signing a multiyear, multimillion-dollar contract that included paying his children's college education. Glenn died in January of 1992 from a brain tumor. His death came after he had completed his second marine corps marathon. The news team and the entire Washington area went into mourning over the loss. Joe Gibbs, coach of the Washington football team during its Super Bowl run, brought one of the footballs from a Super Bowl win to the hospital where we all gathered in the hallways to comfort one another during Glenn's last hours.

Anchors J.C. Hayward and Maureen Bunyan were trailblazers. NBC correspondent Andrea Mitchell and University of North

Carolina School of Communications dean Susan King were street reporters. Bob Strickland, Steven Gendel, Henry Tenenbaum, Patrick McGrath, Pat Collins, Mike Buchanan, and Eldridge Spearman rounded out the street reporting team. All I needed to do was fit in and that meant getting up to speed and a cruising altitude quickly. I couldn't be just okay. Poor performers were not kept around for long. People with promise but not yet ready for Washington's prime time market might be farmed out to one of the Post–Newsweek smaller market stations. I had to be really good. The pressure was immense. I had to pull out everything I had learned under Schottelkotte and that wasn't going to be enough. Jim Snyder often would ask me, "Did you get away with that in Cincinnati?" He used that line a lot in the beginning.

⤙

Jim Snyder could be scary and a great motivator. When he detected that I was getting down on myself, he reminded me that broadcast journalism was still in its infancy, that White journalists like Mike Wallace of *60 Minutes* fame never had formal journalism courses. Wallace had been in theatre. The first White anchors, all of them male, were actually booth announcers, with little education, no reporting or writing skills, who merely read whatever was put in front of them.

I was part of the second wave of African American and female journalists. I was coming in with a graduate degree and several years' experience in a major market. J.C. and Maureen were also experienced and both had graduated from the Michelle Clark Program at New York's Columbia University journalism school.

I belonged in Washington. I had paid some dues, but I was an unfinished product that needed time in Jim Snyder's finishing school. The time spent under Al Schottelkotte, Allen White, and Greg Hahn and watching veteran WCPO-TV reporter Jim Delaney proved invaluable.

I immediately went into the Jim Snyder boot camp. Like Schottelkotte, Jim read over scripts before they went on air. Snyder didn't anchor which meant he had more time to scrutinize the writing and producing. In the beginning, he called me in after practically every news package aired on the 6 PM news. He said my delivery was strange. "You're emphasizing the prepositions! Did you get away with that in Cincinnati?" There were times I didn't think I would make it, but I had been here before in Cincinnati when Allen White challenged my poor writing. I got better. I could get better here if given the time. I had no backup plan. Where would I go?

We called the building where I worked Broadcast House. It was located off Wisconsin Avenue in upper Northwest D.C. I often retreated five floors down to watch my stories on TV sets in the lobby, away from Jim Snyder's glance or voice. My desk was right outside his office. I could get his critique the following day.

I had a wife who gave up a good teaching job in Cincinnati, a young daughter who would be starting preschool in a year; and a mother, in-laws, and siblings asking how it was going and when can we make plans to visit Washington. All eyes were on me!

With one salary coming in, money was a problem, again. The company paid for a hotel and we stayed at the Holiday Inn for about three weeks and then found a cute two-bedroom Cape Cod on Woodbridge Avenue in Silver Spring, Maryland—a short ride to work. I was depending on all the overtime I could get. Jim Snyder reminded me that "Journalists don't punch a clock." Translation, I was putting in for too much overtime.

⤳

Working in Washington sometimes meant working and socializing among journalism giants. In 1976, Ben Bradley was executive editor of the *Post* and another hero of Watergate. My first impression of him came at a reception at the newspaper with Bradley pulling up his trousers and straightening his belt. His hair and clothes were impeccable and I thought, *He must spend a lot of time on his presentation.* His handshake was firm, the voice was authoritative. I took notes. Bradley could have played himself in the movie.

Katherine Graham, publisher of the *Post*, was another journalism star. Jim Snyder introduced us at that same reception. She treated me like a colleague, explaining one of her biggest mistakes was caving in to the Federal Communications Commission and giving up owning both the *Washington Post* and its TV station in the same city.

I had been there two years when Post-Newsweek exchanged WTOP-TV with the ultra-conservative Evening News Association for their Detroit station, WWJ, which was renamed WDIV.

⤳

The Washington Post, while better than most media corporations, wasn't without sin for its delay in hiring minority journalists and its hourglass pace at promoting minorities to editor and columnist positions.

In 1961 Dorothy Gilliam became the first Black female reporter. She's from my hometown of Louisville. She wrote in her autobiography that she often had to take taxicabs to her assignment, but the drivers refused to pick her up. Fifteen years later I experienced the same thing. D.C. taxicab drivers were discriminating against us and leaving African Americans at the curb.

On one Saturday afternoon, I was leaving a youth football game in the upscale Georgetown neighborhood. Like Dorothy, I attempted to hail a cab on Wisconsin Avenue, Northwest, to take me the couple miles to my TV station. At least a half dozen cab drivers passed me by. They had no passengers and never bothered to ask where I was going. I was furious by the time I had walked to my job to anchor the weekend news. I decided to investigate a practice that had been only talked about until now.

I put Black and White colleagues on the street, in some cases on the same corner within several feet of each other. With cameras rolling we witnessed not one, not two, but many cabs, from different companies, pass up Black fare but stop for the White customer. I wanted more proof. I recruited D.C. city Councilman Kevin Chavous, a tall, handsome African American in a suit, to try and flag a cab on Connecticut Avenue in downtown D.C. at midafternoon. Again, lots of cabs passed him by.

‿

Those that did stop wanted to know where he was going. he said "Southeast, D.C.," as I had instructed him to do. The cab drivers said, "Sorry! I'm not going that way." That was illegal. Cab drivers are not permitted to refuse to transport any passengers.

It was part racial and part class discrimination. The cabbies told me they feared for their safety in Southeast DC or Blacks routinely don't tip, or Black people want to be taken to areas far outside the prized downtown area. The shorter and most lucrative routes are located downtown. Poor people can't afford to live downtown and they can't afford to keep paying the fares to get to their homes and apartments across town.

I even put the Chairperson of the DC Taxicab commission, Karen Herbert, on the street to try to catch a cab. The African American woman was in a business dress when she was left standing on the corner by cab drivers who refused to stop and pick up the fare. Chairperson Herbert was irate. "I see your number and I am going to turn you in," she yelled to one driver who refused to stop after waving her off.

In our final demonstration about the blatant racial profiling by cab drivers on D.C. streets, we decided to broadcast the incidents live during the evening newscast. I was reporting live from one side of Constitution Avenue in front of the U.S. District Courthouse. Across the street in full view, I had placed a Black colleague. A few feet away on the same side of the street was a White colleague. The men were dressed the same, both had on microphones and were standing alongside the National Gallery of Art.

This is what we captured on videotape: a taxi driver stops for the Black man but after a brief exchange and refusal turns him down and moves several feet to pick up the White passenger. The Black passenger follows the driver who can be heard on the live microphone and camera, "It is my taxi and I will do whatever I fucking want to do," the driver said. "I was standing there and you saw me," said the Black man.

The Taxicab Commission held hearings, and the taxicab companies promised to abide by the rules and retrain their drivers. We won Emmy Awards for our work. Years later, a rival TV station did the exact same investigation. The cab drivers had reverted back to racial profiling.

Dorothy Gilliam had said she didn't want to complain about her problems in the streets because the *Washington Post* might not hire any more Blacks as a result. I had learned in Cincinnati how to not make waves, but those days and the journalism apprenticeship were over. I had come to Washington to do just that! Make some waves.

I was encouraged by knowing or watching a stable of accomplished Network News correspondents—Black and White—who worked in downtown Washington on M street at the CBS bureau. Hal Walker, Randy Daniels, Ed Bradley, Bernard Shaw, and Michelle Clarke had become regulars on the evening news with Walter Cronkite and then Dan Rather. I once watched the anchor toss to Randy Daniels by introducing him as our "Africa Correspondent." I'm thinking, damn! The brother has to cover the entire continent by himself! Daniels also reported from eight wars and the Iranian revolution. I never missed Bradley reporting from the White House, and later *60 Minutes*, every Sunday night. I got to watch him up close on the grounds of the White House when covering stories there. White House reporters traveled in a pack and I often wondered if the journalists in the front tripped and fell while running would everybody behind them end up on the ground? I knew Ed Bradley wouldn't trip; Ed was the epitome of cool. Always walking, never seeming to break a sweat.

⤳

Bernard Shaw was hired by CBS in 1971 and had a voice from God. Deep and smooth, and there was no pronunciation that tripped him up on air or caused him to pause and lose confidence. He left

CBS because ABC allowed him to become Latin America bureau chief. He retired as CNN Washington anchor but not before calmly reporting live from atop a building in Bagdad while US planes began bombing the Iraqi Capital. I wanted that kind of confidence.

My ultimate goal was to join them at one of the major networks. Why not? When you come from the kind of place where my people started in a tobacco field in Pembroke or a back alley in Louisville, you don't look back. That position had served me well. Leaving home at age fourteen for the seminary! Packing up again and showing up at a TV station in Cincinnati with no funds and no idea what I was getting into, that's me. A man with nothing to lose who is willing to risk everything.

I never took a journalism course in college. The government affairs and history courses proved to be especially helpful in covering the D.C. government and the federal agencies and even the White House. I was able to drill deep into budgets the size of telephone books to find the line-item numbers and programs that mattered most to people.

And coming up with a two-minute reporter package from a D.C. Council budget session that lasted four hours wasn't always easy. TV viewers know when reporters are faking it and really don't know what they are talking about. That's why the beat system is so important: reporters are paid to become well-versed on the issues. Unfortunately, over the years many corporations that bought local TV stations decided they didn't want to invest in beat reporters and investigative units. General assignment reporters became the preferred flavor of broadcaster. Some were really good broadcast presenters. All of them complain regularly of not being given enough time to work their stories and development contacts.

I hung with the print reporters, the journalists from the *Post*, Associated Press, WTOP, and WAMU radio. They had beats and some, but not all, were willing to share some knowledge. I always went out of my way to help the new journalists get through the fog of a new and difficult story.

I had learned in Cincinnati that most viewers were quite comfortable if not impressed with my reporting and Black people in general were eager to support Black journalists. We were there to help and not further hurt them. They liked having a successful, well-educated African American male they could point out to their own sons and daughters as evidence that dreams coupled with education and hard work do come true. Privately, they complained to me that most stories that were fronted by African Americans on the evening news were about violence, crime, drugs, corruption, and incarceration. They were right. In the late 1960s and 1970s, White reporters got most of the plum assignments. The White House, Capitol Hill, and Presidential campaigns, including the political conventions. My appeal to community leaders was, "Trust me! Who would you rather have to get your stories right?" And I promised to expand the coverage of the success stories in the minority communities. It bothered me that the face of poverty and most of the crime was a Black face. An alien to the Washington DC TV market must think there are no poor white people and no street crime in White communities.

꒰

What began to set me apart from other City Hall reporters is that I soon began spending more time on the streets, in the middle- and low-income neighborhoods, where the real people affected by the laws actually lived. I took their stories back to City Hall and demanded answers to their questions from elected leaders. I was a TV reporter: I needed good film, then video and great interviews from real people with real lives and concerns. Other TV stations caught on and began showing up. *Washington Post* reporters divided their time between boring legislative hearings, the press room, and the telephones. I loved the streets and the people in the streets. The ex-offender who was robbed at gunpoint while operating his food truck; the homeless couple with an infant trying to find a place outside the dangerous city shelter; the man who graduated from Howard University law school while homeless who showed me how he negotiated the streets, shelters, and soup lines; The Alliance of Concerned Men and Peaceaholics, two groups that rescued young people from the neighborhood fear and violence.

In 1976, a majority of the D.C. Council was Black. Sterling Tucker was chairman, Arrington Dixon represented the Black, affluent Ward 4 area. Marion Barry was an at-large member with a citywide base that eventually would propel him to four terms as mayor. He was also chairman of the powerful finance and revenue committee.

Polly Shackleton was the oldest council member. White and well-to-do, she represented the rich, predominantly White Ward 3 neighborhoods west of Rock Creek Park. The clergy was represented on the legislative body. There was Douglas Moore, Jerry Moore, and James Coates, all Baptist preachers. John Wilson represented Ward 2, which included downtown and southwest D.C. Dave Clarke, perhaps the most liberal of the Council members, represented Ward 1, which included the historic U Street corridor and the riot-torn 14th Street corridor. Ward 1 was also home to the city's biggest Spanish-speaking communities.

Before the Black flight from the city, which really escalated after the 1968 riots, Washington, D.C., was Chocolate City! When I was hired in 1976, Black people were at least 70 percent of the population.

Realtors made sure Whites were the dominant population west of Rock Creek Park, which ran from Montgomery County in Maryland in the north, down to the Potomac River, which separated D.C. from parts of Northern Virginia. The rest of the District of Columbia was home to D.C.'s affluent, middle-class, lower middle-class, working poor, and poor Black people.

It all made for an incredible canvas for this artist. I was destined to come to the Nation's Capital. but I had a lot of growing, learning, and listening to do.

Residents of the District of Columbia have never been regarded as full citizens of the United States. To this day we do not have a voting member of the U.S. Senate or the House of Representatives. This is no accident!

Article one of the Constitution says D.C. will be under the control of the Congress, not its mayor or councilmembers. It wasn't until the ratification of the 23rd Amendment to the Constitution in 1961 that the city's residents were given representation in the electoral college and thus the right to vote for president of the United States.

All the while, D.C. citizens had been required to pay federal taxes, while other federal territories, including Guam, Puerto Rico, and the U.S. Virgin Islands, have been exempt. The dismissal of D.C. citizens continues today. Of course, if D.C. were suddenly exempt from federal taxes, the gentrification that is now in full bloom would reach epidemic proportions. Property values would climb even higher than they are now. Poor people would have no place to go.

D.C. residents today pay more in per capita taxes to the federal treasury than any state. Young men have been drafted and volunteered to serve in every war the United States has fought. The Vietnam Veterans memorial is easily the most visited war memorial on the national mall in downtown Washington. Scores of names among the near fifty thousand dead, belong to District of Columbia young men.

You can't appreciate the political psyche of the longtime D.C. residents until you come to learn and understand their longtime struggle for home rule. The struggle to become full citizens of these United States. Add to that, in 1976 a majority of the people in D.C. were African American, in a city located below the Mason Dixon line; a Southern city with a slave history.

D.C. was a booming slave depot before the Civil War. Not far from the National Mall, Black people were auctioned. They were held in pens and later chained and herded in front of the U.S. Capitol and White House before they were shipped out to Virginia and Maryland and throughout the South.

It wasn't until 1971, five years before I got here, that Walter Fauntroy was elected by city folk as the nonvoting delegate to Congress. If there was cause to celebrate, I also should point out his taking office was the ultimate evidence of the "taxation without representation" status of city citizens. Fauntroy was a popular Baptist minister, a civil rights activist, and lieutenant to Dr. Martin Luther King, Jr. He was one of many prominent D.C. clergy who protested and marched throughout the South for other people's rights, which also were being denied in Washington.

There were plenty of demonstrations in D.C. for full voting rights. There was once a measure that required a vote by the states, and I was dispatched to Sacramento as the California State legislature voted to support such a measure, but it never had a chance in other parts of the country, particularly the South.

I immediately identified with the District's "us against them" mentality. I often felt D.C. residents weren't angry enough. People should be willing to march, get arrested, go to jail if necessary! Wouldn't that bring more attention to what was happening here? Isn't that what Martin Luther King used successfully to bring about changes elsewhere in this country? I was really tempted, some years ago, to join Mayor Sharon Pratt and several councilmembers in protesting the plight of D.C. citizens by standing on Pennsylvania Avenue blocking traffic until they were arrested. It's what Louisville White activists Ann and Carl Braden would have done.

I feel most new residents to the city don't get it. Gentrifiers often live in the city in new construction or rehabbed neighborhoods, where the 1968 riots took place, while keeping their permanent addresses in home states where they continue to enjoy voting for senators and congressmembers. Understandably, their votes carry more sway in the electoral college where the elections of president and vice president are decided.

Statehood for D.C. would certainly correct this injustice, and there is a persistent campaign with ceremonial figures holding shadow senator and congressmember positions. Jesse Jackson was the first shadow senator.

In 2021 there was yet another attempt at statehood. The measure won approval in the House but never reached the Senate floor. Observers (and I confess I'm one of them), don't think the District of Columbia will become the fifty-first state until some of the current national legislators are replaced. For one, why would Republicans in the Senate vote to add two democratic legislators to their ranks, probably forever tipping the senate majority to the Democratic party? Seven out of ten registered voters in the District of Columbia are Democrats.

This is the most progressive city in the country outside of San Francisco. On that note, two observations: D.C.'s African American population is more moderate than outsiders know. Its White citizens are more progressive. And there are far more conservative Blacks, led by the influential clergy, than people would believe. Black ministers were adamantly opposed to abortion, gay marriage, and legalizing marijuana. Whites overwhelmingly supported these measures that were eventually approved.

In 1973, D.C. won a consolation prize: Congress decided after much lobbying by local folk to give D.C. limited home rule, thus allowing citizens to elect their own mayor and councilmembers, which had previously been appointed at the federal level.

By 1976, I was following Mayor Walter Washington and Council Chairman Sterling Tucker up to the U.S. Capitol every year to explain the city's spending. Congress had ultimate authority over the District of Columbia budget. I remember conservative Republican Committee Chairman William Natcher, of Kentucky, demanding to know why city leaders were spending money for this program and not that program. City leaders sometimes stammered and looked apologetic as they shuffled papers between them, looking for the numbers to justify their positions. I felt embarrassed for them.

I was disgusted that the congressmembers were always southern White men and the city leaders were Black, subservient, with their hands out, never disagreeing with the old men who held the city's purse strings. There were a lot of "Yes, sirs" and "No, sirs" during those D.C. subcommittee appropriation hearings.

⌐

There was a lot of waste and inefficiency in the D.C. government when I got here. Some corruption too. Much of it was left over from the former commissioner form of government, when the mayor, D.C. Council, department heads, and police and fire chiefs were federal appointees. There were hundreds of city jobs where congressmembers could park friends and family members. It became common practice, for people qualified and hardly qualified, to get good national and city government positions after their educations or military service were done.

Walter Washington was finishing up the second half of his one and only term as the District of Columbia's first elected Mayor.

My job was to cover the Mayor and D.C. Council and, where I found it, expose the failings of local government. It was the same mandate I had in Cincinnati, but the challenges in D.C. were mired in past racist, political, and socio-economic disparities. I immediately sized up that the Nation's Capitol was a southern city that while predominantly Black, was still being run by White men in Congress and the White House. D.C.'s business leaders, with allies on the Hill, also wielded major influence. Those were White men too. You don't take on City Hall on day one. I would have been sent packing, I'm sure. The *Washington Post* and *Washington Star* reporters already were established and familiar to people in power who were leaking them stories and offering up quotes for major developments.

I decided to go where I knew I would be welcomed. I went to the streets and poor Black communities. The kind of places I was most comfortable; places that resembled where I grew up in Louisville's west end.

One of my first assigned cameramen was Michael Murphy, a D.C. native, whose knowledge of the Black side of the city was awesome. This man had come up poor and spent time at D.C. Village, a foster facility for homeless children operated by the government. We were young Black men with huge chips on our shoulders and a determination to cover that part of the city east of the Anacostia River. It was referred to as the Separate City, so we gave that name to my very first series of special reports. We moved in with the Barbara Price family in the Stanton Dwellings public-housing project. We never actually spent the night. We were there many nights and most days for almost a month.

We were off the regular City Hall beat. Instead, we documented in incredible detail on camera, the highs and lows of living poor in D.C. Barbara's oldest son, got arrested. I testified on his behalf in court, which helped get him a suspended sentence. I can't remember the crime. It was not a violent offense. He later joined the national guard. The oldest daughter tried but couldn't land a job after high school; the youngest son was a lover of rock music. I easily identified with his not fitting in at the very house he lived in.

Jim Snyder loved the five-part series "The Prices of Anacostia." These were the kind of stories the Washington market was missing. It helped convince him I had been a good bet.

I was just getting started. One of my early dangerous scoops I took viewers into the basement of City Hall. The story came from a veteran D.C. police officer who was close to retirement and couldn't risk bringing such unfavorable attention to the District of Columbia's top elected officials.

Here's how the inside story went.

"Hey Bruce, I need to show you something, but you can't say where you got this!" I would get that a lot in the years that followed.

It was the first time the officer had ever given me a tip, except for an occasional heads-up that "the mayor is on his way downstairs," in case I wanted to grab Mayor Washington for an interview.

The officer walked me to the elevator and pushed the button that took us down to the basement. I had never been to the basement of the District Building and had no idea what was stored down there. Did I mention that this floor was off limits to the public? You had to have a key to the elevator to get down here. In the basement, the cop walked me to a hallway that led to a dark, dusty room. How did he know the place would be empty? He told me he had been secretly monitoring the basement's activity for weeks.

"Watch your step," he said, as he pointed his flashlight at the floor. I couldn't believe what I was seeing. We had walked into a damp dark area and there were used syringes all over. I'm talking dozens.

This was a flop house underneath the mayor's offices and council chambers! Six floors under the city's most powerful offices, and people were gathering down here to shoot heroin. "You've got ten minutes!" With that my police source disappeared.

I practiced a few lines in my head. "You won't believe what my cameraman and I were directed to in the basement of the District Building," I said as the camera panned off me onto the needles on the floor. "That's a wrap!"

I telephoned the assignment desk and notified my people back in the newsroom that they should hold page one at the top of the newscast that night for my scoop.

No one in high office, not the council chairman Sterling Tucker, not Mayor Washington, not the police chief, had much to add to my exclusive report that night. They promised to investigate. Tucker expressed disbelief. We got the same angry reaction from viewers. The basement was swept clean. There was no investigation. No report on who was bringing heroin into the District building and who was shooting up under the seat of the local government.

That retired cop approached me years later with his grandson in tow. He introduced us and thanked me again for the work I had been doing. I said no, I should be thanking you, again!

I was working a lot of overtime. I needed the money but loved the work too. I justified the evening hours away from home by coming up with great contacts and great stories for Channel 9. Jim Snyder reminded me that "Real reporters don't punch a clock!" Translation, he didn't like paying the overtime. In a compromise move, he gave me a new three-year contract. After Post-Newsweek swapped the station with the Evening News in Detroit, I got a really nice raise from Ron Townsend who was promoted to General Manager.

Townsend was the former business manager. He became the first African American GM in station history…likely the only general manager in either company.

Here's what the move meant to me. Madge and I were looking to buy a home in the District, but we had no savings. She was teaching high school in Montgomery County. Together we were doing okay, but there was no money for a down payment. When I shared this news with Townsend, he drove me downtown to the *Washington*

Post credit union. I enrolled and soon after had the borrowed funds to put down on a home at Kansas and Ingraham in Northwest. Ron also signed me to a new multiyear contract with a 50 percent raise. Soon after we moved into our new home, Brandon Bruce Johnson was born. We had a son to go with our daughter.

9/11 taught us that no government building in Washington, D.C. can be entirely safe from a possible terrorist attack. We've got all the evidence we need. This wasn't the case when I arrived in DC.

Covering City Hall should have been a safe beat. Hardly the place for deadly gunfire back in March of 1977. But that's what happened. I was heading there for a scheduled press conference.

My cameraman Peady Shifflet and I were pulling up on Pennsylvania Avenue blocks from the White House and US Capitol when the police radio in the vehicle crackled. "Shooting on the fifth floor of the District Building in Pennsylvania."

Maurice Williams, a twenty-four-year old reporter for WHUR radio, the Howard University station, had already arrived early with Steve Colter, a reporter for the Afro-American Newspaper.

Who could have known that Hanafi Muslims had planned to storm three well-known buildings in Washington at the same time, taking nearly 150 people hostage?

As Maurice stepped out of a fifth-floor elevator, he was shot and killed. Steve was injured. A D.C. Protective Services Officer, Mack Cantrell, was wounded. Officer Cantrell, who was a press-room favorite, died days later in the hospital from a heart attack.

D.C. Councilman Marion Barry walked into the fifth-floor hallway to investigate the commotion and was hit by a shotgun pellet. He stumbled into the council chambers where he eventually was extracted by police and transported to a hospital; later that evening, Barry gave interviews from a stretcher to anxious reporters.

The District Building was one of three landmark buildings seized by the Muslim Sect. Armed with guns and machetes, they also stormed the B'nai B'rith headquarters in downtown Washington and the Islamic Center on Massachusetts Avenue.

We were positioned outside the 13th 1/2 Street public entrance to the District Building. Office workers were still spilling out of the building. Some had walked or run out on their own. Others were being escorted out by police. No one seemed to have the story on what was going on.

Ward 7 Councilwoman Willie Hardy was asking what's going on and suddenly collapsed on the sidewalk. I think she fainted.

Lieutenant Ike Fulwood arrived with Sergeant Richard Pennington. Two of my favorite cops. They brushed past me and went inside, guns drawn. Fulwood would later become chief of D.C. police. He would be in his office at headquarters the night the FBI arrested Mayor Marion Barry for smoking crack in a downtown hotel.

Our live satellite truck arrived and parked in the front and to the left of the District building. I'd be going live from the scene and sharing the crew with CBS correspondent Lee Thornton. I knew Lee from Cincinnati where she had been hired by a rival station, one of their first hires of an African American.

She joined CBS in 1977, becoming the first African American woman to cover the White House.

In 2003, at my induction into the Society of Professional Journalists Hall of Fame, she hugged me and revealed she was the one who nominated me for the honor. I was inducted along with NPR anchor Judy Woodruff and *New York Times* columnist William Safire, who was impressed that I delivered my acceptance speech without notes. I learned to do that by watching CBS correspondent Bruce Morton as we both reported live from Columbus, Ohio when John Glenn was first elected to the Senate.

Lee died of pancreatic cancer in September of 2013. Later that year she was inducted posthumously into the National Association of Black Journalists Hall of Fame.

My friend was flawless for those hours that now seem like minutes outside the District Building. Lee reported for the CBS evening news and I went live many times for our nonstop local live coverage.

The leader of the Hanafi Muslims and architect of the violent attack in the Nation's Capital was Hamaas Abdul Khaalis. Khaalis had once been a member of the Nation of Islam, but after he broke off from the Nation and publicly criticized the Nation in 1973, gunmen broke into their home headquarters on 16th Street Northwest. Seven members of Khaalis' immediate family were killed, including children and grandchildren.

Khaalis was convinced the men responsible were members of the Nation of Islam. He wanted the men arrested, convicted, and turned over to him. And he wanted the movie *The Message* banned because of what he called its sacrilegious portrayal of the prophet Mohammed.

Most of the hostages were at the B'nai B'rith building, which was located on Rhode Island Avenue.

During my live reports I was withholding a lot of information because lots of lives were at stake inside the District Building. I had learned that Mayor Washington had been trapped in his offices on the fifth floor of the building, at the opposite end of the elevator that had brought the two Hanafi gunmen up from the street level.

Highest priority for the police was getting the mayor out safely. One of the officers who helped form a human shield around him said, "You've never seen that old man move so fast!" But there were scores of other people who couldn't get out. They were barricaded inside the Council Chambers behind police officers who had turned tables over and prepared to meet the gunmen should they attempt to enter the double doors that Marion Barry had earlier stumbled through.

Khaalis telephoned my TV station. I looked up on a TV monitor in the field to see anchorman Max Robinson with a phone to his ear.

"You say you are going to kill me too?" That was Max's booming voice coming over the airwaves. Honestly, I'm not sure if he wasn't acting a bit, mining this moment for all it was worth.

From nearby police radios, I could hear that some councilmembers and their staff were hiding in fifth floor offices. No, they were really curtain cubicles, on the fifth floor, at the back of the building. Eventually a fire department ladder truck was backed up to the rear of the building. Food was smuggled in and eventually a ladder was extended, allowing the hostages to climb down safely to the street.

For hours we were glued to that live shot, having to repeat the same information, not wanting to share everything we knew would jeopardize the lives at all three locations. People had already suffered serious cuts and beatings.

The ordeal ended late the following day, thirty-six hours later, after Khaalis agreed to meet with the Iranian, Egyptian, and Pakistani ambassadors.

We were allowed into the fifth floor many hours after police had cleared the crime scene. The place looked like the battle scene that it was. Glass had been shot out at both ends of the hallway. Tables were left overturned in the council chambers.

It would take weeks to return the place to normal and allow people to return to their jobs. Some sought transfers or new positions away from City Hall. Millions of dollars would be spent over the years to redesign the building with state-of-the-art security and offices for each legislator and staff member. A new wing was added to the back of the building. The mayor's office was placed on the new sixth floor that was not accessible to the public.

All eleven Hanafi gunmen were tried and convicted. Khaalis died in prison in 2003.

CHAPTER 7

Who's Your Daddy?

It was June 19 of 1992 and the start of my morning ritual…sipping a strong cup of Starbucks, while on the laptop checking social media, reading the *Post, Times, Journal*, ESPN and clicking through every morning network newscast. I hate the cooking segments. It's hit or miss with the entertainment interviews, but I get it. There are movies to peddle, and the networks need the big names to keep regular folks watching. These morning shows are cash cows. The commercials pay the bills.

My mom was visiting from Louisville. She didn't come often, since her other children and her support system were in my hometown. I'm the only child who ever left home. It's worked for the both of us. I couldn't handle the family drama up close. Maybe I was broken as a child by the tension and violence. Since I had been away, my oldest brother Les and my younger brother David had both been arrested and sent to prison, twice. Robbery, burglary, receiving stolen goods, I think. I never sought out specifics. Didn't really matter. Nobody was killed. My oldest niece, Crystal, *was* shot to death in her own home as she came between two guys who were beefing.

Ma was muttering something to herself in the kitchen. I couldn't see her, she was turned away from me. "Your father died a couple years ago."

What? Did I hear her clearly? Leslie Johnson senior was dead. Why am I just hearing the news?

"No, Les is not your real father! Your daddy was named Robert Richard Marshall!"

Now she was sitting across from me in the breakfast room, holding a crumpled piece of paper. An old newspaper obituary. Ma extended it to me as evidence to support her claim.

I didn't really need proof. She was struggling with a truth that she had been keeping to herself and away from me, and maybe the world, for a very long time.

The only word I can think of to describe my reaction is *stunned*. This isn't somebody else's story. It belonged to my mother and now me. Les Johnson Senior was not my real Dad!

As her news washed over me, I was disappointed and angry at my mother. Why do this to me, why did I need to be told this news now? She explained that it was time! She didn't want my son and daughter to one day run into cousins at some time or place and not know. It didn't make sense to me back then. But years later, the kids would reach out and connect, maybe on Ancestry.com.

I was immediately interested in this Robert Richard Marshall. How and when did she hook up with him? Had he been some smooth talker, athlete, or entertainer who took advantage of her during those times when Les Senior had abandoned us? She and Les had David after I was born, right?

I couldn't imagine my mother initiating an affair, not my mother.

I left her sitting at the breakfast room table in silence. I abruptly excused myself and had to get to work. I was the angry victim, and I was intent on punishing her at that moment.

As I drove into the office, I thought back all those years. Did I miss a clue, should I have picked up on something during the rare infrequent visits from Les Senior? Did he suspect I wasn't his? The ridiculing I took from James Marbry—did he know, or at least suspect? I have more reason to not trust anyone, not even my mother!

At work, I sought out my good friend Gordon Peterson, the main anchor on the WUSA9 (CBS) six and eleven o'clock news. More importantly, Gordo had become one of my trusted friends at the station. He could see that I was upset. "My mom just told me that the man I thought was my father all these forty-two years is not my father!" There, now somebody else knew my sorry story. Turns out I'm a bastard! Gordon steered me away from "me" to my mother's situation.

He wanted to know "what courage" it must have taken for her to keep her secret for all these years. He seemed to have enough compassion for the two of us. Screw that! I wasn't ready to forgive. I stumbled through the next hour or so. I came up with my own assignments, my own stories, which news managers were always hoping would turn out to be exclusives. If I didn't have something by midday, I'd usually take what was available, what was needed for the news team. On this day, my big assignment would be finding out all I could about Robert Richard Marshall!

Ma was in Washington because my daughter Kurshanna was graduating from Wilson Senior High and my son Brandon was graduating from Shepherd Park Elementary School.

By the time I was able to call her from work, I was no longer upset. Ma had been crying. She had called my sister, Ordette, who was living in Cincinnati. Ordette was the only girl in our family, one of four siblings from Ma's marriage to James Marbry, her second husband. Ma told Ordette that she feared she had lost me and I would never speak to her again. That was one of the options that crossed my mixed-up mind, but it did not last for very long.

I wanted to know everything about Robert Richard Marshall. Like the title of the old Bill Withers song, I wanted to know "Who was he and what was he to you?"

Ma said he looked like me. Not that tall. A kind man, the one she should have married, but like her, he was already married with a child. She said he had left high school and joined the Navy.

They began their affair when he drove by and saw her standing at a bus stop. He had a car and that brought immediate status. Robert Richard Marshall had been a waiter at the Pendennis Club, an exclusive social club for White men only. No Blacks or women need apply.

Ma says she never told Robert Richard Marshall about me. He never knew she was pregnant. I never asked if she had ever considered not giving birth to me. Had that even been an option?

How she'd been able to keep my "natural" father a secret from Les Sr., and then James Marbry, I'll never know. I didn't ask because I didn't want to put her through that kind of pain. Frankly, who's to say they didn't know or at least suspect. I didn't look like any of my siblings. Les Johnson's three sons were taller, darker!

One of my mother's two first cousins, who we called Aunt Que, confessed well after my mom had died that they did know and helped keep Ma's secret all those years.

I have often wondered what Robert Marshall would have done had he known about me. Would he have insisted on being a part of my life? That would have meant only problems for his wife and the children they would have together. Would Robert Richard Marshall have been proud to call me his son and boast about the success that I had become? His loss, I've concluded.

I needed to know everything about my dad. I thought it could help me better understand myself, and I had to start with his children, my half-siblings. I would need help to find them and learn if they would even want to know me and share information about our father.

I first contacted my mother-in-law. Madge's mother, Evelyn Williams, worked at the state capitol in Frankfort. She was able to get a copy of Robert Richard Marshall's birth and death certificates. He died on September 22, 1986—six years before I learned about him. Cause of death was lung cancer. He passed away roughly one month before his sixty-first birthday. Every Black man I knew back in the day smoked! How many men were killed by cigarettes because greedy cigarette makers were insisting their products were not causing cancer?

Robert Marshall was born to William Marshall and Armenta Evans of Louisville. My dad's wife was Jenner Marshall and they raised a family on Hale Street in Louisville's west end, not far from where I had attended Shawnee High School. The school's stadium where I'd played football games was only a few blocks from their front porch.

It took a while, maybe a year or so, before I made contact with my new siblings.

My brother Philip, James' oldest son, had done some leg work for me. Using information I had uncovered, we found out that my dad's oldest son (turns out, his second-oldest son) lived on Grand Avenue. Can you believe it! Robert Jr. lived on the street, although blocks away, that intersected Grand Avenue Court where we had lived.

Philip suggested he approach Bobby in person to see if he might want to meet the older brother he didn't know existed.

Bobby had been born less than a year after me. He attended Male High School and later married his high school sweetheart,

Tanner. The Marshall children had been raised Jehovah's Witnesses by their mother, Jenner.

I got to admit, when I first learned this, I felt embarrassed. My only experience with Jehovah's Witnesses was Saturday mornings, when followers would knock on the door unexpectedly to share a scripture reading. We would hide in the kitchen or behind the curtains until they moved on.

When Philip arrived at his home, Bobby and his son Robby were on the roof finishing up an addition to their home. Phil was a captain in the Louisville fire department, and he was in the process of building his own home, so there was an immediate conversation starter: how to build your own house.

Phil introduced himself, ran down a list of people he knew in the neighborhood, in hopes of landing on a name or two that made a connection to give him an excuse to stay and keep talking.

Phil told Bobby that he had a step-brother who shared the same father, and that I lived in Washington, D.C. and wanted to make a connection if that would be okay with Bobby. Had Robert Richard Marshall, Jr. said, "Hell no!" that would have been the end of this story, but he said OK! I could reach out.

To this day, I never asked why he said yes. Was it the same curiosity that I had, or was it his faith? His way of helping put this stranger in D.C. at peace? Whatever the reason, I am so grateful.

I called Bobby. And then I was on my way to Louisville to meet him.

I drove into my hometown in June of 1993, around midnight. My BMW pulled into the curb lane of the downtown Galt House Hotel. I didn't have a reservation, probably because it was a trip made on impulse. The concierge made a call to the nearby Brown Hotel and I was checking into a room minutes later. The next day would be Father's Day, and I drove around in my hometown to mark the occasion.

I knocked on the door of Bobby's house and was far more anxious than nervous about who would be on the other side and what greeting I was about to get. Tanner answered: Bobby wouldn't be home till after five and I should come back. She meant it. He was going to be surprised by how much I looked like his dad, I thought. Tanner looked awfully familiar; Louisville's west end wasn't that big and I probably had met her growing up there.

My next stop was the Pendennis Club, the legendary monument to Louisville's segregated past, and Robert Richard Marshall's employer when he was a young man. I should have been dressed in my best dark suit, white shirt, and silk tie, maybe inquire about joining before revealing my true mission: finding some information about Robert Richard Marshall.

I walked through the doors in shorts and sneakers and with a confidence that must have said I wasn't that impressed with the place after all; I had been to the White House, a State Dinner, and the U.S. Capitol building on many occasions. This child of a domestic, a descendant of Kentucky slaves, had done pretty well for himself, with a lot of help, of course.

The General Manager of the Pendennis Club turned out to be a woman, a Louisville native, and a Catholic school product, like me, and she seemed excited to help me after I told her my story. She summoned an old Black man who also carried the name manager on his name tag. Sensing her insistence on helping me, the old man disappeared, and returned shortly with a photo. There was an image of four young Black men, maybe in their teens or late twenties. They were waiters at the Pendennis Club in what could have been the 1940s or '50s. They had the same white jackets and black slacks

SURVIVING DEEP WATERS

and could have been easily mistaken for a singing group like the Platters or Little Anthony and the Imperials.

"Here he is. Here's Robert Marshall." I looked at the picture and immediately broke into a smile.

"I don't even need you to point him out," I said. "That's him right there…third from the right!" I said to the old man and young woman, who clearly enjoyed my discovery and my first look at what my dad, Robert Richard Marshall, looked like!

"That's him," said the old man.

I left there with a copy of that picture. I certainly looked like him. He was better looking, but I wasn't far behind.

I next visited Robert Richard Marshall's gravesite at the Zachery Taylor Veteran's Cemetery. I wasn't sure what I should feel. I might have said "Hello and goodbye Dad"? I was missing a man I never knew existed until my mom broke the news at breakfast that day. I couldn't cry for a dad I never knew. So, I cried for me as I stood at Robert Marshall's gravesite.

This was the guy who should have taught me to play baseball!

I called Bobby's number and it was a quick pick-up. He wanted to see the brother he never knew existed.

"You must be Bruce! Hi, come on in." He didn't look like our dad, must have taken after his mom. We sat down just inside the door, neither saying much till Bobby said, "You look just like my father." Wow! What was I supposed to say to that? I asked if he had any pictures.

He pulled out a poorly shot photograph of his father and mother. The man in the photo is clearly ill. Thin! I'm thinking he already had cancer. Robert Junior is a good-looking guy, chocolate skin, straight hair, thinning at the top. He looks Ethiopian. Same height and build as me.

• 1 4 5 •

Minutes later we shook hands and I left again. Bobby would report back to his other siblings. In the next few weeks, Curtis would be calling me from his home in Milwaukee; Phyllis, the youngest would also be calling. I knew this was the beginning, but the beginning of what?

My second trip to Louisville was to meet my other new siblings and attend the service of a sibling who was no longer with us.

It was Tuesday, January 5, 1994, much of the East Coast was caught up in a brutal, frigid snowstorm. I was trying to get a flight out of Washington National for Louisville. Most flights were canceled or in danger of being canceled. I had woken up early and had hoped my 7 AM departure would be spared. I was anxious, like when I'm in pursuit of another big story. I had to get to Louisville because Antonio Marshall, my father's youngest child was being eulogized.

Tony had died from AIDS. He was only thirty and lived in Chicago to keep his homosexuality a secret from the rest of the family. The ceremony was to take place at Williams Funeral Home on Broadway, where most west end funerals take place when they don't take place in a church. A week before, Curtis had called from Chicago where Tony was hospitalized with but days to live. I had friends and colleagues who were gay and certainly attended my share of funerals of several who died in the early years of the AIDS epidemic, including radio legend Melvin Lindsay and TV anchor Max Robinson, before infectious disease trials came up with vaccines to prevent inevitable death for anyone who tested positive for HIV.

I was reluctant to travel to Chicago because I didn't want to intrude on Jenner Marshall's space as she shared this difficult time with her children. I had not yet met my father's wife. I explained it to Curtis and said that if it was okay with the family, I would be in Louisville after Tony's body was brought back home.

I thought that no young person needed excuses to leave Louisville and the South; I hoped Tony had found more acceptance in Chicago than he likely found in Louisville.

I got to the airport in a steady rain. It was before the snow and ice hit the ground and there was more than enough time before my 7 AM flight for Louisville and Tony's funeral. Before the day would end, I would meet all of Robert Marshall's surviving children. But this was bigger than that. By learning more about my natural father, I was hoping to learn more about me.

I got to the ticket counter where the agent apparently recognized me from TV and explained how I should have known better before setting out for Washington National. "That flight has been canceled!"

I was numb as I walked back to the airport garage, complaining to myself all the way about how they should have been giving refunds that morning. As I drove home, the heavy snow that had been above the clouds began to hit the ground. It became a driver's nightmare negotiating Rock Creek Parkway on my way back home.

School had been canceled for Madge, a teacher in suburban Montgomery County, and Brandon, at Shepherd Elementary School; they were both at home. Kurshanna was on campus at Howard University. Everybody, it seemed, was where they were supposed to be…except me.

I pulled into the driveway, let myself into the house, went upstairs, started unpacking my stuff, and then collapsed on my knees in the closet in a ball and started crying like a baby. Looking back, it must have been a combination of missing my brother's funeral, a brother I had never met and who certainly didn't know me, and missing the chance to meet the rest of my father's family.

I eventually pulled myself together and called Louisville. To my surprise they told me if I could get to Louisville later in the week everyone would remain. I went to work, anchored the six o'clock news that night. Thursday morning, I was back at the airport for that same 7 AM flight, which was on schedule this time. I was even bumped to first class. How did they know?

It's a short flight from D.C. to Louisville. We touched down just after 8 AM. I picked up a rental car and headed north on the expressway to downtown and the Brown Hotel at fourth and Broadway, which would become my headquarters for this "assignment," to meet anybody interested in meeting me, the illegitimate child, the accidental love child of Robert Richard Marshall.

I chose the Brown Hotel because my mom had worked there cleaning rooms as a young woman. I took pride in flopping down my American Express card to pay for one of their newly remodeled rooms. The excitement was off the charts. A gaping hole in my soul was about to be filled. What a story I had become. Even if nobody else would read or hear about this, I found it to be almost a spiritual journey, an assignment from on high to finish this! Whatever this was.

I dialed the phone number for Jenner Marshall's house. The same house in which she and my father had raised their six children all those years. Curtis answered and could hardly contain his excitement. He couldn't be faking it. We had exchanged pictures by mail. Like me, Curtis seemed to be an outlier in his family. He had graduated from the University of Louisville but couldn't wait to leave, and his compass took him to Milwaukee. He had done really well for himself. He married Janie, a doctor, raised a son, and became active in the public health community.

We would later run into one another in Washington during the Million Man March. I was working. He was part of a bus caravan that arrived from Wisconsin to attend the historic event. He vowed to find me in the crowd and he did. How? I will never know.

In Louisville, we agreed to meet at the Brown Hotel after I got breakfast and a much-needed haircut. I found a young barber not far from the hotel. Black men almost never let a stranger cut their hair, but I was in a fog trusting everything that God put in front of me that day. I tried to start a conversation and maybe bridge the gap with the barber who was more than half my age but to no avail. I left fifteen dollars for an eight dollar cut, feeling like the big fish coming home to find his roots.

At about eleven that morning Curtis arrived at the hotel. There was a knock at my room. Curtis was standing there with a young man who introduced himself as Robby, Bobby's eighteen-year-old son—my nephew!

Curtis and Robby look like Bobby. Brown skin, sharp features.

We didn't know whether to shake hands or hug, so we shook hands and stepped into the room. The real surprise was a huge picture of Robert Richard Marshall that Robby was proudly carrying. Robby worked at Kinkos and would later stop at work to make a copy of that picture for me to take back home to Washington. All three of us were amazed! I looked more like the man in that frame than either of his other two sons. Makes sense to me. I was his firstborn son.

I couldn't take my eyes off his image. Curtis, Robby, and I sat a few feet apart, smiling and trying to fill in the gaps, not knowing what they wanted to share and not knowing what I needed to hear. In that poster, Robert Marshall couldn't have been more than in his midtwenties or early thirties. A really good-looking guy in a dark jacket, white shirt, and knit tie.

He was better looking than the son he never knew. "That's your dad!" I would come to realize that Curtis was always looking to say the most positive thing in the most awkward situation. He seemed very skilled at avoiding and defusing controversy. Was that a learned skill from his training in public health, or did he acquire that from growing up in some difficult times? As I was fixed on the black and white image of our father, I became momentarily proud to be Robert Richard Marshall's firstborn son. Our relationship could become whatever I wanted it to be! I felt wherever he was, Robert Marshall knew what was happening in that hotel room and he approved.

They had also brought a picture of my grandmother Armenta. Robert Marshall's mother. Armenta looked White; she was clearly biracial. Curtis said the word was her father was White. That was a common narrative in Black families back in the day. There was no Ancestry.com and most people seemed okay to let muddled family history remain muddled. Otherwise, what was the point?

Robby would make copies for me to take home. That large poster of my dad hangs in my house today in an upstairs hallway. My mom once asked during a visit, "Why do you have that big picture of your dad hanging up there and not mine?"

I responded, "Because I have known you all my life but I am just getting to know him." She smiled. Ma was relieved that I knew, and she supported my reaching out to my new family. During a subsequent visit to Louisville, I took Curtis by the house to meet her.

The highlight of my visit to Louisville would be dinner with my siblings. All of them. Bobby would be there, and Shirley and Phyllis.

The time and location was left up to Bobby, who at forty-three was the same age as me, and was the man of this family. They picked me up at the hotel: Bobby, Curtis, Shirley, and Tana, Bobby's wife. I got into the front seat and immediately turned to face Shirley. She looked more like her dad than the others. Light skinned, pretty, and distant, maybe even suspicious of me and my intentions. She must have had a special relationship with her father, like me and my daughter Kurshanna. Did she feel her daddy had betrayed her along with her mother by having an affair with my mom, and what must she think of my mother? Shirley couldn't look me in the eye, but I knew she had seen me and seen her father in me.

Dinner was across the bridge in Clarksville, Indiana, not far from where my youngest sister, Phyllis, lived. Everyone, it seemed, was hoping this would convince Phyllis to join us.

I couldn't tell you what I had for dinner. I'm not sure I ate everything. I was overwhelmed with love and excitement from being with blood relatives I had never known. They were as close biologically to me as Leslie Johnson and James Marbry's children, whom I grew up with and knew as my brothers and sister. This was crazy. They would never replace my siblings, but there could be a place for them in my heart and life if they wanted it. I didn't write this script. Mary Pearson and Robert Richard Marshall had.

The conversation was fragmented and a lot shorter than what I'm used to. I'm a talker! Been around the world in the company of some powerful and famous people! Saintly and dangerous people too. I forget it's not a normal existence and most people aren't exposed to that kind of stuff. My siblings were no different.

Shirley wanted to know again, firsthand, how I learned from my mother that Robert Richard Marshall was my father. So, I told the story, again. Did I sound defensive? Perhaps. I added that my mom was a great lady despite the affair with her dad, that she had raised eight kids almost singlehandedly and at age fifty-two earned her degree from the University of Louisville. Hell, I wasn't about to apologize for my mom. She didn't need it.

"What about your dad?" I asked. My reporter training told me they were holding back. "What was he like?"

He was funny, they said; he liked the news, he liked *60 Minutes*, and he read the newspapers. "He woke me up and quizzed us about our presidents and senators," said Curtis. *Are they just saying this for me?* I wondered. "No, really," said Curtis.

I felt awkward referring to Robert Richard Marshall as "our dad." He hadn't been my dad. But then again, he was my dad. I came after Shirley, but before Bobby, Curtis, Phyllis, and Tony! What would he have thought of me? Was I looking for validation? Why would I need it from him?

"He would have been really proud of you.... 'Look at Bruce,' he would have said!" Shirley had the least to say, but later, over the phone, she would warm up and explain that she was tired.

So where was Phyllis? Phyllis is different, they would keep saying. Bobby broke away to call. She would be here and then she was going to bed. And then Phyllis showed up. No, let me rephrase that, she arrived!

Tall, dark, cute as a button. Had she been a model? My youngest sister walked straight to me and gave me a hug, not knowing how I was going to respond. We had never seen or talked to one another. I hugged her back and loved every second of it. We were the first to touch. Bobby, Shirley, even Curtis had kept their distance in their own way.

Phyllis and I wanted to get through the introductions to share our pain. There would be many phone conversations after that night. She had not gone to our father's funeral. She had never visited his grave. She said at dinner, in front of her siblings, the thing she remembered most about Robert Richard Marshall is that he was never there. Never at home, which meant she never expected anything from him, could never have her expectations dashed. There was so much more to share. So little time.

I wanted them to know that I wanted nothing more than to be a small part of their lives. I had been through some tough times and disappointments from the dads in my life—the real and the replacements—but in the end, it's been a good life. Then as if on que, this White guy with a beard walked up to our table to say, "Bruce Johnson, from Washington, D.C.? I love your work; you are the greatest!" I assured my brothers and sisters this wasn't staged. How could I have known?

And then it was time to go. Bobby and I liked one another, but he had to go to work the next day. Phyllis was glad she came. I had so many questions about everything: Had Phyllis been estranged from the family? And what was the relationship between Bobby and Curtis? Shirley would warm up to me. Maybe I would become the sibling that none of them had, but I had no idea what that might look like.

We dropped Phyllis off at her apartment. I would meet her husband, sons, and daughter next time.

Back in the car, Shirley wanted to know the name of the song on the radio. "That's the Righteous Brothers, I volunteered, as though this was a game show. I asked if they ever heard the name "The Love Child," my DJ name at the local WLOU in college. They had not.

We dropped Shirley off. When I got to my hotel room later that night there was a message to call her. Too late, I'll call in the morning. I got her at work the next day. We talked for an hour. It was a different Shirley: she said she loved me, that she was sorry she forgot to say goodbye. She was looking forward to seeing me and talking again. We did.

Back at Bobby and Tana's house, I met the rest of their family. Two daughters and Phyllis' oldest daughter, who lived with them. Curtis and I stopped at Robby's job at Kinko's to pick up my poster.

I got back to my room at the Brown Hotel, exhausted and emotionally drained. I placed Robert Richard Marshall's picture on the dresser where I could see it as I fell asleep. Goodnight, Robert Richard Marshall! Goodnight, Dad!

I left for D.C. the following day but nearly missed my flight. Curtis, Robby, and two of my gorgeous new nieces had come to the airport to see me off. Curtis would be leaving later for Chicago then Milwaukee. I had stopped by to see my mother before heading to the airport and brought her up to date on my entire visit. I left her a picture of my dad. It was the Robert Richard Marshall she knew from another time, when they were lovers.

CHAPTER 8

Marion Barry and Me

IT MIGHT HAVE BEEN IN the summer of 2014. Gray gaffer's tape held together the rear fender of the vehicle, a Jaguar, that had been built by Ford. It wasn't the lean classic Jag of the James Bond movies—the ride the British had been making all those years.

Dents and scratches pocked other sections of the vehicle, giving it the indisputable appearance of a hooptie—a type of abandoned car that young people salvage from junkyards or auto auctions. They would drive it proudly through the neighborhood, as if it were some fancy ride, rather than one wearing ten-day tags because it was unable to pass inspection to secure permanent license plates.

The Jaguar was familiar; I had seen it dozens of times and knew who was behind the wheel. Marion Barry made a U-turn on Pennsylvania Avenue, in front of the District Building. I watched his maneuver, surprised by the car's ailing condition. Barry put it in reverse, backing into one of the parking spaces reserved only for members of the D.C. Council. The former four-term mayor was in his third term as the Ward 8 councilman.

Still the heavyweight champion, getting up off the canvas for one more round. But how much more did the champ have left in the tank? Barry was now approaching seventy-eight years. He slowly climbed out of the vehicle.

At one time the "Mayor for Life" had enjoyed the luxury of chauffeur-driven Town Cars and Cadillacs. He was in the twilight of his political career and I thought him too old and too prominent to be driving a hooptie.

"What's happening, Bruce?" Barry said. He always looked forward to seeing me. We always had information to swap about the comings and goings in his city. It wasn't always the case when he was a lot younger and I was a "pit bull" reporter, as he liked to say.

He deliberately ignored the Fox 5 News reporter standing nearby, hoping to snag a quick interview with him about unpaid parking tickets. It was a story that hardly measured up to my scoop of Marion Barry being investigated for not paying his taxes.

"What's the deal with your car, Mr. Mayor?" I asked.

"I had a small accident. It's no big deal," he insisted.

Barry's driving was infamous; anyone who had been in the car when he was driving could attest to that fact. He had myriad minor accidents. Once, he even received a ticket for driving too slowly.

"Mr. Mayor, somebody has keyed your car," I said as we continued talking on the sidewalk in front of the District Building.

"What?" he responded, as if surprised.

"Who could have done this?" I asked.

"I don't know; it's the kind of thing that happens when you live in the ghetto," he said.

I grew up in the projects. He was right. But cars also got keyed in upscale neighborhoods like Georgetown in D.C.

He was in the middle of a running feud with a girlfriend. It began when the two were at the 2008 National Democratic Convention in Denver, where then-U.S. Senator Barack Obama received his first nomination for president. Barry was a delegate and had taken a woman a few decades his junior to the event. One night, in their hotel room, he requested a certain sex act. She declined. He threw her clothes—and her—out of the room. She slept in Barry's rented Cadillac, which was parked in the garage. Weeks and months later they were still at it.

A colorful figure, Barry's personal life, particularly his relationships with young, good-looking, stylish women, were the talk of the town and still happening long after his accomplishments had faded from his sixteen years as a revolutionary game-changing mayor of Washington D.C. The man, at times, was brilliant! Other times he left me asking him directly, "Are you serious?"

No African American mayor of any city had set out to do more for his people than Marion Barry. Marion brought minorities into city government jobs—not just on the front lines but as middle- and upper-middle managers and at cabinet level. Many of those appointees were the beneficiaries of civil rights laws, college educations, and affirmative action efforts. Barry created a summer jobs program guaranteeing part-time work for every teenager in public or private school. But in time he became his own worst enemy. Four terms, sixteen years in office, was probably two terms too many.

I wanted to be both his friend and the good journalist who broke all the big stories out of the Marion Barry administration. We both discovered from the beginning, you can't always be friends in politics and media unless you both have very short memories.

Ambition is the fuel that drives most successful people in Washington. Marion Barry and I were no different. Poor boys who came to town determined to not be ignored...to do some good and remain relevant after we were done.

For me and my upbringing under Louisville's system of segregation, oftentimes when Whites are in charge and Blacks are at the receiving end, it's hard to siphon what's direct or even indirect racism or just a different viewpoint. In public and private organizations, including newsrooms, oftentimes they are one in the same. Systemic racism always will provide cover for indifference or a difference of opinion.

Marion Barry developed his viewpoints on race from an earlier time, a brutal time to be born in the deep south. In Mississippi, a place I had only heard about and feared and vowed never to be caught there by night or day.

As a civil rights leader, and later D.C. Mayor, Marion Barry wouldn't hesitate to use race as a weapon—a call to arms for Black constituents, a battering ram to put White people on the defense. From my view as a veteran broadcast journalist and more importantly as a Black man in America, he was often right, but he used race often to cover his own inexcusable behavior. He knew Black people wouldn't abandon him. In private conversations they expressed disappointment. But they shook their heads while continuing to vote for him.

Marion Barry was never accused of stealing money. He wasn't a thief. A number of his cabinet members including employment services director and campaign manager, Ivanhoe Donaldson and former Deputy Mayor Alphonse Hill, did go to prison for pocketing taxpayer funds.

Ambitious prosecutors weren't convinced! They suspected Barry was using a controversial minority set aside program as a cover for white-collar crime, kickbacks, influence peddling, and more! They couldn't have been more wrong! A Black businessman, contractor, and Barry supporter, John Clyburn was put on trial three times. He was acquitted in one case and juries failed to reach verdicts in two more cases. Clyburn is brother to Congressman Jim Clyburn, the powerful Democrat and member of the House leadership team.

Here's what was true. Every D.C. developer, Black and White, was donating to Barry's subsequent reelection campaigns. That's how business and politics came together in D.C. Still is.

Some of those Black businesspeople became rich through those minority government contracts, including BET founder Robert Johnson, real estate developer Donald Peebles, and entrepreneur David Wilmont. Wilmont and his legal wingman, Frederick Cooke, were among Marion Barry's closest friends and longtime advisors. Cooke, a D.C. native and Howard law school graduate, was Corporation Counsel under Barry—a position which eventually became Attorney General. Wilmont was a Georgetown University law school grad and former dean of the school. He and Cooke were forever on speed dial, at a pro bono rate, when Barry ran into personal headwinds of any kind, including divorces. Critics complained their close relationship with Barry resulted in the kind of access on all levels that competitors would kill for. Of course, far more White businesspeople, already rich, became more wealthy when Barry was mayor. Abe Pollin, Oliver Carr, Robert Linowes, Steve Harlan, and Donald Graham are but a few of the names that wielded influence while perched at the Greater Washington Board of Trade.

In the end some of those same wealthy business people, White and Black, were refusing to return his phone calls. One complaint I heard was Marion had made it impossible to be caught helping him.

At the start, there was no way I could have become friends with Marion Barry. He *was* often the story I was after. The center of gravity—political and otherwise—in D.C. The District of Columbia was my beat! Marion Barry was D.C.! He described me early on to friends as a "pain in the ass."

He would invite some of his staunch male supporters to stand in the back of press conferences to react out loud to some of my tough questions about services that were falling short in poor communities. The biggest and loudest complaints came as I was seeking answers to rumors that Barry was using drugs and hanging out in places like "This is It" and the Camelot Show bar Strip Club; but also in private homes while in his government-funded private car with a D.C. police security escort was parked outside until well into the morning hours.

I was tough but wanted to be fair. I knew some White influencers, including cops, resented his popularity among Blacks and progressive Whites. They resented his arrogance and assumed I resented it too. I didn't! I covered a lot of arrogant men, White and Black. Ivanhoe Donaldson told me before his death that "Marion always assumed he was the smartest person in the room."

Barry, like all good politicians "played" reporters sometimes to win favorable coverage. Black reporters got special attention when he needed us most, comparing our known newsroom struggles to the country's racial history. Barry, Jessie Jackson, and some others expected us to promote their messages and mute their shortcomings that could have made news. It was a constant struggle.

I didn't want to be the Black journalist who took down an important Black leader unless that leader was engaged in the same kind of conduct that would take down any public figure.

I had colleagues who left the business rather than repeatedly be assigned to follow up newspaper stories critical of Black leaders. The systemic racism, the not-so-subtle comments in newsrooms pushed some good minority journalists out the door.

Viewer criticism is another issue. It's increased tenfold with social media. Aren't Facebook, Twitter, and more built for negative comments from anonymous people who wouldn't dare put their real names or faces behind their comments?

Live, in-person retaliation is different. It can be downright scary, especially if you're caught on the street defenseless! I once was threatened with a beatdown on the street for a story I couldn't recall, but one in which the angry man insisted I omitted his account of what happened. People had been killed. He says my story included police comments but not his account of what happened. I don't recall the story. I asked the man why he didn't reach out to me with his concerns. I'm always willing to correct a mistake. An advantage and disadvantage to being a local city reporter...I was always available. But I don't go out much to mingle with large crowds especially if there is booze or weed, and I always know where security is standing guard as well as where the nearest exit is.

I have always sought to protect my immediate family. I rarely flaunt my wife and children in public view, and certainly not on my social media pages.

Marion Barry had a different take. By the time I arrived In Washington, he'd already had his sights on becoming mayor. He needed the perfect wife to smooth his rough edges and calm worries about his bachelor lifestyle. He found the perfect wife in Effi Barry, his third attempt at marriage.

I covered Barry's upset win for mayor in 1978 over the incumbent, Walter Washington and D.C. Council Chairman Sterling Tucker. Barry admitted that a TV debate that I hosted with some tough questions helped his performance. "Stumbling fumbling government" is how he described the Walter Washington administration. In a display of unheard-of media savvy, Barry called cameras to a government warehouse, where food for the poor was allowed to spoil. He failed to acknowledge that, the day before, I was the reporter who uncovered that warehouse story.

It was in 1979, in the D.C. Council chambers, where Supreme Court Justice Thurgood Marshall, the first African American to serve on the highest court, administered the oath of office. Barry's elegant wife Effi stood at his side. The former Effi Slaughter of Toledo, Ohio, was born to a sixteen-year-old unwed mother. She never knew her Italian father.

Justice Marshall's presence cast the inaugural with a patina of historic significance. I was standing in awe but a few feet away from the civil rights icon, who ended the ceremony with, "You're in," to Mayor Marion Barry.

This is why I was meant to be in Washington, D.C., where national figures brush alongside us local folk at City Hall, the local grocery store, or a popular restaurant. If that doesn't move you, stroll the national mall or tour a museum or historic civil war battlefield at nearby Manassas or Gettysburg.

An inaugural parade put a ribbon on Barry's inauguration. He was joining a court of dynamic Black mayors in cities through-out, including Richard Hatcher in Gary, Indiana; Carl Stokes in Cleveland, Ohio; Kenneth Gibson in Newark, New Jersey; and Coleman Young in Detroit, Michigan.

We cheered the new mayor, and I wanted Marion Barry to be successful. I wasn't going to be forced to take sides as some White managers in the newsroom viewed us with suspicion. Are we with the watchdog journalists like them or with the brothers? My answer would have been both. I had an obligation to report any story fairly. I also had a responsibility to make sure minority voices that had been unheard or unsolicited were now heard. I insisted in editorial meetings that my White colleagues come to the same conclusions, and that meant some of them had to change.

African American reporters like myself were forced to fight constantly to ensure our voices were heard—that our stories carried weight and were not routinely pushed to the last few minutes of an hour-long newscast. One of my executive producers began the practice that D.C. stories were penciled in last before even hearing from me in the field.

⌒

I was reminded daily of the meaning of that West African proverb: "Until the lion tells the story; the hunter will always be the hero."

A big part of me needed Barry to succeed. My mother in Louisville loved him. I brought her to Washington and showed her off at social gatherings that I attended or hosted, knowing the mayor would be there. My in-laws tagged along to the annual backyard cookout at the mayor's home in southeast with Effi Barry. The mayor represented my aspirations, in a parallel but equally dangerous universe. And because he looked like me, and the people he served looked like me, there eventually evolved a special connection.

Marion Barry made covering City Hall fun. It was the center of local journalism that competed every night for time on the local and national broadcasts. I made it more interesting by not confining myself and my camera crew to the wide corridors of City Hall. My day could easily begin or end in the streets, on a street corner, in a housing project, or a school to tell my stories where the impact would be felt most, the community.

Eventually, other news operations caught on and began hiring the best reporters and dispatching them to the streets as well. Sam Ford, at the competing WJLA (ABC), is an example.

The City Hall beat became a coveted broadcast beat. The shy rookie showed up at great peril, although I made a point of reaching out to new arrivals, assisting them with the basics of the story.

During the early days of Barry's first term, no one would have forecast that he would eventually become a member of the club everybody dreaded—local and national elected leaders who landed in serious trouble, including prison.

From the beginning, he had put together an all-star team of former activists and holdovers from the Jimmy Carter administration who were not eager to leave town after a single term in office.

He told me he had to desegregate just about every agency in city government. The two biggest fights, and maybe the longest, were changing the fire and police departments. When he took over as mayor, both were practically reserved for White males. No Blacks, no Hispanics, and no women need apply.

Isaac "Ike" Fulwood called Barry a change agent. A native Washingtonian, Fulwood joined the D.C. Metropolitan Police Department in 1964. Twenty-four years later, in July 1989, Barry appointed him police chief.

"When I came on the department, Black officers barely rode in cars. And you didn't see Black supervisors," Fulwood told me during an interview. "When Marion came in, [he] said that has got to go."

"When they sent a list over to promote people, Marion would ask how many of them are Black and if they would say, 'None,' Mayor Barry would say 'Then there won't be any promotions,' continued Fulwood. "He knew there were qualified Blacks. That fight went on for years, perhaps Barry's entire first term. But eventually changes were made."

Racial tension in the D.C. fire department was even worse. Burton Johnson was already in place as the city's first African American fire chief, but he had been in the department since 1943 and had had to wait more than twenty years to rise above the rank of private. That pattern, a *Washington Post* editorial noted, was not uncommon for Black firefighters. During the years he labored in the department, Johnson attended American University, Ohio State University, the University of Maryland, and Purdue University. There might not have been a more qualified fire chief in the entire country.

Barry may not have appointed Burton Johnson, but he made sure every fire chief in the Barry administration was Black. He essentially ensured the District government was representative of the city's population. That meant, when it came to jobs, Blacks were always at the head of the line. By some estimates, the number of city employees ballooned from about 28,000 to nearly 40,000 employees.

There was a time when Black people couldn't even walk through the front door at City Hall to pay their water bills. Under Marion Barry they would soon be running the water company.

Mayor Barry and I both got help in buying our first homes in the District. He got the reduced interest rate that Independence Savings and Loan gave to its well-connected clients. Other financial institutions offered the same perks to their high-profile clients.

My first home was a $75,000 purchase at 5300 Kansas Avenue in Northwest. Lois Dyer, a colleague, D.C. native and expert on all things Washington, had pointed me to the area and the house, a semi-detached, and mere fifteen-minute drive to work. A really good, middle-class neighborhood, called Manor Park.

Ron Townsend, the TV station's first African American General Manager helped me acquire my house. He drove me to the *Washington Post* credit union, had me sign up as a member, and then walked me through applying for a loan of several thousand dollars that I used as a down payment for the house. No White manager had ever offered to do as much for me. I don't know they did as much for any employee. Ron would later become the first African American voted in as a member of the Augusta National Golf Club?

At times, our first home became a clubhouse for local journalists. Milton Coleman of *The Washington Post* decided we would celebrate one of my birthdays with a party, at my house. He moved the furniture so we could pack close journalist friends, Black and White and every hip Barry administration official, into the center hall, living room, dining room, kitchen, and basement.

Eugene Robinson of the *Post* came. Penny Micklebury of WJLA TV, the rival ABC station, was there. She later successfully sued the station when she was passed over as news director; the position had gone to a White male with far less experience. Mike Davis of the old *Washington Star* newspaper also showed up for the party. WTOP was represented too.

City administrator, Elijah Rogers, was the top city official there, until the mayor himself arrived, sporting a cowboy hat. I made sure the Metropolitan Police Department's Fourth District station had a marked cruiser out front, not for security purposes, but to impress my working-class neighbors; they marveled at how the new TV reporter on the block had a party and Mayor Marion Barry was there.

All that celebrity really had little effect; across the street a couple of young guys were running a thriving curbside reefer business out of their mother's house. The traffic to the corner seemed nonstop. They didn't appreciate the disruption in curbside sales the night of my party.

"Why are you living in this neighborhood?" I was asked one evening. "How much money do TV reporters make?" When the radio was stolen out of my Austin Healey 3,000 convertible while parked in front of my house, I immediately suspected my young drug-selling neighbors. I had no proof, but there, I said it!

Five years after that first real estate purchase, I cashed in, using the profit to purchase another house in need of serious repair but now worth considerably more in D.C.'s Colonial Village, which is located along the city's platinum coast.

Marion Barry stopped by the new house for a couple of cook-outs. It helped that my new neighborhood was located in a Black, upscale, voter-rich Ward 4 section of town. It's a haven for Black educators, lawyers, judges, doctors, and business leaders. Most of the folks are graduates of Howard University, although Morehouse, Maryland, and some Ivy League grads are sprinkled in. The neighborhood, like the rest of the city, has been heavily gentrified.

Christopher Barry, Marion and Effi's only child, became a fixture around my family. He and my son Brandon were the same age and attended Tot's Development Center, a preschool for the children of Black families. The founder, Clarise Davenport, made no secret that Christopher Barry was her favorite and Bruce Johnson's son, Brandon, was her second-favorite student. My home telephone number was the first one Christopher memorized.

After winning a third term, Barry was in trouble, politically and personally. I remember as part of a victory lap, he wanted to tour a public housing complex in Southwest, D.C. It should have been a photo-op showing residents were still madly in love with him.

I got to the complex before Barry and interviewed a dozen tenants who complained about the need for repairs. During the campaign, Barry had promised changes.

As he stepped out of his police-driven Ford Sedan, I whispered to him, "These people are really upset with you."

"Fuck 'em! They didn't vote," said Barry.

He knew the remark wouldn't make it on the news that night. Not because he didn't say it, but my cameraman was not nearby to record it. He could come back later and claim I was lying or made it up. He had done that before.

During the latter part of his second term into his third, his behavior had become bizarre to everybody around him. There were instances, like the time he chased a woman around the conference table in his office. "I have never had a lesbian before!" The woman, a leader in the LGBTQ community, relayed the story to me. She remained a Barry supporter till the end.

People noticed when the mayor dropped in at the Camelot, a downtown D.C. strip club. He'd spend a little time on the main floor or walked upstairs to talk with Grace Shell, one of the performers. When Barry showed up uninvited at her home early one morning, it became news. He told me on camera he was there to talk with her young son. She said on camera, in an interview, arranged for me by her irate boyfriend, that she had not invited the mayor, and her son was too young to know or care who Marion Barry was.

The mayor later told me while laughing, "I was really interested in her roommate." The roommate, Kelly was not a dancer, but she was incredibly attractive according to Grace Shell's former boyfriend, nevertheless....

One night during a live appearance on our broadcast show called *After Hours*, I watched anchor our Gordon Peterson interview the mayor, who was decked out in a tuxedo and bowtie, coming from or going to an important event. Peterson asked Barry directly, "Are you using drugs?"

Surprised and angered by the question, he wore a look that said: *I want to kick this White guy's ass!* That's how Barry would later explain the encounter to me.

"No, and I resent you asking me that," he eventually replied to Peterson on TV.

Years later, during a period of deep reflection, that same Marion Barry told me, as we stood on Pennsylvania Avenue looking east to the U.S. Capitol, "I wasn't the first or the only elected official to use drugs recreationally." Interestingly, that confession came on the same spot where, years later, he would park his hooptie.

On November 18, 1990, I was at home watching TV when word came through on a rival TV station that Mayor Marion Barry had been arrested in a drug bust at a downtown hotel. I still had a shirt and tie on hours after work. I leaped from a basement chair and rushed to work. Every journalist in town was doing the same thing.

Barry's closest advisors seemed the most surprised by his arrest, including D.C. Councilmember Anita Bonds, a longtime friend and political advisor.

"You know Bruce, it was surreal for me. I wasn't aware of the mayor having a problem like that. I always thought that he drank too much. I didn't know what signs to look for. He told me, 'Anita, don't you think if I had a problem, I would do it around you, you're a friend.' And I'm like, 'Okay.'"

"If you haven't been in it, you don't really know." Anita and others were prepared to launch Barry's reelection the following day when he was arrested at the Vista Hotel.

"I was devastated," said Bonds.

She wasn't alone. An entire city was devastated!

The night of the arrest, while lights were on and every news-room desk occupied, I got the big tip. Assignment Manager Pat Casey picked up the phone. Casey was brash, confrontational when he felt he needed to be. A good, old-school newsman. "Johnson, somebody on the phone, and he only wants to talk to you. Says he has information on the Barry arrest!"

We had been at work only a few minutes pounding the phones to confirm that Mayor Marion Barry had been busted at a down-town hotel. I had rushed to the station from home after seeing the newsroom cut into regular programming with the headline. No one had details.

Casey and I decided to give the caller a codename. Here, I'll call him "the Falcon." It's not the actual name we agreed to.

My source told me that Barry had not stumbled into a sting operation. The drug bust had been set up by the FBI and a couple D.C. detectives with the sole purpose of catching Barry using drugs. That was my first live hit on air.

The Falcon obviously watched my report and called back with more. The FBI had used Barry's former girlfriend, Rasheeda Moore, to get him to the Vista Hotel room where they videotaped Barry smoking crack.

Damn!

I rushed on the air with the new information. By that time, it was clear that I had the ball; the majority of our news team began asking what they could do to assist me.

There was one more exclusive: the girlfriend's name was Rasheeda Moore! Never heard that name before. The FBI had brought her and her kids back to D.C. from California. The FBI babysat the kids at an undisclosed location while she lured Barry to the hotel where she got him to smoke FBI-supplied crack.

The Falcon's information put us far ahead of the competition that night. By the time the evening was over, Barry had been released on his own recognizance to return to his home in Southeast. His son, Christopher, had been brought home by the preschool director, Clarise Davenport, who had to cover the boy's head to protect him from photographers.

The day after Barry uttered those famous words, "The bitch set me up," at the Vista Hotel, the Falcon was instructing me to go to a nondescript motel in Northern Virginia. I grabbed cameraman Greg Guise and my associate producer Jody Small.

Minutes after we arrived, an FBI agent walked past Jody and me, his arm around this woman, not tightly, but clearly guiding her to a waiting car in the parking lot. At first glance, I thought they could have been a legit couple, not married but dating, maybe even a side piece, hooking up at midday.

The woman was dressed in black with a big hat that covered her eyes. I'm not sure what drew Jody's suspicion. But her instincts were on point. She yelled out in her soft voice, "Rasheeda!" That was enough for the government's key witness to turn in surprise to see who could have possibly recognized her.

The FBI agent sprang into action, clearly pissed that they had been discovered. He wasn't sure how much danger we posed to the operation. He moved quickly to the car, where he turned at me and yelled, "FBI! Get the fuck out of the way!"

I took a position behind the vehicle in its direct path, preventing him from backing out of the parking space. I was more nervous than scared but determined to buy time for Greg to come running from the other end of the parking lot. The agent shouted at me again. I knew I was about to get into a load of trouble if other agents arrived on the scene.

"Show me some identification. How do I know who you are?" I shouted, before yelling, "Bruce Johnson, Channel 9 news!" I wasn't fully sure why I was volunteering information that he wasn't asking for.

My cameraman was finally in place at the rear passenger side of the car. Greg was able to get on the right-rear passenger side to capture images of the woman in the big hat and sunglasses as the car backed out and burned rubber as it sped off.

We were pumped. We had gotten our video. It made page one that night on the newscast. It was a brief moment—we had to slow the video down to make it last more than the seconds it took to take it. But it was an exclusive! That's what I had come to live for as a street reporter. It's what my viewers and colleagues had come to expect from me.

All that went down in the summer of 1990.

National figures, like activists Jesse Jackson, Jr. and the Reverend Al Sharpton, were at the courthouse. Nation of Islam Leader Louis Farrakhan had to get a higher courts permission to attend the trial after the government tried to bar his attendance, claiming it could add to tensions.

The mayor had claimed he had been targeted by the government. Just another Black leader singled out for investigation.

"I thought they were scoundrels to do it that way. To set Barry up to smoke crack," explained Anita Bonds. "In fact, in court, we were prohibited from using entrapment as a defense."

Reporters wondered aloud on camera if there would be violence in the streets as a response to the FBI setting up Barry. I felt that reporting was irresponsible because I knew police were the source of the reports. None of my contacts were predicting violence. It never happened. News managers were preparing for it. I'm convinced some of those who remained in the newsroom were looking forward to it.

The out-of-town protestors worried me most. I don't recall the names of the national groups. I didn't recognize any faces. I had covered combustible events that could explode in a second. I had no hint that I would soon become a lynchpin for such an event.

I was used to being singled out for "working for the man," being a pawn in the conspiracies to take down Black leaders. I was constantly asking myself, *Was I being used? Had I been an unwitting pawn?* I certainly hope not. I pointed out every chance I could that the government had supplied the crack cocaine that Marion Barry had smoked—that some law- enforcement figures opposed their entrapment of the mayor, not to mention threatening Rasheed Moore with jail, on pending charges, if she didn't cooperate.

This crowd outside the court room wasn't local. They didn't know me or my work. But someone pointed and then outed me as part of the media. In seconds I was surrounded by an angry mob of African Americans screaming words I can't remember. They scared the hell out of me. I wasn't sure how to get away; the more I backed up, the more people seemed to cut off my path out of there. How would this end? I was being crowded, then bumped, and getting dizzy.

Suddenly, out of nowhere, I felt this huge hand reach for my arm through the hostile bodies. That arm forcibly pulled me away from the crowd. It was a uniformed cop who pulled me some feet and into a nearby police cruiser. It wasn't a D.C. police car; but a Special Police vehicle assigned to D.C. protective police Sergeant Mayfield, who knew me from his guard post at the District Building. The Protective Services department guards several local government buildings. One of its officers, Mack Cantrell, had died from injuries he sustained in 1977 when Hanafi Muslims stormed the District building.

Sergeant Mayfield didn't ask where I wanted to go. We didn't stop until he pulled into the circular driveway in front of my TV station. He opened the door. I stepped out from the passenger side and thanked him. He could see I was okay. He pulled away. I was grateful.

Was the Marion Barry prosecution racially motivated? Perhaps. I've known racist cops, prosecutors, judges, politicians, and journalists since the beginning of my career, going back to Cincinnati.

The FBI had conducted surveillance on civil rights leaders, including the Reverend Martin Luther King, Jr. There were tons of files that had been kept on other individuals. Agents or FBI collaborators had been placed inside selected organizations to facilitate investigations, but these facilitations often really amounted to unbridled harassment.

Barry knew that history. He knew he had done drugs with the people who testified at his trial under oath. He was arrogant and seemed to flaunt his ability to stay ahead of local police, the FBI, and his own associates who, when caught and confronted with jail time, were no longer willing to cover for the mayor.

Marion Barry would have walked out of room 727 at the Vista Hotel had he been sober enough to suspect a setup. Rasheeda invited him up, for what, if not to rekindle their prior sexual relationship, of which sex was certainly a major part. On the FBI tape, she and not Barry suggested they do drugs, at times persistently, and when he begged off saying he didn't do that anymore, her girlfriend was at the ready and responded in short order to the Vista hotel with the crack.

The Falcon had claimed there was sex between Barry and Rasheeda Moore on the video shot by the FBI. That appears to have been false information. Prosecutors denied it when we reported the claim. The video shown in the courtroom does not show sex between the two. I never asked Barry about it. In his book, he doesn't claim they had sex. He only says prosecutors were not going to allow us to see everything that's on the video.

One of the last tips from The Falcon came after Barry's conviction. I was told to go to the basement of the FBI field office in Northern Virginia and I would find an invitation that had gone out to field agents who worked on the Marion Barry case. There would be a recognition event and agents would be coming in from the field. The FBI was really proud of its work.

I took a veteran WUSA9 cameraman, Frank McDermott, with me. Frank was a smart and fearless cameraman and journalist, but he also needed to be a White cameraman! I was tenacious, but if this turned out to be a setup, I felt more comfortable having a White colleague along to back up this Black reporter's story. I was always aware of the strengths and weakness of my support team in the field. There were several stories when I insisted, I needed a "Brother" for backup.

Frank dropped me off in front of the building. It might have been conspicuous if we both went inside. I never want to put my reporting team at risk of anything out on the streets. I went inside. As instructed, I hit the elevator button for the bottom floor. Once there, I spotted a cigarette machine, right where my source said it would be. I reached my hand to the top and pulled off the printed invitation. We aired the new information with a picture of the invite on our newscast that night. There was more backslapping in the newsroom from coworkers. My sources say that FBI field celebration at the Northern Virginia field office was canceled.

Meanwhile, Marion Barry was undeterred. The morning after his arrest and release from custody, he was calling a meeting of his department heads. This was the day everybody had been preparing for Barry to announce his candidacy for reelection.

The late police chief Ike Fulwood had told me he was incensed and let his boss know he wasn't coming to the meeting. "As I have always said to him, I have a certain amount of respect for you because you made me chief and you never mistreated me personally. But you let everybody down when you did that because you had moved the city in a certain direction and it was just off balance that you allowed this to happen."

Barry served nearly six months in federal prison when most other first-time offenders would have gotten a suspended sentence. He wasn't convicted of the crack charge. The jury of ten Blacks and two Whites couldn't reach a unanimous verdict, because of the entrapment no doubt. Barry was convicted of another drug possession charge. Again, any other first-time coke offender would have gotten off.

⤙

In 1992, when Barry was released from federal prison in Loretto, Pennsylvania, more than three hundred people in cars and buses were waiting to meet him. I was there too with my cameraman. We had been embedded in the caravan from Washington, D.C., organized by the Reverend Willie Wilson, pastor of Union Temple Baptist Church in Anacostia. The rumor started circulating that he was going to run for mayor. But that was two years away. He couldn't sit idle for that long. He also had to test the waters. Had people forgiven him, truly?

I should have known he would go after the one seat he knew he could win easily. It didn't matter that the seat was occupied by Barry's friend and ally: Wilhelmina Rolark. She represented Ward 8 on the D.C. Council. Barry challenged Rolark. It wasn't close. He eventually won 70 percent of the vote.

Two years into his term as Ward 8, Councilman Barry took aim at his old job. Marion Barry defeated Sharon Pratt, to win a fourth term as Mayor. It would be his final term before deciding he couldn't win again and settled for being the Ward 8 legislator representing some of the city's poorest citizens, and staunchest Marion Barry supporters. Much of his final years were spent doling out wisdom, accepting the love and gratitude of many, and ignoring lasting critics, who dwelled on what else could have been.

↵

In 2014, Marion was approaching eighty. His health had been failing, with quick trips to Howard University Hospital. It was where he always went when he didn't want the media to know how sick he was from a number of ailments, including diabetes.

I should have been prepared for the call I got Saturday night, November 23, 2014. I had just gotten home from anchoring the 11 o'clock news on WUSA9 TV on CBS.

"Bruce, he's gone," a woman staffer said, in tears, from Greater South Community Hospital, not far from Barry's home in the city's Southeast quadrant. I recognized the voice, a longtime friend and political operative from his circle of friends and associates. But it took a minute to wade through the tears and barely audible sounds she was muttering. Finally, I got it: Marion Barry had just died, and I was the person the mayor would want her to call with the story. She hung up, unable to say anything more. I was stunned.

I called Bill Lord, the news director for WUSA9.

"You want me to go back to work and go live from the newsroom with this?" I asked him, knowing a story didn't get any bigger. Bill said it was so late, staying on Twitter would suffice.

I posted: Barry had collapsed on his front porch. His volunteer driver was with him. A call to 911 got him to the hospital in minutes, but he had been in cardiac arrest. At seventy-eight years old, Marion Barry was gone. The tweets went viral.

"Bruce, has somebody hacked your Twitter account?" a familiar voice from a female Barry supporter was asking on my cell phone. She couldn't even say his name or ask the question, *Has Marion really died?* I wanted her to know my cell phone had not been hacked.

"No, it's true. He's gone!"

Marion Barry had been knocked down more times than most people. He always seemed to get back up punching, refusing to be defeated.

I witnessed that political stamina firsthand. I covered him for almost four decades. No other broadcast reporter had that record of longevity. Certainly, none knew him better!

He would agree. Here's what he wrote in his autography *Mayor for Life: The Incredible Story of Marion Barry, Jr.*, which I didn't read until I started writing this chapter: "Best Wishes to Bruce Johnson. One of the few journalists in America that is honest. You have let your job get in the way of Our Friendship. Marion Barry 06/17/2014." That was slightly over five months before his death.

He was right.

I was the only journalist invited to speak at Marion Barry's funeral. He planned his own homegoing ceremony that ended with his casket being driven through all eight Wards of the city. The outpouring when it reached Martin Luther King in Ward 8 can now be compared with the community outpouring I witnessed for Muhammad Ali's casket in my hometown of Louisville. I was moved that Marion Barry chose me to be the only journalist to speak at his funeral.

I was on stage with his son Christopher and his widow Cora Masters Barry. There were local and national clergy there. The ceremony went long.

The funeral was carried live by all the local TV stations. That meant I was on everybody's TV set that morning and C-Span, which was broadcast nationwide.

I tried one last time to explain Marion Barry to the rest of the world. I shared a story that I had been told by the former Ward 2 Councilman, Jack Evans.

Evans was one of several candidates in a crowded field trying to unseat an incumbent Marion Barry. Evans wanted to understand the unwavering poor and middle-class African American support for Barry. He asked an old Black man following a candidates' debate, "What's the attraction to Barry?"

The old man said, "Okay, I'll tell you. If there was a dollar left there on that table, I know Marion Barry is fighting for me to get a piece of that dollar. I can't say that about the rest of y'all."

The applause and laughter let me know they knew that I "get it." I understood the loyalty to Barry. He never stopped fighting for African Americans at all levels. A lot of our heroes have weaknesses.

Gentrifiers may wonder, along with tourists, how D.C.'s elected leaders, Black and White, voted to honor Marion Barry with the placement of a prominent statue in front of the John A. Wilson Building on Pennsylvania Avenue, blocks from the White House, U.S. Capitol, Washington Monument, and memorials on the Mall. Folks who have been in the District of Columbia, who lived through some astonishing years, know the entire Marion Barry story.

Other cities and towns have their own imperfect political figures who left huge footprints and incredible histories. In my opinion, there may never be any one as substantial as Marion Barry.

CHAPTER 9

Get Here If You Can

"I'M REALLY AFRAID FOR YOU and your brothers. Y'all never been through something like this." Ma was dying from pancreatic cancer. It was almost spring in 2006. She had summoned me and two of my siblings to her hospital bedside.

We were grown men but we would always be Ma's boys. She was attempting to preside over perhaps one more family meeting in which she issued one last set of instructions.

⤻

Ma had surrendered! To her medical team, her faith, and to what we her sons felt should come next.

Mary Johnson-Marbry had buried two ex-husbands, James Marbry and Leslie Johnson. She had buried her mother Ivo, who returned ill to Louisville, after spending her adult life somewhere else, leaving her daughter and son for Grandma Millie to raise. Ma buried Grandma Millie in 1965. Everybody needed Mary to be there for them in the end. I was certainly going to be there for my mother in her remaining days even though like she said, I had never been through something like this.

It was a Monday in March and she was sitting on the side of the bed in her room at Baptist North Hospital. At her summons, I had flown in that morning from D.C. and arrived at the hospital for a final meeting between her oncologist, her nurse, and a social worker from hospice care.

Ma was fully dressed and looked pretty. Like a woman without a care. What did she know?

My younger brothers, Doug and Phillip, were already there. If there had been a conversation at her hospital bed before I got there, the room grew silent upon my arrival. I had come as much for my brothers as for Ma. I always wanted to be there for my younger siblings, be the older brother that I never had. Phillip had been a great big brother to the Marbry kids—Ordette, Don, and Doug—and a great younger brother to us Johnsons. I could see this was taking a toll on him though.

Ma had given him power of attorney, which made sense. He had been her rock. The one everyone turned to in Louisville. A captain in the fire department, Phillip was also finding success buying rental properties and fixing them up using skills he'd learned from his late father.

Now it was time for that meeting that every family at some point was going to have. Leslie Junior and Michael's absences were noticeable. I knew Don and Ordette were having a tough time dealing with this moment; we were in constant contact.

It was time for the meeting to begin.

Kate, the hospice social worker, had a great smile, combined with an easy disposition and quick wit. She knew exactly what to say and when; she also knew what not to say.

Once the doctor started speaking, Ma's eyes were fixed on him in a manner that seemed to say, "I know you have done all you can. I'm grateful for the time I've been given with my boys."

Sure enough, the doctor began with, "We've done all we can. To continue the chemotherapy would just make you more sick. We are going to concentrate on making you as comfortable as possible. I'm going to sign you out. There is no reason why you have to stay in the hospital." There, it was done.

Ma listened attentively even though she had already heard this in private from her medical team. "Well, if you think that is the best treatment," she replied. There was no sign of disappointment, no visible fear or anger. Maybe Ma had surrendered. Was she on pain medication that put her in a fog, unable to go where anxiety and fear would be waiting? There was no self-pity in this woman. No "why me?" Only 10 percent of pancreatic cancer patients survive past five years. My mother was nearing the end of a single year after her initial stage-four diagnosis.

I couldn't help but ponder what was really on the other side of all this. Is there life after death, like I had been taught by the Catholic church since I was a child? It made sense all those years, but now I was asking: When one dies, is it like falling asleep and never waking up again? I couldn't wrap my head around that thinking, but is that any more baffling than a God who always has been, creating all this?

I wanted to climb in bed with her, assure her that this good son wouldn't leave her side. I didn't but promised to be there till the end.

I asked the doctor if we could step aside. "Does she realize she's dying?" I needed to know.

"Yes, she knows."

"How much time does she have?"

"Maybe a couple weeks."

We thanked the staff, gathered her things, and walked alongside her wheelchair as Ma was escorted out of Baptist Hospital East for the last time. How many times had staff made this sad trip?

We piled into the rental car and made the trip to the hospice wing of another hospital, Baptist North, which was a thirty-minute drive outside of Louisville. I drove. I'm the oldest, so I get to drive. It's the way it's always been.

We set out for Baptist Hospital North, a short drive away in LaGrange, Kentucky.

You can't get there without passing the landmark State Reformatory. The legendary medium-security prison in LaGrange was familiar to everyone in the car, except me. My brothers Les and David had both done time there, twice. Les had resorted to robbing liquor stores after he lost a job as the manager at Southwick housing project. He tells a story of getting too close to the tenants. David was part of what seemed to be a petty criminal enterprise that included stealing then fencing items from places where they worked.

How many times had my mother visited LaGrange to see her sons? "A lot," she replied as we passed the ominous entrance. How many of my childhood and high school friends had done time there? "Too many," came the response. How many were still there for drug convictions that emanated from time spent in the Cotter Homes and Southwick Housing projects? How many were nonviolent offenders who were sentenced under the same mandatory minimum sentences imposed in crack cases that I covered in D.C.?

David died on September 16, 1998, on my oldest brother Les's birthday. He had heart issues while serving his second sentence at LaGrange, but after he had done his time, it was colon cancer that killed him. I was able to visit Louisville one last time before David passed. We rode through the old neighborhood and reminisced about playing on the same basketball team at Immaculate Heart of Mary school. And when I discovered I could no longer "take him," beat him at wrestling because he had grown to outweigh me by about fifty pounds. David could have been the best football player in the family if he had stuck with it. He said he didn't like the way the coach talked to the players. When kids don't grow up with a father, they can become frightened when a man screams at them.

A piece of my mother died with David. He was the youngest of the Johnson siblings—my favorite and the one I had promised to help raise and protect—but then I left for the seminary. I came home for David's funeral with my daughter Kurshanna. Madge and I had been separated for a few years.

David was forty-six—two years younger than me. By then, I had more than twenty years of experience as a journalist. David had never settled on the one thing he would do in life. He was married, two daughters and granddaughters but one grandson—who wouldn't see him grow old.

Ma volunteered in her only comment about LaGrange reformatory as we put it behind us on the road, that she was proud that most of her sons had avoided prison. She certainly did her best, beginning with enrolling us in Catholic schools. I was thinking that I'd been lucky—fell into some mentors but also maybe more persistent and willing to put up with more abuse to get what I wanted.

This may sound strange, but for many years I had dreams in which I woke up in prison. No matter what status I achieved, in my reality, I was destined to be arrested, caged, and sentenced to life without parole. Had this segregated and racist society done this to me? Was it merely a part of this Black man's psyche? There has never been a sense of entitlement. No reason to believe that one day I too

could feel free, comfortable, or even privileged. As a broadcast journalist, I had covered every kind of Black male—poor, rich, middle
class, smart, and dumb…cuffed and led off to prison.

We pulled into the parking lot of Baptist North just before one
that afternoon. I dropped Ma off at the entrance, where staff already
was waiting with a wheelchair. Phillip and Doug went inside while I
parked the car alongside a motel that was built for families to stay in
while spending what time was left with a loved one in Baptist North.

The hospital was divided into two hallways: one leading to the
acute-care facility; the other leading to the hospice wing where people went to die. I choked up thinking no one would leave there
alive. Not my mother, no one.

The brochure said my mother would receive continuous skilled
care without the aggressive diagnostic tests and treatment. They
knew her time was coming. There were no limits on visiting hours.
We could come anytime we wanted, day or night, seven days a week.
I dropped everybody off and parked the car.

By the time I got back to the hospice wing, Ma was already settled into her room. A nurse, a pleasant Black woman, was already
talking to Ma as if they had been friends for years. Did she mean
it, or was it part of her training? How does she not take this grief
home at night?

I wonder how many people know about or ever get the chance
to consider hospice care?

It was a big single room. Ma had wanted a roommate. She had
always had someone to talk to during her other hospital stays, someone who appeared in worse shape. It made her feel needed. This
time, though, she would be alone. That didn't sit well with any of
us. Had there been somebody in the bed next to my mother?

"We got to get you ready for bed," the nurse said.

I asked if the couch could be pulled out for a bed, in case I want to spend the night. It could. The nurse and Ma continue their routine. Phillip, Doug, and I appeared to be in the way. There was nothing for us to do. Medicare would pay the entire bill. Papers had already been signed.

Ma said she was hungry; she'd not been able to hold any solid food down for days. It was the cancer. The tumors were wreaking havoc on her digestive organs. "I want some bottled water!" It was one of those orders from Ma to her boys. She'd also not been able to hold down liquids, but we went next door to the Cracker Barrel restaurant to get water, as the cafeteria was closed. The nurse suggested some ice, maybe ice cream.

After we brought back her ice and ice cream, Phil, Doug, and I had to excuse ourselves. There were important decisions to be made. We went next door to Cracker Barrel to get some lunch.

My mother had converted to Catholicism as a young woman but was married twice outside the church. Still, we insisted that it was going to be a Catholic funeral at Immaculate Heart of Mary. We decided she would be brought home to "our church" to be eulogized when the time came.

I would call Father Ed Branch, in Atlanta, her former pastor and a lifelong family friend who had been on standby for months to deliver the eulogy. Father John Judie, the current pastor at Immaculate Heart, was more than willing to help plan the mass and repast at the church and school.

The Johnson-Marbry family was small, maybe a few dozen people at most, and Ma didn't have a lot of close friends outside her family. Mary Ann O'Callaghan would be there with her family.

Ordette would clean and prepare Ma's little house for visitors off Cane Run Road, just outside Louisville. She would also write the obituary for the service and newspaper article. Doug was put in charge of notifying all family members and friends.

When we left the restaurant forty-five minutes later, we had a good plan. I felt closer to my brothers than ever before. This is what Ma would have wanted.

When we returned to her room, Ma was in bed, covered and clearly worn out.

"How do you feel?" Why did I keep asking her that, and what did I mean—physically, mentally, spiritually? All of the above. She raised an arm and pointed out how wrinkled it had become. Ma's vanity was still there and she looked so cute but fragile to me. I'd crawl in bed and hold her if they let me. She must weigh next to nothing! Her phone was on a table at the bed. Her new medication had arrived. Time was running out on my stay; it was approaching two-thirty and Phil needed a ride back into Louisville to pick up his son, Cedric, from school. I wasn't ready to leave. My brothers could visit Ma every day, all day if they wanted to, but my time there was precious. I'd come a considerable distance and at some expense too. I wanted and needed every minute I could get with my Momma.

Instead, I settled for a hug and kiss on the mouth. "I'll come back Saturday, Ma, and I'll spend the night on the couch."

"Okay," she said. I moved to get another hug and kiss. The three of us were now headed out the door.

Goodbye, Ma. I love you, Ma.

I was still planning to fly back to Louisville on the weekend. Exhausted and mentally and emotionally drained, I did what I always do when I need to reboot. I would first get away to my safe place in Lewes, Delaware, a two-hour-and-fifteen-minute drive from my D.C. home.

I bought a place on the rebound after the near twenty-year marriage to Madge. We separated while Kurshanna was in her second year at Howard University. Brandon was entering seventh grade at Saint John's College High in D.C. Madge and I agreed at the start to never openly complain about the other—to always put our children first. I will always thank my first wife for allowing our son to live with me. I was determined to be the father to Brandon that I never had. I wasn't perfect, but I think he would tell you I was always there and putting my children first. Madge and I both dated and never tried to sabotage the other's relationships. Our families remain close.

My car knew the way to Lewes. It was an easy drive, about two hours and fifteen minutes.

I never worried about wakeup calls there because there had been no clock bound to my wrist and ankles like in D.C. where I had now been a TV reporter and anchor for three and a half decades. Loved the work, but the job takes a toll.

Ma had loved the place. Nothing fancy: three bedrooms, garage, wooded area all around, and the beaches along the Delaware Bay and Atlantic Ocean were but a few minutes away by car.

My plan was to get back to her hospice bed in a day or so. The house in Lewes was supposed to be a vacation spot for my siblings as well. They loved the experience when they came to visit; Lewes, Delaware, was due east of D.C. Where the Delaware Bay met the Atlantic Ocean. It sat on the Delaware Bay at Cape Henlopen Park. No one loved this spot on earth more than my mother.

"Bruce, does any other state have this much water?" Like a child, Ma had once begged me to help her walk through the thick sand at Lewes Beach on the bay so she could flop her chair at the water's edge and permit the salt water to wash over her tired feet. We both must have thought this was a long journey from our poor beginning in alleys and housing projects in Louisville.

The landline phone rang and I decided not to answer it. They could leave a voicemail. I enjoyed coming to the beach alone. I often heard my wealthy friends talk about having such a place on the Outer Banks, the Hamptons, or Martha's Vineyard.

I had never heard of Lewes, Delaware. Rehoboth Beach, Dewey and Bethany Beach, sure, but not Lewes. A coworker, Robin Small, from the television station, suggested I take the two-and-a-half-hour drive east to where the Lewes–Cape May ferry crosses the Delaware Bay to Cape May, New Jersey.

I took the advice and immediately felt an attraction after traveling down Savannah Street onto second street in the center of this colonial village. It was like I had stepped into a time capsule. A charming Mid-Atlantic town on the bay and a stone's throw from the Atlantic Ocean. The best hotel was called the Inn on the Canal; there was no computer at the front desk when I checked in the first time years before. The spring, summer, even winter months would become my cure-all for any ailment! I could bike, do yoga, swim, eat great seafood, and soak up some sun on any choice of beaches. I loved to flop under an umbrella with a good book for a few hours of me time.

I had introduced Ma to my girlfriend. She and Lori hit it off from the beginning, maybe because Lori, like my mom, was a single mother. She had a young daughter, Carolyn, from a long-term relationship. Lori would join me in Lewes on her days off. She worked as the production manager for WJLA TV(ABC), a competing station. We started dating at Channel 9, but I wasn't interested in getting married a second time. Lori and I agreed if we were going to be an exclusive couple and maybe more down the road, we couldn't work at the same TV station collecting a check from the same company. She nearly doubled her salary when she left Channel 9 which had passed over her for a promotion to a job she had been doing for many months.

Seven years after my separation and divorce, Lori and I got married in a Catholic ceremony. It was a destination wedding in South Beach, Florida. Her parents, sisters, uncles, and aunts were there. My mother and three of my siblings were there. My son Brandon was my best man. My daughter, Kurshanna, and Lori's daughter, Carolyn, were maids of honor.

Lori was Catholic and that may have sealed the deal with Ma. My new wife had already convinced me to go back to church with her at Saint Augustine's. The Catholic church had never recognized my first marriage outside the church.

The phone rings again. "The nurse says you should get here if you can!" It was my brother Phil's voice. He was already back at the hospital outside Louisville. "Something will always bring you back home if nothing but death in the family." That old man's saying in Rocky Mount, North Carolina, would remain in my head for the rest of the day.

As I rushed to get dressed in Lewes, my anger and pain became a volatile mix. It didn't seem right. Death never does.

I told Phillip I was on my way, as though he could put off the inevitable. I felt guilty for being in Lewes. I had planned to fly back to Louisville the next day to spend the night with Ma. I had promised.

I picked up my cell phone to break the news to Lori, back in D.C.

"Can you book a flight for me back to Louisville? Any flight, from Dulles, National, BWI, any airport. Okay?" I closed the blinds, drew the curtains, turned down the thermostat. brushed my teeth, ran a towel over my face, and saved the shave for later. For a second, I glanced in the mirror. My face didn't betray me. No emotions registered. How should I feel? My mother was dying four states away.

It was still early by my watch. Friday morning, just seven AM.

I was doing seventy in Maryland. Farms lined both sides of the two-lane highway. Produce stands had popped up every other mile. I can still see my mother peering from the passenger window, taking in the view. Farms were absolutely alien to us growing up deep in Louisville's projects and west end neighborhoods. Cows and the smell of manure and chicken farms were as foreign to us as the smell of fish, the ocean, and the bay.

I dialed Lori again. "What about the flight?" She had booked an afternoon flight on Southwest Airlines, from BWI airport.

An hour into the drive, as I passed through Denton, Maryland, halfway home, I lost control. I had been stuffing my grief. I pulled off to the side of the road and cried. An emotional explosion, and then it was over.

I pulled back onto the highway. And then the thought of losing my mother, my only parent, slapped my heart again. I'm a bastard! The tears stain my face. I could not pretend this wasn't happening. My body started to ache! On Route 50, I crossed the Chesapeake Bay Bridge.

Sailboats so far below looked like mere toys in bath water. The scene reminded me of how small I was, of how little control I really had over anything.

I began to hope that my mother would be able to let go soon and find the peace that had eluded her all these years. Morning rush hour traffic met me as I approached the beltway surrounding D.C. commuters heading to work, school, or whatever.

I reached for the car phone to get an update from Phillip. It was a call that I both wanted to make and feared making at the same time. "How's she doing?" I asked. "I have an afternoon flight. I'll be there by four-thirty." Silence greeted the urgency and anxiety in my voice.

"You can take your time," he said. "She's gone." My head hit the steering wheel. Tears poured out. On March 31, 2006, I became an orphan.

Days later at my mother's funeral, I spoke for the family as we gathered at Immaculate Heart of Mary Church. Madge was there for support. I had attended her father's funeral and would be there when her mother later died. Lori, Carolyn, Brandon, Kurshanna, and her son, my grandson, Shawn, had flown to Louisville with me. Also in the church, where I had spent so many hours, decades ago, were my brothers and sister, nieces, nephews, cousins, longtime family friends, and the O'Callaghan children. Ma had helped raise these White people. They had not forgotten her. I recall that despite her college degree, Ma continued to babysit their grandchildren in her old age.

Father Ed Branch gave the eulogy. In my remarks I insisted that everyone stand and say out loud, "Goodbye, Ma. We love you, Ma. We are going to Miss You, Ma!"

Before I left town to fly back to Washington, my brothers and sister and I were sitting in the living room of Ma's house and they were placing bets on whether I would be coming back to Louisville to visit. I didn't weigh in on the discussion. Privately, I thought about that old pig farmer's words in Rocky Mount, North Carolina.

CHAPTER 10

Crack

AN AMBULANCE PULLED UP AND double-parked outside an apartment building not far from the intersection of East Capitol Street and Benning Road. A wailing siren was always a signal that something bad was up in these parts of southeast D.C. A shooting, a violent beatdown, a drug overdose.

The people, the neighborhoods, reminded me of my early neighborhood growing up in Louisville.

The crowds on the corners, the clothes, the music that spilled out onto the streets. The smell of soul food billowing from a carry-out or open apartment window. There is a strip mall on the corner, with mom and pop stores always going out of business to be replaced by new ones, which won't be here for long either. The Shrimp Boat Restaurant is a landmark. The fast-food eatery sits on an island at the intersection. It's now owned by an Asian family, which was not uncommon in these parts. The fast food, cooked to order, was good and affordable, but only family members were employed here. The money is passed through bullet-proof plastic, a reminder that carry-outs and liquor stores were ripe for robberies. Credit cards and steady jobs with benefits are not easy to come by in these parts. A thriving drug market fueled the underground economy over here.

You can throw out the government's statistics. Lots of people in Southeast D.C. have no disposable funds—money they could afford to lose, like in the stock market. But people dependent the underground economy do have discretionary dollars. In some cases, serious money with choices to make about where to spend that discretionary income for needed goods and services; entertainment and pleasures.

I spent a lot of hours observing, reporting on, and acquiring some knowledge of how crack dollars drove the buying and selling in some of D.C.'s lower income communities. The period was between the early 1980s through the 1990s.

Commerce was brisk if you knew where to look and what to look for. Weekdays and nights, but especially on weekends, business was booming. I figure at least half of the population in some neighborhoods was out of work or not looking for steady work. Steady work would mean earning money that is taxed by the government. It meant having regular working hours and supervisors more interested in their promotions than yours.

"There are two kinds of people out there: people who are making money and people trying to take their money." Those words from a sixteen-year-old! I met Dwayne Jones inside the District of Columbia's Youth Reformatory in Lorton, Virginia. He had started selling crack while in middle school before dropping out. The money and what it bought became far more important than school, which had done nothing to change his tough circumstances at home. More on Dwayne later in this chapter.

I would describe these communities in my TV broadcasts in the manner I had been taught. It was unfair but journalists always reached into our bag of familiar terms to appear well versed on what we were covering. "At-risk children," "high-crime neighborhoods," "hard-core unemployed," "single-parent households" were phrases that conjured up negative stereotypes of Blacks who lived here whether or not the labels fit them. Those overused labels were Tweet language to assure most other viewers: You have nothing to fear because you don't live amongst these people. Eventually, with time, I would find some of the better stories were from the community folk who didn't fit the stereotype we helped perpetuate. The single working mom who produced the valedictorian; the dad who wasn't absent and was there for his kids and others in the neighborhood who didn't have dads; the working people hoping to get their twenty-plus years in before retirement; and community activists who marched after every child or teen slaying to insist before it became fashionable that "Their Black Lives Mattered" too.

The constant battle for me as a reporter was not only to seek the truth and present both sides of an issue, but I also had to decide how much of the truth I wanted or needed to reveal while putting the story in a two-minute reporter package that a show producer has allotted. Stories from these parts were often treated as a nuisance rather than worthy of the status quo's attention.

The truth is that lots of rents were paid with money generated by a thriving crack-cocaine drug businesses in these communities. Cooked meals, bad food, comfort food, groceries, entertainment, electronics, cars, sneakers, dress shoes, and nice clothing were paid for with drug money. Haircuts, hairdos, private-school tuition, vacations, jewelry, and personal loans were made possible with drug money. The demand for drugs wasn't just in these parts. It came from all over the city. It crossed geo-socio and economical lines, but the revenue from drugs—specifically crack—transformed lives in these parts in ways that couldn't be missed.

The emergency responders from the start of this chapter were part of that demand.

Their ambulance had double parked, siren off, lights still flashing. The EMTs (emergency medical technicians), one Black, one White, exited the vehicle with gear, a dual-head stethoscope, and blood-pressure cuffs tossed over their shoulders. But they were not there to save anybody; they were there to buy crack! The gear included their own crack pipe.

A source who is now in recovery told me the story. He was inside the apartment when the emergency responders walked in.

They had been expected by the young man on the other side of the door. There were already eight to ten people inside his apartment. The EMTs had walked into a crack house. No one seemed bothered by their presence. My source says the drug dealer who may or may not have actually lived in the apartment (it didn't matter to anyone there) sold some crack to the EMT. His companion watched anxiously as the drug was placed on top of the pipe and lit. The two each took a long, deep inhale on the dope before falling back into a synchronized nod.

Inside a crack house, you don't want to know who else is in the room. Later, should someone ask, you were never there! You didn't see anyone and you didn't hear anything! Your life might depend on it.

It's not like the barbershop. No one cares about your favorite football team or how good the Georgetown Hoyas might be this season. Take care of your business, and then get out. Robberies, shootings, beatdowns, police raids, anything could and would break out in these places.

But my source says no one could ignore the EMTs because they were in full uniform: dark blue shirts and slacks, the D.C. Fire and Emergency Medical Services insignia patch on their shirt sleeves.

And in yet one more stunning move that every zonked-out body in the room witnessed, after taking a hit or two on the crack pipe, the EMTs took one another's blood pressure! They were checking their vitals!

A call came over their portable radio. It was time to leave. To return to their government jobs of saving lives! They left the apartment, jumped into the double-parked ambulance, turned on the siren, and sped off down the street toward Benning Road and East Capitol Street.

Selling crack was enticing employment for scores of people in D.C., young and old, male and female. There were skilled and unskilled positions in every organization. Selling crack was an equal opportunity enterprise too. Independent dope dealers could ask for an agreed-upon amount on credit. No money down. This was called a Tick or Tika. Anything you earned above the dealer's fee was yours. There was an immediate agreed-upon contract that if you failed to deliver on a tick because sales lagged, you got sick, or even robbed, the consequences could be severe for you, maybe even deadly.

News director Dave Pearce once said to me, "A lot of us would be selling drugs if not for the fear of getting arrested and going to prison." Maybe! I was bothered by seeing the many people strung out on crack. My boss didn't have to look at that! Pearce was conservative, White, and he lived in suburban Maryland. He didn't have to cover the human fallout from the crack epidemic.

By the early to mid-1980s, this may have been Chocolate City, but D.C. could have been an acronym for Dodge City! Crack cocaine had turned parts of the nation's capital and other large cities into the wild, wild west!

Violent Jamaican gangs came down from New York City with huge supplies of crack cocaine and they were hell bent on controlling the crack markets. They brought in semi-automatic weapons and their calling card was shooting rivals in the lower back, leaving them paralyzed from the waist down. I would report on neighborhoods marked by the young men, left unable to walk and confined to getting around in electric-powered wheelchairs.

One of my cameramen, the legendary Kline Mengle, recalled that "sometime during the 1980s I was working the 6 PM to midnight shift and I "videotaped" five separate homicides in six hours." And that wasn't far from the norm.

One of my other trusted cameramen, Mike Murphy, recalled that he kept a record of the killings he covered over a three-year period. "There were eighty-six, seventy-three, and eighty-three separate killings, and that didn't include the hundreds of shootings that left people wounded!"

People grew tired of the constant body bags filling their TV screens at dinner time. They stopped watching. We stopped showing body bags, and the killings kept on coming.

"This has got to stop. They're killing our babies." I could write the scripts for local clergy before getting to the scene. I knew what their reactions would be.

I felt that White people saw the violence and drug activity as a Black problem. Some Black people viewed the activity as an embarrassment as well as tragic and a result of drugs and guns being dumped in poor Black communities. Many Blacks, like me, had lived in the same places now under siege. Parts of Louisville's west end were undergoing the same carnage.

Isaac Fulwood, former chief of the Metropolitan Police Force often talked about the lasting impact the media and D.C. had on the crack era.

"The war on drugs, no matter how you paint it, is a war on Black people, because most of the people we locked up were Black."

I sat down with Fulwood, after his retirement as police chief, when he was serving on the federal parole commission. He passed away in 2017. I made sure to pay my respects at his wake.

In what may have been his last interview about "Operation Clean Sweep"—the department's military-like assault on the crack organizations—Fulwood said, "We didn't do anything up in the White community. Why not? Because of the violence associated with the street-level drug activity in the Black community." "In Wards 7 and 8 at the open-air drug markets, you had violence associated with it. So police had to go in and do what they needed to do to address it."

The disproportionate police response to D.C. drug enforcement also applied to marijuana. Fulwood added, "Even before the D.C. Council passed a bill to decriminalize and later legalize marijuana use, 93 percent of the people arrested for marijuana charges are African American. Whites don't use marijuana? (of course) They are using it. But police don't go up in the neighborhoods and police the same way. Because the (White) community wouldn't tolerate it."

I shifted my reporting to the single women and working couples who went to work and had to live on the lawless streets. They most feared whoever had the guns. They became the law in a city where handguns were outlawed at the time. The elderly were especially afraid, hiding inside homes that they had purchased decades ago and hoped to leave to their children and grandchildren.

I felt pressure to fix everything wrong with media coverage. I couldn't. Black, Brown, and female managers were rare. Some cultural diversity would have helped; people like me who had come from the ghettos and barrios. White news managers looked at this shit as Black people's business and it was up to Black people to fix it. Where are the ministers, the after-school basketball programs, where are their parents they would ask in meetings? They didn't have a clue as to the impact of race and class in these issues. Or did they? While conservatives were playing the blame game; progressives were just as irritating and complicit with their silence in meetings. It's easy to care about the children; the others got far less sympathy.

Cops on the streets in Southeast D.C. were being sent to the police and fire clinic for psychological evaluation after witnessing or being involved in the trauma fueled by crack. My camera people and I were merely sent back out there every day with a slap on the back and words that suggested, "Keep up the good work."

My camera crews and I never fully recovered from reporting on children who died out there, on the streets, in their own homes.

Young Mark Settle's life ended suddenly late one afternoon in a drug dispute inside his own home. Mark was twelve years old. Skinny, fast with a quick smile, I was told. I know he was street-smart, like me. You had to be when you're growing up in public housing, whether D.C. or Louisville, Kentucky. You learn to sense danger and when to run away from it. But when it's inside your own home, you often have to stand and fight. You will lose but hope to survive to fight again.

The call came crackling from the police scanners on the assignment desk in the middle of the newsroom. "Report of a juvenile shot, 37th Place, southeast!" We sprang into action, me and several camera people who didn't wait to get the assignment. We know the area well and spring into action, maybe three or four of us at once. When a child is shot, it becomes our top priority. Anybody else, it depends on the circumstances. How old? Where did it happen? If it's the suburbs, a well-to-do city neighborhood, we're on it. If it looks like it might be a White victim in an upscale neighborhood, we send the cavalry! As many news crews as possible. Most news managers would deny that!

It took us a good half-hour to get across town to the scene, which could have taken twice that long had we obeyed the speed limits, which we hardly ever did. Mark Settles had been shot to death in the kitchen of his family apartment. I was left to imagine what the scene looked like inside, as was often the case. One cop tipped me off to a gut-wrenching detail that I wasn't allowed to report then and there: Mark had been shot by his own kin, an uncle, who apparently killed Mark's German Shepherd as well. The dog had tried to protect his young best friend.

Outside, police, some of them with shotguns, continued to arrive on the scene. I can still visualize them as I write this, running up a hill, squad cars parked in disarray, motors still running with doors ajar toward Mark's unit as though they expected more violence. A child slaying bothered the cops too! Some officers had grown up in the very same neighborhoods, attended the same schools, and performed on the nearby athletic fields. A few would volunteer that they had become cops to make a difference.

There were just as many who seemed to thrive on the action. Some were military veterans who were given extra points and moved to the front of the recruitment class because of their service to country. I saw no proof that combat duty made one a better street cop. But lots of police officers equated their jobs on D.C. streets to war and vowed they would be the ones returning home that night. I never felt the danger and I saw no evidence that uniformed police officers were under assault. Undercover or plainclothes detectives—that's a different story!

I went live from the scene for the 6 o'clock news. We framed the shot so viewers could see Mark Settles' apartment unit a half block up the hill beyond the yellow police tape.

Interviewing people in the crowd was a big part of what I had to do to get ready. My job was to bring this brutal reality to your affluent dens and upscale neighborhoods. If you watched TV while having dinner, all the better. I wanted people at home to be as upset and angry as I was. Maybe then, they'll demand some changes.

Most reporters, White and Black, stood by and watched or later followed me to interview the very same people. It was easy to spot the journalist who was afraid or hated being there.

The local folk knew I wasn't here to judge. They recognized me and seemed interested in how I would put my reports together. "He was quiet, playful, and could have been one of your friends that you could depend on," said a crying boy who appeared to be Mark's age.

I asked, "A nice young man? Ever talk about problems inside the home with family?"

"No," another kid volunteered. "He was nothing but twelve years old. So, he was my friend." Mark's friend nearly collapsed from his tears and grief into the arms of an adult standing alongside him for support throughout—maybe also to monitor his comments to me. We made eye contact. I had seen that look before as I worked the crowd trying to make sense of what had just happened. Some people watching me and my cameraman knew more than they would ever let on.

I filed my report and then went to the nearby elementary school. "The community has a lot of drugs floating through and the children have to learn very early on, it takes a lot to survive!" That came from Mark Settle's school principal, who seemed defeated or broken from having lost another student.

Mark had been a member of the church choir and played on the neighborhood school football team.

At a subsequent press conference, I asked the question that every reporter wanted to ask but didn't: "Chief, was the boy involved in drug activity?"

"Yes," said Larry Soulsby, the D.C. police chief at the time. He refused to elaborate. How did he know and what would have been the motive? Meal money, sneakers, tee shirts? If Mark was selling drugs, it didn't let the rest of us off the hook for why he didn't have better, safer options.

We often stayed too long and drank too much while taking turns telling what we were seeing and feeling out there on the streets.

I was brought to Washington, D.C. in 1976 to cover the new majority African American government in a majority Black city. A half-decade later, a majority of my stories, the planning, and the time were spent on the crack-cocaine epidemic.

I can't overstate the fact that D.C. was obsessed with buying and selling crack and spending the money the illegal enterprise was generating. It had to have been billions!

In June of 1986 at the height of the crisis, the country finally got the message. The illegal drug activity was claiming unsuspecting pleasure-seeking victims at every level. That's when University of Maryland basketball star Len Bias collapsed in his dorm room in the early morning hour, then died of cardiac arrest at Leland Memorial Hospital not far from the College Park, Maryland, campus. An autopsy concluded Bias died from an unadulterated dealer-level quality of cocaine.

I was quickly put on a plane for Boston with cameraman Greg Guise. Len Bias had just been drafted in the first round by the

National Basketball Association Boston Celtics. Red Auerbach, the famed coach of the Celtics would be in his office at the Boston Gardens and available to talk with me on camera.

I recall it was late at night when we arrived in Boston to be escorted across the iconic parquet floor, and up a set of stairs to Auerbach's office in the famed Boston Gardens arena. Once seated, while my cameraman Greg Guise was setting up his camera and lights, I took it all in—where I was and who had graced the franchise and city with so many titles. On the wall was a framed inscription that read, "Experience don't mean shit." It was signed Bill Russel—the legendary Celtic center. Russel was also a member of Kappa Alpha Psi! A fraternity brother!

As his coach entered the room I said, "Wow, Bill Russel. I'm a big fan." Red Auerbach took a long puff of his cigar, looked at me, took another puff, then said, "You don't look like a big anything!"

Ok! Guise couldn't stop laughing at the remark. I was actually flattered. The ice was broken. I would have a line for this yet to be written memoir, but we were there to talk about the loss of Len Bias. Coach Auerbach told me, "You have no idea what the loss of this great athlete will have on this franchise. A player of Len Bias's impact comes along once in every generation." *Damn!* I thought to myself.

I interviewed dozens of coaches, parents, and grandparents about young people lost to coke and crack. None of the interviews got the kind of national attention as did the interview with Red Auerbach. That bothered me. The country would eventually pass a tough law that treated crack offenses far more harshly than powder cocaine offenses. The bill resulted in mass incarcerations of African Americans from the communities I had been covering. D.C. inmates would be sent to federal prisons across the country because they were federal inmates.

My TV station and the others were obsessed with covering the crack epidemic. The local Fox station in D.C., renamed its 10 o'clock newscast "City under Siege," and viewers, especially Black people, tuned in religiously. Was it because that was all we were airing? The video was better than any the television cop shows were offering.

When D.C. cops were conducting all those raids on suspected crack dealers in the streets or in peoples apartments—most of the time in southeast communities—and houses, my cameramen and I were there. In the beginning, we were embedded in the cars with police. In hindsight, this wasn't a good idea. It wasn't good for objective journalism.

We were not on the same team. They had a job to do. We had a different job to do.

Looking back, I think that every time we stormed into those apartments with police, we were probably violating people's rights, certainly their expectation of privacy. The warrants never read, "… and Bruce Johnson and his camera crew should be allowed to accompany police to capture as much incredible videotape as possible."

The video was exciting but revealed that almost nothing was gained in those raids. No large amount of drugs or weapons were seized. No crack kingpins were ever taken down. I wondered where are the people who were really getting rich off crack. The stunned and maybe fearful occupants never posed a threat. People wanted to get away from the police and not confront them. Bit players they were! Not once did I sense a violent outcome for anyone, not us, not the occupants of the homes and apartments, not police. This was reality TV, and we were part of the production. And not once did the occupant of the apartment order us out!

No need to imagine what the reaction would have been had we busted uninvited into a White family's apartment or house in one of Washington's upscale neighborhoods on Capitol Hill or west of Rock Creek Park. A thousand-dollar-an-hour attorney would have been calling the general manager of the TV station demanding that I be fired while threatening to sue if any second of the video made air.

Cameraman Kline Mengle and I once found ourselves uninvited inside a woman's apartment where a police informant had made a drug buy. Cops had stormed in to arrest her male friend and toss her home inside out looking for crack. They found a small amount of drugs and a gun under a sofa cushion, which we caught on videotape.

The woman's baby started crying. When no one else picked up the toddler, I did and gently patted her back and bounced her in my right arm, much like I had my own daughter at that age. *This is no place for children*, I was thinking, while not feeling so above all this! The baby wouldn't remember this, and the mother with some luck will discover a resolve to never put her child in this situation again. Perhaps! Poor children are unfairly exposed to things that all children should be spared. I handed the toddler to her mother who was busy and nervously answering questions from police. She wasn't the target; her boyfriend or the guy who was using her apartment to sell drugs was. Drug dealers often were setting up shop in somebody else's home.

"Yeah, friends come by sometimes and smoke," she said to the police, not knowing she probably shouldn't be saying anything to them or me. She volunteered, "I smoke sometimes too, but I've been slowing down."

I wasn't above using drugs. I sampled powder coke a couple times at parties, though I was terrified of serious substances after my acid trip in college. Using drugs was not just about having a good time; it was also about status.

Crack was a poor people's powdered cocaine, wasn't it?

For those who don't know, crack is the crystalized form of cocaine, and it's much more accessible.

In the 1980s, powder coke gave way to freebasing, which brought a quicker and more powerful high. Freebasing coke meant smoking it in its pure rock form with a flame, usually from a cigarette lighter. One user told me "everything was made better by freebasing. Your sex drive and stamina were off the charts." If you had minor illnesses such as a headache or cold, they swore freebasing was the cure-all.

Freebasing led to crack. Water replaced the chemicals in freebasing coke, which could at times be dangerous and even explode. The crack epidemic took off because it was cheaper and led to a quicker and better high.

Crack quickly became the affordable, preferred drug of the masses that hooked anyone who tried it. Problem is, there is never enough crack. "The moment you've smoked it, all you are obsessed with is how to get some more," said a friend and former colleague.

Crack infiltrated my WUSA9 (CBS) newsroom. While doing research for my book, I learned that one of our veteran police reporters bought and smoked crack! Only newly hired station employees are tested for drugs. The reporter, whose name I won't reveal, happened to be White and he didn't risk exposure and his own reputation to hit the streets to buy crack. So he and one of our best video editors, who also happened to be White, would dispatch a couple of Black cameramen into the streets to make crack buys for their use.

One cameraman shared this incident with me. He had been assigned to cover an upcoming football game between the Washington Redskins and the Dallas Cowboys. He had a reservation for a Friday departure from BWI (Baltimore Washington

International) airport for the Sunday game. He would never make it. The cameraman, who was Black, said the news reporter and editor had given him money to purchase crack.

It wasn't the first time. The deal was the cameraman would make a buy, keep a portion of the rocks for himself, then turn the lion's share over to the police-beat reporter and video editor before flying to Dallas. As with a lot of drug purchases, plans fall apart; the White guys were left empty handed when the Black guy started smoking his share of the crack and then crashing with a female acquaintance at her apartment. He was zonked out and useless for the entire weekend. The flight to Dallas never happened. He missed the Cowboys–Redskins game.

I found some heroes out there during the crack wars. Brig Owens, a retired player for the Washington football team founded Super Leaders and asked me to serve on the board of directors. The goal was to take a large number of students, train them in conflict resolution and leadership skills, then send them into their schools to change the norm. Drugs may be in the surrounding communities, but they weren't to be tolerated in Spingarn, Eastern High, or any school where Super Leaders have chapters.

George Rutherford, the principal at Fletcher Johnson Middle School, was one of my heroes. Doc Rutherford's school was blocks from East Capitol and Benning Road and I watched him wage war to save his students from drugs and violence. Test scores were secondary to keeping his boys and girls alive and safe. George Rutherford and his staff at Fletcher Johnson were convinced that one person and certainly one principle could make a difference. I learned that junior high was often too late to save some youth.

A CRACK DEALER AND TEEN KILLER

Dwayne Jones dropped out of school in the eighth grade. Nobody came looking for him. No parent at home. No truant officer alerted by the school. He was already getting high and hustling, selling drugs.

I interviewed Dwayne while he was serving time for murder at the Lorton Reformatory, which was located in Lorton, Virginia.

"So, you chose the streets and drugs over school?" I asked.

"Yes."

"Did you talk to anybody about that? Parents?"

"I couldn't talk to my parents about stuff like that. The only person I could talk to was my older brother and he was already locked up." Dwayne was sixteen when he got his first gun. You don't get a gun unless you're prepared to use it.

"Where'd you get the gun?"

"From a friend."

"Did you carry the gun with you all the time?"

"Just when I was going hustling, or going to the go-go."

He said he carried the gun to the go-go (clubs) because some people were jealous that he was hustling. He was also getting robbed. "I usually got jumped three or four times a week, but it didn't faze me none cause I knew I could get back at them."

Dwayne was still sixteen when he killed another teenager, Melvin Allen Pickett. "Why did you kill him?"

"'Cause he tried to take my money from me. He had threatened my life a couple times and I told him he might as well go ahead and get it over with now because my turn would be next." I'm thinking to myself, *Is this the one time that Dwayne killed somebody or was he really an assassin?* The more violent crack organizations had runners who doubled as hitmen. They were always armed with a semiautomatic. Dwayne had no remorse for the killing of another young man.

"Did he plead for his life? Did he ask you to spare him?"

"Yeah, he was like, 'I'm sorry man. Can we forget it this time? It won't happen again.' But I told him it had already happened, so he might as well just go ahead and suffer the consequences.... I got some buddies out there who do the same thing I do. They ain't going for nothing if somebody runs down on 'em."

He was right! In one trip to Southeast D.C. with cameraman Kevin King, I spotted a group of teens and what had to be preteens hanging out the windows of an apartment building.

The signs all pointed to a street-level drug-selling operation, and I suspected at least a few of the males were packing. There was a time when reporters were given time to research and produce incredible stories for air, especially during a ratings period when television news operations were doing their best work at whatever the cost to draw the most viewers. Advertisers paid top dollar to the top stations. This was before the internet. TV news was still king. It was during sweeps period that we did our best work.

On this late afternoon or early evening, Kevin and I were looking for a scoop. We wouldn't find it back at the office. It was getting late, and we were tired of cruising the area for hours with no specific plan, but we hoped we would come across something interesting; something that hadn't been shown on TV news before. I wanted a story with impact, to show how dangerous it had gotten out here for everybody, including cops, who liked to remind us that their goal every day and night during the crack epidemic was to make it back home at the end of the shift. Single mothers were trapped. If they worked, they only earned enough to pay for childcare, food, and rent; they couldn't afford to move to safe, higher ground. Those who didn't work were fighting the streets for their sons and daughters.

I told Kevin to park the car. I was wearing a suit. He was in jeans and a sweatshirt. The two of us getting out made us look like undercover narcs, and I never put my crew in jeopardy. I used to remind them, "You can get scared when you see me scared!" When I was afraid, I would never let them know. I got out of the parked car and slowly, but confidently, proceeded up a hill toward the group that guarded the apartment building and whatever they had stashed inside. I counted at least ten people, but I wasn't nervous. Most drug dealers, even the young ones, are not looking to add more trouble on top of the usual mayhem that comes with this line of work. I had never felt a drug dealer would shoot me for just getting in the way.

I asked who was in charge. It was important to identify, recognize, and respect a chain of command.

A good-looking kid who might have been fifteen or sixteen stepped up and said, "That would be me."

After explaining I wasn't a cop but a news dude looking for a story that would help explain how dangerous it was out here, I didn't have to spell it out that it was a story about the crack wars. I explained that I knew I was dealing with businessmen and my being there might be interrupting their enterprise. I said that I had forty dollars in my pocket and would be willing to give it all over if someone was willing to show me a gun and explain on camera why he was packing. Of course, I agreed no faces, no names.

They huddled up with their backs turned away from me. Kevin King was still in the car. I'm assuming he'd be ready to speed off if I came running if this all went off the tracks. I never turned my back on the group. In just seconds, the leader came up to me and said he would do it.

I signaled to Kevin, *Let's go.*

The kid who had been selected for my exclusive interview could not have been much more than twelve or thirteen, and he could not have weighed 125 pounds soaking wet.

We were rolling video. No face, no name. The camera was pointed to his shirt that was soon lifted to reveal a 38-caliber revolver. No match for a semiautomatic weapon out here, but if he could aim and fire at a stationary target, somebody would be going down, and maybe for good.

"So where did you get the gun?"

"From a crackhead."

"And what did it cost, what did you give him?"

"Some crack!"

"Are you prepared to use that gun if you have to?"

"Yeah."

"Are you afraid out here?"

"Yeah, you're gonna be afraid. Police out here and they're afraid. Everybody's afraid."

"Okay, that's it right."

"No names, no faces?"

"Right. Thanks."

That was the end of my exclusive interview.

The group of young gunmen and I assumed they all were armed, turned and walked back to the building where others had perched in windows to watch or more importantly guard us from danger.

Kevin and I turned downhill to the news car. Once inside, I took a deep breath, let go a sigh, and said out loud, "That went well."

My exclusive interview would air in a week on Channel 9 during a sweeps period when every TV station was competing for viewers. You could hear a pin drop in the newsroom when that kid was talking and his gun was filling the TV screen.

THE GARRISON TWINS

It was April 8, 1998. Lawrence and Lamont Garrison had made their mom, grandmother, and uncle incredibly proud by completing their studies toward college degrees from the historic Howard University in Washington, D.C. The Garrison twins had always been the primary focus of this Northeast D.C. family. Growing up in a tough neighborhood known as Trinidad, they had been kept on the straight and narrow. They attended McKinley Tech High in pressed shirts and trousers. Sometimes they came to school in bow-ties. No pants hanging below their butts like the local losers who cut classes early and often. The twins were smart. A classmate recalled for me that they took advanced college-prep courses.

After high school, Lawrence and Lamont landed coveted internships at some federal agencies. They also worked part-time jobs. Their uncle Junior came up with a used car, which they enjoyed working on.

It had taken six years, often going part time, to complete work toward Political Science degrees, but the journey was worth it. Karen Garrison had built two fine young Black men who would make any parent proud.

And then it was gone.

Days before their twenty-fifth birthdays, DEA agents pounded on the door of their row house while the family was stretched out watching TV. This was a raid. They had a warrant for the arrests of Lawrence and Lamont Garrison. The boys had been named as part of a thirteen-person conspiracy to sell crack. They had never been arrested before—never gotten as much as a traffic ticket growing up!

To this day, the Garrison twins, their mother, friends, and college professors, everybody who knows them, say they are innocent.

When they were taken into custody there were no drugs, no large sums of cash, no wiretaps, no video.

"Everything is not what it seemed. We thought our system of jurisprudence was fair, but it's not," said Lamont Garrison.

The nightmare began many months earlier, when the twins were taking their uncle's damaged car to a body repair shop in Capitol Heights, Maryland, outside D.C. The shop was owned and operated by a convicted drug dealer by the name of Tito Abea. His business was under surveillance by the FBI and a joint federal–regional drug task force.

When Abea was arrested, he struck a deal with prosecutors. If he hadn't made the deal, he would have received a mandatory crack sentence that would have put him away for life. Abea named thirteen co-conspirators, Lawrence and Lamont Garrison among them. Lawrence told me, "Only thing I'm supposed to notice is that he fixed the car, that the paint matched, and things like that! That's all I'm supposed to notice. I'm not supposed to notice they were bringing drugs out of the shop. I never noticed anything like that."

Karen Garrrison wanted to refinance the house, get her sons a good attorney, but Lamont vetoed that plan. He would accept the public defender appointed by the court to represent him and his brother. They were innocent, he said. A judge and jury had to believe them.

Karen Garrison reached out to me for help. She had seen my work on TV. All the network TV operations and major newspapers had received the package of information she had compiled but turned her down. The story needed an entire investigative team to sort through the records and interview witnesses. I had never gotten anyone out of prison or had charges dropped against an innocent person. I had shed some light on what appeared to be injustices or just bad things happening to poor Black people. I might have made some people feel better knowing that somebody cared, but one of my biggest regrets was not being able to get Lamont and Lawrence out of this trouble. I felt I was going to prison with them.

I wanted Ed Bradly of CBS *Sixty Minutes* fame to take the story. Or what about Georgetown University's program that had some success having sentences commuted and innocent people freed after years in prison?

Karen Garrison admitted from the start that she had put her boys through some stuff. They were left for her mother Angel and Junior to care for when Karen had to go to prison.

As a young woman working as a hairstylist, she'd accepted a job from Isaac Tingle, a noted heroin dealer, that paid her $250 per week. "That was a lot of money back then." Her job was to travel to several locations a few times a day to collect money that heroin addicts had paid to Tingle's street dealers. Eventually, Karen was counted on to tabulate large sums from the heroin trafficking. If you visited D.C. back in the 1970s and '80s, you couldn't miss the heroin traffic along the city's riot corridor on 14th Street. Junkies by the dozens, if not hundreds, gathered at 14th and W Streets near Dottie's Carryout. At least three or four times a day, each time the high wore off, they reappeared on the corners waiting for the heroin man to buy packets of the brown stuff that the men and women addicts would shoot up. In the arms, legs, necks, any part of their bodies that would support a syringe and needle penetration.

She was named as a co-conspirator when Isaac Tingle and others were arrested. Garrison was considered a bit player, but she was sent to a federal prison in Lexington, Kentucky, to serve a two-year sentence. Karen Garrison says while in prison, she made it her life's work to make sure the twins never got involved in drug trafficking. She was equally determined to stay on the straight and narrow herself.

Their professors at Howard University paraded to the courthouse in Alexandria, Virginia, to testify on behalf of Lawrence and Lamont Garrison. At my suggestion, the family hired a retired D.C. narcotics cop, Jim Bradley, to investigate. Jim concluded the Garrison twins were not involved in drug dealing at any level. He told me on camera for my story that "They were just two smart, fat boys who liked to work on cars."

The judge refused their attorney's request to sever the Garrison case from the others. The judge's action meant that Lawrence and Lamont had to be seated at the start of trial at the table with the co-defendants when guns and drugs were brought into the courtroom and submitted as evidence. From that point on, Karen Garrison knew her boys stood no chance of acquittal. "When we saw the evidence and the judge refused to separate the boys' case, we knew the conspiracy charge belonged to all of them," she explained.

In the end, the jury convicted everybody who refused a plea, including the Garrisons. Tito Abea got thirty-six months. Lawrence Garrison was sentenced to fifteen-and-a-half years in prison. Lamont got nineteen-and-a-half years; they added four years because he took the stand to try and explain to the jury that he and his brother were innocent and had never met their co-defendants other than Abea.

Karen fainted in the courtroom at sentencing. She then spent subsequent years trying to get attorneys to appeal the sentences and the media to cover the story of what happened to her boys.

I went at it alone, although others reporters got onboard in later years when the harsh mandatory, minimum crack sentences were revisited. Powder cocaine convictions for first-time offenders usually meant probation, unless you were Marion Barry. He got six months.

I interviewed Lawrence and Lamont several times, beginning when they were still being held in jail in Northern Virginia, before they were separated. Identical twins cannot do time in the same prison facility. They went years not able to see, touch, or talk with one another.

I contacted jurors to explain their verdicts. There had been no FBI wiretaps, no drugs seized from the Garrison home, no undercover drug buy, no direct testimony from anyone but Abea.

The first juror told me by phone, "We didn't actually see a direct link to their wrongdoing but we felt it was a strong case for conspiracy. The Garrison twins were simply in places where innocent people should not be. That's what juror number three told me, "If they got a combined thirty-four years it was certainly higher than anybody else got. They were at the bottom of the pyramid. The sentence was completely out of proportion to the crime."

It was a crack-cocaine mandatory minimum case. The judge and jury had no say in the amount of time that came with the convictions. It was all part of the national crime bill, the response to the crack cocaine war. President Bill Clinton had signed the bill in 1994. Then-Senator Joe Biden was a major sponsor, but the truth is, the Congressional Black caucus and local elected Black leaders, raised little if any opposition to the harsh sentences that were applied disproportionately to Black defendants because of the violence associated with crack. Black people wanted something done about the violence, but they didn't offer any alternatives.

The Garrisons each had a few years reduced from their sentences eventually after lawmakers began to admit crack sentences had been incredibly unfair.

I was determined to keep their cases in the sentencing-reform conversation all the time they were incarcerated.

Lawrence and Lamont had spent two and three times the years in prison, respectively, that it took to earn their Political Science degrees from Howard University. What was the biggest adjustment, I once asked early on? Lamont told me, "Time!" How to do the time, how to fill the time with someone telling you what to do and when to do it." A lot of hours were spent in the prison library helping other inmates appeal their cases. Because they were identical twins regulations meant they could not be held in the same prison. That meant two separate trips to two different places and, sometimes it meant visiting different states for their family.

Every time I left the prison, I was hit by the thought that their time, their minds, could have been put to such better use! Lawrence and Lamont and so many of the others didn't belong in prison for all those years. I would have lost my mind in prison. On the set of "Off Script," Lamont said "I didn't have a life sentence. I knew that one day I would be returning to society. You gotta prepare for that. It's nothing else to do in prison but prepare. We went to penitentiaries in our travels and most of the people we saw were Blacks who for little or nothing got life sentences!"

Karen Garrison is now a grandmother. Lawrence and his wife gave her that gift upon his release after they got married. Since his release, he and his twin brother Lamont had joined their mother as staunch advocates for sentencing reform.

But the Covid-19 pandemic would have a say, and it was cruel and painful. Lawrence Garrison passed away in January of 2021.

Bruce Johnson with Oprah

On set with DC Congressmember Eleanor Holmes Norton

On set with Senator Cory Booker and former NAACP head Ben Jealous

Bruce Johnson looking very much like a child reporter, in the early days

Getting my hair cut off by wife Lori during chemo for Non-Hodgkin's Lymphoma

Reporting on the election of Pope Francis from the Vatican

BJ reporting from the field with the crew back in the day

Interviewing the late legendary Georgetown University basketball coach
John Thompson, first African American to win a national NCAA title

With colleagues Mike Buchanan, Pat Collins, and legendary news director Jim Snyder,
who hired us and built a news dynasty at WTOP which later became WUSA9

Mary Johnson-Marbry, better known simply as Ma!

In studio with CBS NFL sports anchor and close friend James Brown

Bruce Johnson's proof sheet as a young reporter

In dining room TV studio during the Covid pandemic and lockdown

Reporting at the White House

With former mentee, now CBS morning news anchor and star, Gayle King

With the late Washington TV anchor and close friend Jim Vance

With the late civil rights icon and congressman, John Lewis

What's left of Grand Avenue Court where Johnson, Ma, and his siblings once lived

With Marion Barry

In studio last year

At Ben's Chili Bowl Wall of Fame

Sacred Heart Seminary

Reporting from Paris, France on one of many overseas assignments

CHAPTER 11

What Didn't Kill Me Made Me Stronger!

SOMETIME IN LATE 1989, I began to secretly duck out of the newsroom before the six PM news. Some total strangers were waiting for me, twice a week, at a strip mall in Rockville, Maryland. These were not news sources feeding me important news tips. This was bigger and there were no excuses for being late.

I was always a little late. The last one to stroll into the room hoping not to be recognized—hoping not to see a face that I knew. The session would be over in a couple hours. In the beginning I really didn't want to be here. Not for a single minute, but I needed this! I needed to stop drinking! I hadn't been able to quit the booze on my own. Drinking had stopped being fun, a pleasure, a stress reliever. It had become more than just a problem. I was afraid of how this was going to end. I had plenty of examples of where it could end. I wanted to live!

It wasn't a long drive; just a few miles north on Wisconsin Avenue, but rush-hour traffic made the arrival unpredictable. The room was always full, and I could feel the sympathetic glances aimed my way. This would go on for several weeks.

I was in an alcohol-rehab program that was run by Suburban Hospital in nearby Bethesda, Maryland. There were stories behind every person seated in the room. Men, and some women, majority White. I'm guessing middle- to upper-middle class, but I couldn't be sure. I unfairly profiled everybody in the room. I'm sure they were also trying to figure out how I ended up here.

I had voluntarily entered the recovery program after making a unanimous call to Suburban's 24/7 hotline. Actually, I had made a few calls over several weeks but always hung up before committing to come in for an interview and examination.

Some of the people in the room had the decision made for them. A drunk-driving arrest, family intervention, or threat of losing the job filled a lot of the seats next to me. We had the submit to taking an oral drug called antabuse. The clinical name is disulfiram and it works by not allowing the body to process alcohol. It produces a really bad reaction if you try to drink alcohol on Antabuse; but that didn't stop a few people from trying.

I wasn't there to try and figure out if I had a drinking problem. I had surrendered before setting foot in the room. I had grown up around booze and drugs and seen what happens when a good fun-seeking drinker turns into a dangerous drunk. People get hurt. People sometimes die.

In the beginning, I was embarrassed that I couldn't fix this— stop drinking on my own or at least control the time, the amount, and type of alcohol I was consuming. In the end the drink was like the prize waiting for me after a great day of reporting, but also at the end of a really bad day.

Eventually I started avoiding the bars and restaurants. Too expensive. Too risky, and I knew cops waited outside the popular watering holes like the Dancing Crab and Babes. I retreated to a well-stocked bar in the basement of my home. A cigarette and smoke at the end of the day. I told myself I had earned the right. It was yet more evidence of another success I had achieved. I worked the phones talking to news sources and colleagues, which added to my cover for what was really happening in the dungeon.

There was no epiphany! No one incident that made me seek help. I was suffering on many fronts. Physically, mentally, and spiritually. Over time I just got really tired of feeling sick and tired! Slow to start my mornings, impossible to get to sleep. Too many to do things on the weekend with the wife and kids that fell through.

Tanqueray and tonic was my preferred drink, but I tried everything! When I was in Russia on assignment, I drank Vodka. If we were vacationing in the Caribbean, it was the best Rum. If I was impressed with somebody and they were drinking scotch, I became a scotch drinker for a while. I recall a friend and popular television anchor once telling me that I should drink soda water with my gin. It can't be smelled, he insisted. I did but he was wrong. I was told by a colleague, one morning at work, that the alcohol could be smelled coming through my pores. Her personal observation put more fear in me than the death of a colleague years earlier.

In 1978, Paul Henderson of WJLA-TV (ABC) was twenty-six years old and a rising star in Washington TV. He was far more polished as a broadcaster than me. It was four AM when his car went out of control, struck a pole, and flipped over at Georgia and Missouri Avenues. The police report says he was traveling alone and may have fallen asleep at the wheel. Perhaps!

In January of 1985, another colleague, reporter Kelly Burke of WRC-TV pleaded guilty to driving under the influence after an accident that killed twenty-nine-year-old Dennis Crouch, one of his Poolsville, Maryland, neighbors. A judge ordered Burke to produce a documentary on the consequences of drunk driving. A more serious charge of homicide with a motor vehicle while intoxicated, was dropped.

It would be four years after the Burke case when I turned myself in for outpatient treatment. I don't credit anything. It was God's grace. Most people don't seek help and most of those who do don't recover.

Still, I was embarrassed to seek help. I paid out of pocket to Suburban hospital. I didn't want anyone at work to know, so I didn't put in a claim with my health insurance company. Only my wife knew. Twice a week I listened to staff explain why some people can drink socially and others like me cannot. I wasn't interested in drinking socially, not really. Never liked the taste of hard liquor and was never a beer or wine drinker. I did like getting slightly high. A buzz lightened every boring moment. It made a great time even better! But over time, some years, the alcohol stopped working. It turned on me. I hated not being in control. Not able to quit after one or two drinks. Truth is one drink was never enough, and two drinks meant, time permitting, there would be a third drink or more.

There was another reason to quit drinking. I didn't want to end up like the other men in my world who weren't able to put their lives and careers back together because of a drinking, drug, or mental-health issue or a miscarriage of justice. Life isn't fair. I saw that in the beginning as a child. A lot of the men I wanted to look up to hid their insecurities in a bottle. Marvin Gaye, in the book *Divided Soul*, was quoted as saying he could never shake the feeling of inadequacy. I know that feeling. It's destructive. But I learned that what other people say or think about me is none of my business. Why listen to their taking of my inventory? What's my opinion of me? Black culture in particular frowns at therapy and support groups. I believe in therapy for anyone who needs it. That support group in Rockville did for me what I could not do for myself. And I've learned to take life a day at a time. I get to reboot every morning. The past is gone. The future is not yet here. I'm living in the here and now. Do the best I can, and leave the rest up to God.

A few weeks into the Suburban Hospital program, I became comfortable. The fear of being outed was replaced with the anticipation of seeing friends who I only knew by their first names. If someone recognized me as the guy on TV, I was ok with that. I had stopped running away from me!

◡

I stopped smoking at about the same time I stopped drinking. Quitting cigarettes was harder!

Two friends—Courtland Mulloy, a *Washington Post* columnist, and Jim Vance, the legendary news anchor at NBC4—were also determined to stop smoking. Jim was a two-pack-a-day smoker, one menthol, the other nonmenthol. He told us over brunch one Sunday that he was undergoing hypnosis to try and quit smoking. After Max Robinson, Vance was the most popular anchor in town, with the ratings to prove it. If Jim was giving a hypnotist a try, so would I.

I made an appointment for the coming week. I had a pack of Benson & Hedges menthol in my pocket when I arrived at the office, not far from the National Cathedral in upper northwest. I said a quiet prayer before going in, knowing I didn't have another plan if this didn't work, and I had no reason to believe it would.

The hypnotist clicked on a tape recorder, pulled out a watch, and began talking. I don't remember what he said. I was sure this wasn't going to work. Never felt an out-of-body experience. When it was over, he gave me the recording and told me to play it as many times per day as I needed, as long as it was in a quiet room where I could relax. In hindsight, I'm thinking he was training me to meditate.

I paid the fee. It might have been a hundred bucks. I would have paid a lot more if it came with a guarantee. I got to the car and immediately lit up a cigarette, more out of habit than needing one at the time. I took a puff and felt something was missing. I didn't recognize the taste. The smell bothered me. There was no sense of relaxation that came from the usual smoke. After that one puff, I threw the cigarette away. I haven't had a cigarette since. I celebrate the time I stopped smoking on Thanksgiving Day too. The cigarette habit was harder to break than drinking.

Here's what another former smoker told me he learned. The urge to smoke for those addicted to cigarettes only lasts for forty-five seconds. And then it's gone. He said we can get through forty-five seconds, right? What he also said is that the forty-five-second urge to smoke will hit an addicted smoker many times a day, but it lessens the longer you are able to resist and eventually quit smoking.

I wanted to get that information to President Barack Obama, who had been a smoker for years when he entered the White House. There would be enough pressure on the country's first African American president. I wish my mother had lived to see it. I wish Barack could stop smoking. I feel the same way about comedian Dave Chappelle. Before Covid, we met at the District's Duke Ellington School for the Arts, where Dave is the most famous alumnus. In an interview he told me the millions spent to renovate the school for Black students was a tribute to America. I liked that. My exclusive reports on conditions at Ellington helped secure the funding for the extensive renovations. Now if I could just get Dave Chappell to stop smoking cigarettes.

Since my people were old enough and allowed to work for wages, cigarette companies and liquor stores everywhere have done all they could to keep poor folks puffing away and drinking. It became an entitlement. We work hard; we can afford some of life's pleasures.

We were the last to get the news. This stuff can kill you. Smoking and drinking have hooked and taken out a lot of people that I really care about. Jim Vance died on July 22, 2017, of lung cancer. Before that, Jim and I promised one another to meet at least once a month for dinner at the Cafe Deluxe Restaurant on Wisconsin Avenue. It was about the same distance to our workplaces. He wasn't old enough to replace the father I never had, but his wisdom and humility made our meetings special and much needed for me. He said often that he too looked forward to our dinners. There was no agenda. Just two Black men with more years behind us than ahead. In the time we had left we would talk about anything we wanted. This was the time and place to sort it all out. To try and quiet all the noise that could creep into our heads. We knew all the slogan's "Don't let someone live free inside your head." "The mind can be like a bad neighborhood." Could either of us afford righteous indignation?

The unscripted chatter and laughter often lasted so long that staff was cleaning up for closing, and people were interrupting our conversations to tell us how much they appreciated our work, our longevity.

We sometimes shared a dessert. I had never shared dessert from the same plate with another man. Nothing was off limits. Most of Jim's history with cocaine had already been documented. He announced on the air to viewers the times he was leaving to enter treatment at the Betty Ford Clinic. He told *Washingtonian* magazine about the time he put a gun to his head and considered suicide. Did depression lead to drugs or did the drugs cause the depression?

Despite his local fame from TV, Vance repeated over dinner how he once accompanied a drug associate to the Summit Hills Apartments in Silver Spring and drove right into a Montgomery County police sting. Jim was lucky that night. The cop looked at his identification and then told him to "Get the fuck out of here, Vance."

In recovery, Jim readily shared his story with anyone who needed to hear it. He helped start recovery meetings in the Columbia area of D.C. And while he struggled with his own sobriety, Jim Vance was known for introducing other addicts and alcoholics to meetings.

When we shared over dinner, there was no need to dress up for live audiences or taped interviews. We weren't being judged. There were no hidden secrets. I told him everything. Whatever was bothering me. We talked about our marriages, our women, our children, and of course, our jobs and the impact race had on our careers and the country. Like fellow anchor Max Robinson, Vance was certain racism was in this country's DNA. The evidence is there.

No need to pretend or sugarcoat details. We were not capable of judging one another. I loved this brother. Jim was nearly a decade older than me; he was the big brother that I never had. But he also knew he could confide in me and he appreciated the fact that whatever I said to him was said out of love.

My friend Jim Vance was seventy-five years old when he died of cancer. He had been the face of NBC4 for nearly forty-five years. Despite all his success and the millions of dollars he earned in that time, Jim suffered from immense insecurity. He told me more than once that his biggest fear was always that Max Robinson would return from network anchoring to reclaim his spot at my workplace, WUSA-TV. Max had been the Washington market's most popular anchorman before departing for ABC. Max had died in December of 1988. Jim had his own legacy. After starting as a reporter in Philadelphia, he came to Washington in 1969, paving the way for coming journalists like me who were just entering college with no clue that TV journalism jobs would even be possible to us upon graduation.

Near the end, I visited Jim and his girlfriend, Christina Eaglin, at his home in Silver Spring after he was no longer able to report for work on the anchor desk. His workload had been cut entirely. No more trying to at least anchor the cash cow eleven PM newscast. He was rail thin and taking part in clinical trials to try and stave off the cancer. I can't help but recall that after every dinner at Cafe Deluxe, Jim would light up a smoke as we stepped outside. His spanking new Corvette parked illegally at the stop sign. There never was a ticket on it. Cops must have known who that car belonged to.

It isn't until September of 2017, that Jackie Bradford, his long-time friend and station general manager was able to organize an incredibly moving and uplifting service for Jim at Washington's historic National Cathedral. Jim and his wife Cathy had been separated, but his wife, adult children, his colleagues, and city leaders wanted a public memorial service, even though Jim had insisted that a smaller party among co-workers would have been fine. I disagree. My friend deserved a sendoff fit for the other notables who were eulogized at the cathedral, including former presidents. The cathedral is also a local church to many D.C. area residents. Retired local anchors Gordon Peterson and Paul Berry were there. Jim and I were members of Kappa Alpha Psi fraternity. His frat brothers from Cheyney State University in Philadelphia were on the program. They volunteered vintage Vance stories from back in the day. It was kept light, at times really funny, as Jim would have wanted.

I'm glad Jackie Bradford didn't listen to Jim's directive before he died. Funerals are for those who are left behind. We need some closure, a place to park all these memories, the good and the not so good.

I had no way of knowing, no signal that after saying goodbye to Jim, cancer would come looking for me. Jim helped me even after he was gone.

⤙

Nobody wants to hear they have cancer. I had already been through some stuff. I had no choice but to turn to God and the medical team at Medstar Georgetown University Hospital if I was to survive this latest life-threatening illness.

It was the spring of 2018 when I first learned that I had Non-Hodgkin's Lymphoma. It's a cancer that can develop in the network of vessels and glands that are spread throughout the body. The lymphatic system is part of our immune system. I knew it was a blood cancer and that was all. My first question was how could this happen? Nobody in my family had this disease. My mom had died from pancreatic cancer; my natural father from lung cancer. Only two-hundred-thousand people in the entire country have this type of cancer. Why was I so lucky?

I had kicked cigarettes, booze, and beaten a heart attack years ago; that heart attack nearly took me out at the age of forty-two. I was on assignment on July 2, 1992. It was a hot and humid D.C. afternoon and I had just wrapped a really good story about some young guys who explained why selling drugs made more economic sense to them than signing up for then Mayor Sharon Pratt's summer jobs program. As I headed back to the station to file my report, I felt a tightness in my chest that I couldn't massage away. Within minutes my cameraman, Mike Fox was pulling into a fire station and yelling at paramedics that "I've got Bruce Johnson in the car, and he's having a heart attack."

The emergency room staff at then-Greater Southeast Community Hospital saved my life. Doctor Joseph Robinson was head of cardiology and just happened to be on duty when I was rushed in. They stabilized me, then summoned a medivac helicopter that flew me to the Washington Hospital Center where Doctor Robinson and Doctor Hector Collison went to work to save my life.

A soft clot blocking my left anterior descending coronary artery was removed when a tiny compressed balloon was inserted and threaded to the spot to clear the clot and the artery. The balloon angioplasty was a success. What had been excruciating pain subsided.

It would take months of rehabilitation to get my strength back and many more months to restore damaged heart muscle and get my ejection fraction to where Doctor Robinson would stop worrying about his patient and friend suffering heart failure or another coronary.

Racquetball had replaced Happy Hour after I gave up drinking. That was two years before my coronary. My new love, running, would replace racquetball.

In 2000, I completed the twenty-six-point-two-mile Marine Corp Marathon. I beat half the men my age. How many people run a marathon after a heart attack?

So, as I reflect on my history of comebacks and waddle through a pool of self-pity over the cancer diagnosis, *What next?* I recall asking God.

The response was, "This is next." Non-Hodgkin's Lymphoma.

My discovery that something was wrong came when I looked in the bathroom mirror at our beach house outside Lewes, Delaware.

I discovered that a mass of flesh was growing alongside my tonsil. It was at the back of my mouth where the tongue disappeared into the throat. I had been experiencing a sore throat for some time and not really feeling at the top of my game.

One morning I said to my wife, Lori, I need to go to Georgetown University Hospital to check this out. I can't say for certain why I wanted to go right then. But something bigger than my usual judgment said "Let's go." Was it the same voice that, against my nature, said "It's time to let your cameraman know, you need to get to a hospital. You're having a heart attack." It turns out that voice was saving my life again. God ain't through with me yet!

Here's the good news! The overall five-year survival rate from NHL is roughly 70 percent. It drops to 60 percent after ten years. Early detection is always better regardless of the cancer.

Just because you get to the emergency room doesn't mean you won't be kept waiting for extended periods of time. In my case it was an awful six hours consecutive hours of waiting. I was put on a bed just off the emergency room. Everyone who came in to look into my mouth had a different opinion. "It's no big deal, we can put a needle in that, nothing serious." Then finally, I said to somebody, maybe an intern, "Do you think this could be cancer?" *Bam!* I said it, the first person to properly diagnose my own illness. Shortly after that an oncologist comes in with his student attached. He doesn't acknowledge my suspicion, but he didn't have to. His says he doesn't want to do a biopsy there in the emergency room, but I should come to the office tomorrow. He suspected oral cancer. I'm thinking, *What else could it be?*

A biopsy was conducted, and doctors were so sure it was oral cancer that they were moving quickly to schedule me for surgery and possible radiation. I was warned my broadcasting career could be in danger. I likely would need physical and speech therapy.

Then a few days before my scheduled surgery, I got the call. The biopsy revealed it was Non-Hodgkin's Lymphoma! As scary as that sounded, it would mean chemotherapy and not the knife and radiation. My case had already been forwarded to Doctor Bruce Cheson, a prominent oncologist who specialized in my disease.

"Fortunately, yours was still localized to the neck, which is not what we usually see." That was the first reassurance I had heard. It came from Cheson in our initial meeting in the famed Lombardi Cancer Center at Medstar Georgetown University Hospital.

This wouldn't be a cakewalk. My white blood cell count was already low. I probably could not withstand the regular chemo cocktail that is given to NHL patients to attack their cancer.

I would become only the second of Cheson's patients to undergo this special treatment. "For you, we're trying to take out some of the toxic drugs and insert more targeted drugs." My response was "Sure, okay."

Cheson had a demeanor that would calm any pilot trying to land a twin engine plane with both engines on fire—which might explain why he was playing and singing in a band made up of other oncologists. They have a videotape and were good enough to perform at the House of Blues nightclub in Chicago.

I was sixty-eight years old. That seemed young, but not for most Black men, including the dad I never knew. He never saw sixty-five. I had adopted a healthy lifestyle decades ago, but was it too late? Nobody could explain how I contracted this type cancer.

My boss at work, Richard Dyer, the president and GM at channel 9, seemed to take my illness really hard. He had a meeting in his office with the station manager, Michael Valentine, and the HR officer, Amanda Levi. She teared up as I did when Dyer started describing the journey I was about to embark on. Right on cue, I went into a coughing spell that wouldn't stop. It was another symptom of the cancer.

Everybody knew I would have to say something on air to viewers. I didn't want to read from a script. I would speak from the heart—that's where I'm best—during one of the evening newscasts I anchor. Maybe not at six; but at seven PM during my "Off Script with Bruce Johnson" broadcast.

I would then go to social media to chat with friends and fans. The thousands on our FB pages became my support group. If I didn't post updates, they would ask how it was going. There was already a Facebook Non-Hodgkin's Lymphoma support group. I'm an active participant to this day.

Here's how the announcement went on air. I almost didn't make it through my remarks.

"I'm going close tonight on a personal note," I said. "I'm going to have to step away from 'Off Script' and anchoring the six o'clock news and reporting here at WUSA9. I have cancer. A week ago, my biopsy came back and I tested positive for Non-Hodgkin's lymphoma."

Boy, was that hard. Jim Vance, after he'd been diagnosed, was able to get through his announcement on air and that might have helped get me through. My good friend had shown me how to do this!

"Uh, I begin chemotherapy soon," I continued, "so I'm going be away some weeks, maybe a bit longer. I do plan to be active on social media, and you can find me there and I'll look for you there. Have a good night, a great weekend, and I'll see you." That was a Friday. Lesli Foster, my six o'clock co-anchor had phoned my daughter who arrived at the studio with my second grandson just as I was coming off air. It was a welcomed sight. I hugged them both. I think I may have recorded some remarks with Lesli for use later on the eleven PM newscast. I was emotionally drained. But I had one more major public appearance before I could submit fully to this battle with cancer.

In a week, I would be the commencement speaker at my alma mater, Northern Kentucky University. Doctor Cheson had wanted to begin chemo treatments immediately. I was determined to keep that commencement promise. I try to never let down young people. The university was also presenting me with an honorary doctorate degree.

Lori and I flew in to Greater Cincinnati Airport, which is across the Ohio River in Northern Kentucky. It was a Saturday. My voice had gotten considerably worse, with the graduation ceremony now but hours away on a Sunday afternoon on the campus in Highland Heights, Kentucky.

I would deliver two speeches to 20,000 people at two commencements at the BB&T Arena.

I told the graduates and their families that I was the first in my family to graduate college and, like them, I attended NKU fulltime while working a full-time job. My degree encouraged my siblings and my mother to go to college, and her degree came after raising eight kids.

"So be an example to your family first," I said. "Reach back for one, then reach out to your community and then someone who doesn't look like you, reach out past your comfort zone into this diverse world; that's where you get the biggest bang for your buck. It's the kind of diversity you have seen right here on this campus. You are ready for that diverse world. The question is, are they ready for you? I'm betting on you."

Lori and I left the ceremony and headed straight for the airport. We arrived back in Washington that Sunday evening. Neither of us got any sleep that night. The next morning, I underwent my first chemotherapy session at Georgetown. I was there for hours. Each drug had been formulated just for me. A witness was called in to confirm each one in front of me. A catheter went into the left arm. My heart rate was monitored throughout. There was a tightness in my chest that subsided after a while. My body was accepting the chemical invasion, whose mission was to attack and destroy the cancer cells.

Lori was quiet, which meant she was nervous. "Are you nervous?" she asked. Then responded before I could answer, "I'm nervous," she volunteered. I told her I was more anxious to get started.

I was going to share the experience on social media. By putting myself into reporter mode, it became easier to ignore how much serious trouble I was in. I had Lori shoot video on my iPhone. I had to do this in one take. After all, it was a "look live" report from behind a curtain in the chemo-ingestion center.

I made a connection with one other patient, in part because he was sitting in the waiting room at the Lombardi Cancer Center, wearing Pittsburgh Steelers gear in a Washington football team town.

Sean Davis had stage-four Non-Hodgkin's lymphoma. He had been battling the disease for years and credited the clinical trials and Doctor Cheson with keeping him alive. "I just try to stay positive as much as I can," he told me.

His son, Sean, was a safety for the Pittsburgh Steelers. A second son was graduating from the University of Maryland and looking to make a pro football squad of his own.

"As a husband and a father, Bruce, you can understand this. My house is in order. I couldn't say this in 2010. My whole mission in life now is to make sure I put not just my immediate family but my children's children in a good spot."

As of this writing, we stay in touch.

I kept my word to keep viewers and social media fans and followers abreast of my progress. I let them into my world on the good days and the bad, including when the self-pity set in. But I also wanted them to see me fighting cancer. Prayers and a positive attitude work.

When the cancer started to take my hair and I started to look as sick as I was, I decided to surrender, give my hair away. With camera rolling in our kitchen, Lori cut off all of my hair. I became bald and would soon show the video to the world.

Turns out cancer allowed me to come clean with who I was becoming: a veteran broadcast journalist far closer to the end of a career than a beginning, and it was okay to start looking the part. I had been coloring my hair for years. I was becoming comfortable in my own skin. Besides, half the Black men in my fraternity are bald. That's true of the old and young.

I thought about my mother's battle with pancreatic cancer. Not once did I ever hear her complain. When I came home from the seminary to visit my grandma Millie, who was fighting diabetes and lost both legs in the process, I never heard her complain.

I was scheduled to undergo six chemo treatments, which was reduced to four treatments as I continued to respond well to sessions. The growth at the back of my mouth alongside my tonsil started to disappear almost from the first treatment. I would ask Doctor Cheson how they arrived at six treatments. His response was reassuring and the kind of honesty I had come to appreciate as a reporter. He said "It was arbitrary;" there is no exact science that says it has to be six treatments. After a fourth session, a CT exam showed no more signs of Non-Hodgkin's Lymphoma. I was cancer-free. I would need to be examined every few months for two years. I was grateful to Doctor Cheson, Lori, my children, Sean, and Lisa Davis, but I was mostly thankful to God. I had been given a reprieve, again!

Not even a serious bicycle accident was going to stop my return to full-time work as a broadcast journalist. I don't know how to gradually return to living. I began riding my Cannondale Super Six again, the bike you might see in the Tour de France race through the Swiss Alps. I was back in the saddle after I had agreed to Doctor Cheson's request to chair the 2018 Lymphoma Research Ride. It was the least I could do for the man who helped save my life. Bruce Cheson is also one of the founders of the annual local Lymphoma ride, and no one raises more money for the cause. But as one of my good friends once said, "There is always drama where Bruce shows up, and quite often he's in the middle of that drama!" That's fair. Consider this….

During one of my training jaunts in Rock Creek Park, I had a terrible accident. It was in the middle of the day. Vehicular traffic had been stopped by signs and workers doing road repairs. I turned onto the parallel pedestrian pathway to move around the delay. As I came off the path and dropped back down on the street pavement, past a manned temporary barricade, the bike collapsed under me. It came apart and I was tossed over the handlebars, face first into the road.

I'm sure there was a concussion. Might have even blacked out a second. Pictures taken by onlookers showed me sprawled out on the pavement, bleeding at several places on the face, arms, and knees. My helmet was still on, my glasses shattered; but my bike was now in two pieces. The frame had broken. All that held the front tire and handle bars together to the rest of the bike was the brake wires.

A Montgomery ambulance crew was summoned. They helped me into the back of the vehicle, and they also agreed to transport my bike to nearby Suburban Hospital, which always seemed to be nearby when I needed them. I suffered a broken nose and a cut that required stitches; a broken finger that required a cast over the entire right hand; and a terrible gash under my nose and above the mouth that required the skills of noted plastic surgeon Doctor Wendell Miles to close in the two weeks before I was due to report back to work and appear on television.

I made it back to work on my scheduled return date, looking very much like I had just stepped off the battlefield. Family and colleagues shook their heads when I explained the cast and other visible injuries. I was just glad to be back at work.

The news team at WUSA9 gave me a standing ovation when I returned and looked every bit like a linebacker who had gained twenty pounds from the steroids and time off. It would take a couple months to get back into game shape.

CHAPTER 12

Black Lives Matter, For Now

IN MAY OF 2020, LIKE most of America, we were prisoners in our homes and apartments. Reporters had been ordered out of the newsroom and warned not to attempt to come back to work inside the building until a vaccine was found for the coronavirus. Except for essential workers, the city and federal governments were being run by people operating remotely.

My dining room had become a makeshift broadcast studio. A spaghetti of wires draped across the dining room table and floor, portable bright lights, a live video camera atop a plant stand with four books for added height. There was one laptop to display the 6 and 7 PM show rundowns, and a second laptop to show a teleprompter, which was being scrolled by someone back at the TV station on a three-second delay. Show producers had to cue me via cell phone to start talking three seconds before viewers actually could see me talking. I needed two iPhones, and two iPads for a single broadcast. And WUSA9 insisted on attaching an ethernet cable to my personal router on the second floor of my house, to save the station money on its internet bill.

It was a new and difficult time for everyone. At times I felt myself becoming mentally and physically ill from the stress. I don't recall a single day that went smoothly from beginning to end. There were times we were just trying to get on and off air with whatever stories we could get to or imagine. God bless Zoom and Skype interviews. But *Who needs this*, I thought more than once. Adding to my worries was that my age, race, and health history put me more at risk for contracting Covid-19 and perhaps not surviving! Several times a day I reported the grim news. How many more people had contracted Covid? And why were African Americans the most likely to get the virus and die from it? Health disparities were the likely reason, said scientists, but that wasn't the entire story. African American workers were on the front lines as essential workers with the most exposure to the disease. We worked in the food stores. We drove the buses, responded to calls for 911, and worked in the nursing homes and hospitals.

A Black employee at a giant food store in Silver Spring, Maryland contacted me to complain that she was sent home from her job because, on her own, she decided to report for work wearing a mask over her mouth and nose. At the time we were being told not to wear masks. They wouldn't help, and a scarcity of masks would jeopardize our emergency healthcare workers who needed the masks while caring for Covid-19 cases in the emergency rooms. I told my TV viewers about the Giant employee, on air and on social media. She was merely taking a step to protect herself, her customers, and her children at home. It wasn't long after that—maybe one full day— that Giant foods was reversing its prohibition on masks and offering all employees their choice of face coverings, including shields, throughout its stores.

I also pointed out what doctors were telling me before scientists and government leaders caught on. Working class and poor Black and Brown people live in crowded housing. They couldn't quarantine in small homes and apartments. If one person in the family contracted the coronavirus, everybody in the house was going to get sick. Anyone with preexisting medical conditions was far more likely to die. I sought out medical experts every day to solicit suggestions on what local health authorities should be doing. This pandemic caught everyone off guard it seemed. Even the country's most famous epidemiologist, Doctor Anthony Fauci, made mistakes. In the beginning, he advised us not to wear masks; perhaps the biggest single bad advice. Later the order was that everyone had better cover up.

Reporting and anchoring remotely from home was broadcast purgatory. A slitter of joy might have come from not having to wear a tie, dress pants, and shoes. For a moment I toyed with the idea of doing one newscast in my underwear just so I could write about it later. I didn't have the nerve to do it. Viewers and channel 9 staff complimented the anchor set in my home, which was mostly Lori's idea. A background of French doors leading into a center hall with staircase, and beyond that, across the hallway into the formal living room, a lit floor lamp, and a gorgeous vase sitting on top of a hand-carved wooden bench that came from a boutique in Rehoboth Beach, Delaware.

There is no way I could have gone on air and stayed on air each night without my wife stepping in as volunteer stage manager, floor director, and onsite executive producer. This was in addition to her own job as a coronavirus contact tracer for the D.C. government. While I was reporting, anchoring the news, and writing commentaries in the dining room, Lori was set up a few feet away, working in the sunroom.

I couldn't leave the house to gather and report the news. Executive Producer Carrie Hernandez reminded me every day that she needed my voice and my contacts to get stories, expert opinions, and advocates on air during the lockdown. I totally understood the stakes.

Throughout much of 2020, there were only two stories that mattered most to every American no matter where they lived. The coronavirus pandemic and the brazen police slayings of African American citizens—all of them unarmed. George Floyd's suffocation from the knee of a Minneapolis cop, pressed into his neck proved to be the tipping point.

Derek Chauvin, a police sergeant, would be sentenced to twenty-two-and-a-half years in prison after a Minneapolis jury of Blacks and Whites, male and female, convicted him of the murder. I have no doubt the outcome would have been different had it not been for the videotape of the crime that sparked protests on six continents and sixty countries.

People quarantined in their homes had no choice but to watch the cop snuffing the life out of Floyd. It was often described as a modern-day lynching.

Only bystanders were not cheering on the law-enforcement-turned-vigilante justice. We saw and heard on video Black and White witnesses urging, then pleading, then demanding that Chauvin stop and that cops under Chauvin's command intercede rather than continue their aiding and abetting in the crime.

George Floyd died on May 25, 2020, in Minneapolis. By June 5, my birthday, people were in the streets filled with outrage. D.C. Mayor Muriel Bowser had ordered the public works department to paint the words Black Lives Matter over a two block area of 16th Street where the boulevard ends at Lafayette Park across from the White House.

But for the pandemic, I would have insisted on being in the streets too. I grew frustrated watching reporters from every station.

Local, network, and cable channels—their reports looked the same. This is the story everybody was covering: a Black man killed by a White police officer! Black people in the streets demonstrating and to a smaller scale, rioting! It's a Black story, correct? Got to get interviews with Black people, preferably a Black Lives Matter leader and don't forget the Black clergy! I literally saw our reporters walk past scores of WHITE people marching to get that BLACK interview. Here's what upset me. There were hundreds of WHITE people marching in step with their Black brothers and sisters! Young White people came as no surprise, but how could we miss the great story that was unfolding right before our eyes. I'm looking at hundreds of old and not so young White people in the streets, carrying signs that say Black Lives Matter! Around the country and the world, there were hundreds of thousands of White people supporting "Black Lives Matter" demonstrators.

For years, African Americans have been complaining about police killing Black people at rates that far exceed our percentage of the populations and those Black people are more likely to be unarmed. Black Lives Matter demonstrations started back in 2012 after unarmed seventeen-year-old Trayvon Martin was shot and killed in Florida by a security guard, and again in July of 2014 when Eric Garner was choked to death by NYPD for selling illegal cigarettes on a street corner.

When I was able to talk live to our young reporters, I had no choice but to say for every viewer to over hear, "I need to hear from some of those WHITE people out there!" I needed our reporters to find out what moved them to the streets in the heart of a pandemic. We knew the answer! George Floyd's murder was the tipping point.

White people all over the world were pouring into the streets at some risk to their own health to protest the police killing of another ordinary Black person? Ahmaud Arbery had already been killed in Georgia; Breonna Taylor in Kentucky; but the timing of George Floyd's slaying made all the difference.

It happened because the detailed video with sound was replayed 24/7 by all media during the pandemic and worldwide stay-at-home orders.

There was now undeniable proof of what Black people had been complaining about for years. There are bad cops out here and not just a few. They are using their authority as intended to keep us in place, and when they see fit, to arrest or even kill us. That's how Black people viewed the George Floyd video.

My teenage neighbor, who happens to be White, explained it this way. "There was no wiggle room." White people who had been willing to give cops the benefit of the doubt in previous killings could no longer dismiss what their eyes were telling them."

I sensed and hoped that I was witnessing something big. A shift in attitude about law enforcement. There have always been bad cops, just like there are bad priests. It's taken this long for some people to realize it. But I'm not yet convinced a majority of White people share the opinion of many Black people about the institution of policing. Maybe Derek Chauvin and a few others were just bad cops that needed to be dealt with!

My view is that it doesn't take a lot of bad cops to destroy police community relations. I compare them to pedophile priests who are shielded by superiors and moved from parish to parish—their victims shamed into frustrated positions of "Can't beat the system. Nothing will change." Police departments need major reform and it can't happen from the inside. "Defunding" police isn't going to happen. The term is a bad one that has become a useful weapon of BLM critics.

What can happen is a reimagining of not just police, but of all public safety. Police have had too much authority, too many responsibilities, and few consequences for improper or criminal conduct.

The news media needs change too. I watched too many reporters unwilling or unable to pursue stories on the streets and the corridors of power. It was never made clear who was responsible for the rioting that accompanied the peaceful Black Lives Matter demonstrations. Catch phrases like, "The peaceful demonstrations turned violent." No, they didn't! I saw two separate demonstrations. One was organized and peaceful; the other was much smaller, a fraction in size; disorganized and hellbent on destroying property and stealing merchandise.

More than once I was disappointed to see reporters not skilled enough to pivot toward something far more interesting than the obvious details we already knew. For example, a TV moment that was lost came when a young White demonstrator stepped into a Fox 5 reporter's live shot to say "I just want to tell police to stop killing Black people." Isn't that why the reporter was out there to explore what brought such people to a demonstration during a pandemic? Rather than solicit further explanation from the protestor, the irate reporter turned away from him to face the live camera to continue his monologue. I couldn't tell you what came out of the reporter's mouth after that. It was a lost opportunity for some great spontaneous television.

I don't think it unreasonable to insist that reporters be more than mic holders or presenters during live shots. My advice to young people I mentor is "Never waste the viewer's time." What will they miss if you're not in the picture and on the scene? If the answer is "Not much," you're not reporting. You're in the way!

If something wasn't happening in my live shot, if I didn't have information that the viewer couldn't get on his or her cell phone in an instant, I was wasting the viewer's time. One of my favorite camera people, Danielle Gatewood Gill, knew when it was time to move, when nothing else was happening at our location and I had run out of things to say. Go to where the news is happening! Take your viewers as close to the action as possible.

In April of 2015, during the demonstrations and riots following the Freddy Gray killing in Baltimore, an irate group of Black residents was gathering in West Baltimore. A few feet away were dozens of city and state police. Reporters were across the street doing their live shots with the protesting crowd used as mere props in the background. I grabbed Gill and said, "Let's go." We waded into the middle of the protesting crowd to launch an impromptu press conference. "What is it you want? Why are you out here?" The leaders began listing their demands, which amounted to jobs, housing, better schools, and recreational facilities. It all made sense. "But what about your elected leaders?" "Are they aware of what you want?" The top elected leaders in Baltimore were Black. "Fuck the elected leaders!" was the on-camera response to my question.

During the Black Lives Matter protests, I knew young reporters were listening to news managers and producers, some of them new, who also mistakenly saw the demonstrations as a Black event and a time to air Black grievances. I've always said show producers don't train reporters in the field. Few should be sent to cover a riot. After bad judgment and bias, there is nothing worse than a journalist who is intimidated by an assignment. You don't always have to be brave, but reporters do need to be curious!

Support for Black Lives Matter went through the roof after George Floyd was murdered. With the demands for police accountability and racial justice, TV stations produced public service videos declaring their support. They sent sales teams out to sign up businesses eager to buy air time during Black Lives Matter specials that would air—including a march on Washington to commemorate Doctor King's 1963 "I Have a Dream" speech. D.C.'s Mayor Muriel Bowser had opposed the march because it was bringing thousands of high-risk senior African Americans to Washington, from hot states where the Covid-19 infections were highest. I did a commentary and interviewed African American physicians who advised Black people not to come and put their health and lives in danger. A fraction of the people did come. My station devoted hours to its live coverage, breaking away to air paid-for commercial spots.

Widespread support for Black Lives Matter has waned considerably since the summer and fall of 2020. The Pew Research Center says in June of 2020, overall support for BLM was at nearly 70 percent. By the beginning of the fall, it had dropped to nearly 50 percent, although African American support was well above 80 percent.

I could feel it in my conversations with White and Black friends and associates. My White friends felt they had answered the bell against racism and a criminal cop. Most of my neighbors, White and Black, had Black Lives Matter signs in their yards at some point. Not as many remain. If White people were outraged at Derek Chauvin and saw his slaying of George Floyd as the worst case of police brutality, they're feeling better that peace in the streets has been restored and one bad cop has been dealt with.

Doctor Martin Luther King addressed the contentment of good White people who sought to quell the street demonstrations that King had brought to Birmingham. From the city jail he wrote, "You deplore the demonstrations taking place in Birmingham but your statement I am sorry to say, fails to express a similar concern for the conditions that brought about the demonstration."

Police Sergeant Derek Chauvin's killing of George Floyd was but a symptom. The effect of systemic racism allowed in a police department that had been supported for years by the White status quo.

I would further add that diversity alone at low- and mid-management levels in police departments or media or law offices or medicine doesn't eliminate racism. There have to be consequences for bad cops and consequences for racist behavior in the workplace

There has been recent progress and Black Lives Matter deserves much of the credit. Their calls for defunding police started the reforms that are leading to reimagining how police can best serve every community going forward. Cops are leaving, retiring early, and some potential recruits are reconsidering. That may be a good thing. As basketball legend and humanitarian Kareem Abdul-Jabbar once told me, "Not everyone is cut out to be a police officer. That's why you and I are doing something else."

In media, TV corporations have doubled down on their minority hiring and they needed to. It's long overdue. I haven't seen this type of commitment since the early 1970s when I was hired as a newsroom assignment desk assistant. "We took our eyes on the ball," said one veteran broadcast executive.

Dave Lougee, a former news director of a rival TV station that tried to hire me is now president and CEO of The Tegna Broadcasting Corporation. Lougee says 50 percent of the company's hires since 2020 have been minorities. That's commendable, but what was it before Black Lives Matter and George Floyd? Tegna has a twelve-member board of directors. One of the members is African American as of this writing. The corporation owns TV stations in fifty-one television markets, each with a general manager or president. Two of those properties are headed by African American general managers. Other broadcast corporations have similar numbers. Minorities and women are prominent in front of the cameras. Not so much in newsroom management and upper- management positions where important decisions are made—where cultural diversity and diversity of thought is important.

The gains made in the last year and certainly from the civil rights movements of the late 1960s and '70s cannot be taken for granted. When the marches stop and people are no longer made to feel uncomfortable, they revert back to their comfort zones, hiring people they know or feel most comfortable working with. Those gains came at great sacrifice from advocates and minority journalists in front of and behind the cameras. Some of those gains were made or allowed to happen reluctantly.

Despite my success that includes twenty-two Emmy awards, journalism and community hall of fame honors, I feel that if our progress isn't guarded and recalibrated, history could repeat itself. That history shows that at times when segments of African Americans are moving forward, serious and often dangerous undercurrents are forming to turn back the clock.

What we have seen is that many White people have not learned how or been willing to share space and power with Black folk.

Here's some context: after Barack Obama's election in 2008 and reelection four years later, the perception among White and Black Americans was that racism had softened. On the night of Obama's historic win as the country's first African American president, I was in the newsroom and turned to one of our expert analysts, the late Ronald Walters, a noted political scientist from Howard University and the University of Maryland. Walters had been a Jesse Jackson delegate to the Democratic Convention in 1988 in Atlanta. Jackson was running for president. I asked Ron what Obama's election meant for Black people. He pondered the question. "Okay, I'll tell you. Not much, if you're asking if it will mean policies that benefit Black people." Ron said Obama's election would make us feel better (about being Black) and give us an incredible example to show our sons and daughters, but that's it.

President Obama confirms that he was on a tightrope for much of his two terms in office when racial controversies came up. In his book, *A Promised Land*, he reveals that he saw a huge drop in his White support when he publicly supported noted African American historian Louis Skip Gates after he was arrested at his home by a White police sergeant James Crowley who was investigating a suspected burglary. Obama says the loss in White support was bigger than any other single event in his eight years in office saying, "It was support that I'd never completely get back."

I regret that my mother didn't live to see Barack Obama elected president and later in 2020 Kamala Harris voted in as the first African American female vice president. But Mary Johnson-Marbry would have agreed with Ron Walters. A former domestic worker and later college graduate, she would have warned Barack that White America didn't want a president with a Black agenda. She would have been incredibly proud but worried there would be a backlash to Obama's election.

Her concerns, and old Black people are always concerned, are supported by a University of Michigan poll that found opposition to affirmative action and integration may have increased since 2008. One explanation is if the playing field has been leveled, there is no need for such policies and programs, but another reason might be that many classes of Whites never learned or intended to live and share power with Black people. And they certainly did not intend for Black folk to move to the front of the line.

Some of our ancestors did move up from the bottom after the Civil War, during Reconstruction. But the vast majority of African Americans—like my great-great-grandparents Jim and Unc Buckner and their daughter, Millie—died really poor.

On January 6, 2021, I was one week into my retirement from WUSA9 9 (CBS) in Washington, D.C. I was watching live TV as a mob of mostly White men stormed the U.S. Capitol in an effort to disrupt a joint session of Congress and overturn the presidential election in which Joe Biden defeated incumbent President Donald Trump. Georgia, with an incredible Democratic voter mail-in campaign, had become the first Southern state in modern times to vote out a Republican president. Arizona too. Motivated Blacks and other minorities had registered and voted in droves in urban areas. Biden helped himself by winning back northern states—Wisconsin, Minnesota, Michigan, and Pennsylvania—that Trump had seized four years earlier from Hillary Clinton.

Trump had convinced supporters who came to Washington to protest that the election had been stolen. No way Democrats found enough voters in Georgia and enough Republican-leaning White suburban women in Wisconsin, Michigan, and Pennsylvania to defeat the incumbent president. In fact, Democrats won the White House and Senate precisely because of President Trump. Republicans seeking reelection everywhere else on the November ballot fared nicely.

Journalists and pundits speculated from the anchor desks at all hours of the day and night about what was really driving the mobs who stormed the Capitol building fighting with overmatched

Capitol police and responding D.C. police officers. So why did so few reporters bother to ask the protestors?

First off, there were few reporters on the ground at the point of the attacks outside and inside the US Capitol. Newsrooms had been reducing staffing during and even before Covid-19. Some journalists were laid off. Others, including me, had to take a furlough day. Did budget constraints prevent news operations from spending the money to allow reporters to follow the protestors back to their home states? The country deserved more than a few Twitter soundbites, which amounted to a few utterances about taking our government back.

We later learned some of the rioters were military veterans and active police officers.

The mob claimed to support the men and women in blue. The Capitol police officers union says 140 officers were injured fighting the mobs. Officer Brian Sicknick died after trying to defend the Capitol. At least three of the officers later committed suicide.

Police never used lethal force. I talked with colleagues, Black and White, about their restraint. Some surmised the outcomes might have been different had the rioters been Black Lives Matter protestors storming the U.S. Capitol. Perhaps! But Black Lives Matter was founded by African American women. Storming the US Capitol or any building by force had never been their modus operandi.

On January 6th, one protestor, Ashli Babbitt, a thirty-five-year-old White female Air Force veteran, was the killed. Shot by a plain-clothes Capitol officer who guarded House Speaker Nancy Pelosi's lobby, with gun drawn and chairs barricading the door. Babbit was fatally wounded as she stepped through a broken window.

Republican Senator Ron Johnson said he never felt threatened in the insurrection, which is antipodal to what Democratic House members felt; Johnson explained that he would have been concerned if the mob had been made up of Black Lives Matter or Antifa protestors.

And there you have it.

One of the people eventually arrested for his alleged role in the Capitol riot was Ryan Samsel of Bucks County, Pennsylvania. Samsel, a thirty-eight-year-old White man, was accused of using a barricade to push a Capitol police officer outside the capitol, briefly knocking her to the ground. Prosecutors said Samsel helped the officer to her feet and said, "We don't have to hurt you. Why are you standing in our way?" The Capitol police officer later collapsed while arresting a second rioter. She was taken to an emergency room where she was diagnosed with a concussion.

Samsel subsequently complained that while he was being held at the D.C. jail, he was beaten by guards. I know that D.C. jail. I'm assuming the guards were Black. Maybe looking for some payback.

As a journalist who happens to be African American, I would have asked each of the protestors, "What is it about this country, the United States, which has given you so much, that has made you so angry? What has this country done to you?" I believe this is the only explanation; they're angry because they feel the country has done too much for people who are not like them. I heard from a young White man in Luray, Virginia, who felt that "too many benefits were going to people not doing enough for themselves."

African Americans hear that as code for lazy, undeserving Black people are getting too much help from the government.

It's been about "race" since 1619, when a reported twenty or so kidnapped Angolans arrived from Africa in chains at Jamestown. And contrary to grade school lessons, this country's Civil War over slavery didn't end or settle anything on April 9, 1865, when

Confederate General Robert E. Lee surrendered to Union General Ulysses S. Grant.

I think it was best explained by the writer Ralph Ellison, who said in an address at Harvard in 1949 that the outcome of the Civil War "is still in the balance, and only our enchantment by the spell of the possible, our endless optimism, has led us to assume that it ever really ended."

The most precarious threat today is from the White man who has been made to believe he is entitled by birth to opportunities and a status that he feels are slipping away from him; if he hasn't attained a certain level of economic security for himself and his family, it can't be because of increased competition or his own diminished skillset and his job has left the country; it's because someone else, likely with help from government policies, has been given an unfair advantage. Translation: something has been denied or taken from him. He might be willing to share what the country has to offer, which is a lot, but he must get his first. He thinks "White Privilege" is a racist slur that certainly doesn't fit him. He is likely working class or even poor; but he does feel entitled.

Martin Luther King never demanded that Black people be moved to the front of the line. As he stood on the steps of the Lincoln Memorial in 1963, he did ask that we not be relegated to the back of the line because of our skin color.

My ancestors had bought my ticket to Washington D.C. with their free labor and sweat on the Buckner Planation in Pembroke, Kentucky over one hundred and fifty years ago.

In 1976, we were more than qualified to be working in our newsroom. Most of us had been recruited by Post–Newsweek, the *Washington Post* company, after serving apprenticeships in smaller markets like Cincinnati. We arrived in Washington with graduate degrees which could have made us over qualified if compared to other White reporters. Because of the Black Lives Matter protests, broadcast companies have been forced to once again recruit the best minority talent and where they can't find the skilled candidates they're being challenged to train people to be able to move up.

In almost forty-five years as a reporter and evening anchor at WUSA9, the three corporations that bought and sold the TV station hired only one African American News Director, between them.

Dave Roberts was a senior vice president for production at ESPN as of this writing. He arrived at WUSA9 in 2000. He lasted but a few years and left the Gannett Corporation when he balked at a cost cutting mandate that forced our veteran anchor Gordon Peterson to leave the station.

Robert's position proved to be the smart one. The day Gordon Peterson went on the air for the rival ABC station, that station went from dead last in the market to second place. WUSA9 went from second place to dead last. The next twenty years under Gannett would prove challenging on multiple fronts. Although I did land some incredible assignments, break some great news stories, and make a lot of money. It was sometimes fun and often professionally rewarding, but never easy and without stress!

The Gannett Corporation had bought channel 9 from Detroit's Evening News corporation in August of 1985. "You could have done a lot worse," said legendary news director and friend Jim Snyder. Gannett then went through its news directors about every two to three years. Each one under obvious pressure to win. Some were better than others and maybe deserved more time. Some of my news directors should never have been considered for the job.

Rob Mennie was one of the first Gannett choices to lead the once iconic "One and Only TV9." He made it clear from the start he was cutting all ties to any past glory we might want to build on. Mennie was White, young, and pretty sure of himself, but with only a couple years' experience running a news operation in Dayton, Ohio. There were problems from the start.

In his first address to the WUSA9 news team, Rob said we were going in a different news direction. Our coverage would reflect the change. He then gives us an example of what that meant.

He said if there is a baby deer stuck out on a frozen lake and at the same time there is a shooting in the projects, where do you send the one camera crew? Mennie's answer was, "To the deer stuck on the lake. Most people will want to know and see how that story turns out," he said. I couldn't believe what I was hearing.

The room of broadcast journalists was silent. No one, including this reporter, dared challenge openly what we had just heard. We feared being labeled malcontents, a problem for our new boss. But we were hurt and bothered by his insistence.

I had earned my stripes covering the poor and working Black communities in North and Southeast D.C., where most of the project shootings took place. Those Black lives mattered to me and Black viewers and to many of my colleagues.

So for me, a slaying of somebody in a public housing project or nearly anywhere was always going to take precedence over a baby deer stuck on the ice. Maybe I would direct the baby deer assignment to our social media team.

I stuck my head in Rob Mennie's office and told him I thought it was a bad example that he had laid out.

Mennie conceded he could have given a different example to make his point.

He later was more direct when instructing our health reporter and a producer on who he wanted to see profiled in a breast cancer story. He told them suburban viewers wanted to see a Montgomery County, blue-eyed blond woman.

Rob saw some ratings improvement and quickly used the one good ratings period to move up to Gannett corporate. Much of the stations on air promotions were centered around the country hit song, "Let's Give Them Something to Talk About." I think the promotion had more to do with our success than our choice of news stories. We never came across a deer stuck on a frozen pond.

There have been only three African American presidents or general managers at channel 9 in my near four-and-a-half decades here. That translates to one Black general manager for every fifteen years.

There was one female news director. Betty Endicott was hired by the Evening News Corporation which owned the station for roughly fifteen years after Post-Newsweek and before Gannett bought the station. Betty lasted only two years before being replaced by Dave Pearce, a White male out of Providence, Rhode Island.

A majority of the newsroom staff was young and progressive. Dave Pearce was clearly conservative and I appreciated the political and social debates we would have in his office behind closed doors. Maybe that's why he felt it was okay to keep me off the roster to cover an upcoming hurricane story. No reporter wants to sit out a big story, including sports and weather, that's certain to generate big ratings.

When I noticed that my name wasn't on the list to cover the storm, which would have meant overtime pay, I stuck my head in the news director's office to ask why.

Dave Pearce said to me, "You're not covering the hurricane because your hair doesn't blow in the wind." I stepped back and explained that I could sue him for that explanation. He didn't seem worried. Maybe he was just trying to be funny, but my name never made the list. I wasn't assigned to cover the storm.

Dave Pearce by most measures was a successful news director. He held the job for over fifteen years. He made me one of the highest-paid reporters in the country. When I complained that I hadn't been sent to the White House to cover a story, he sent me to the White House several times. He agreed to detail me to the programming department to travel the world to report and help produce one-hour documentaries that aired in prime time after *Sixty Minutes* on Sunday nights.

Moscow, Paris, Stockholm, Budapest, Tokyo, and Dakar. We compared life for the residents of those capital cities, including how they were allowed voting representation in their national legislative assemblies while District of Columbia residents were denied the same rights here in the United States. In Paris, I pointed out the city's Mayor Jacque Chirac actually was elected president of France.

By the mid 2000s, traditional broadcast operations appeared to be on their heels or in full retreat because of the hard-charging social media wave that was siphoning off viewers by the boatload: why sit around and wait for the 6 PM and, especially, the 11 PM news when you can get it on your cellphone, which is with you at all times?

Gannett was a newspaper company first, and like all newspaper companies, including *The Washington Post* and *The New York Times*, Gannett was on a slippery slope and sliding fast.

The company had been incredibly slow to adapt to the change. I had a personal Twitter and Facebook account before the company launched its own. Cecil Walker, a former CEO, didn't seem to see the urgency.

The changes were coming at a head-spinning pace. Corporate managers wanted young and cheaper staff who had never touched a manual or electric typewriter.

And they wanted a younger audience. If we could identify them on social media, we could convert them to broadcast viewers. I never bought it. *A different audience totally*, I'm thinking. *If you're engaged with me online, why would you want to stick around for more of the same engagement on air?*

In the middle of all the change, a tall curly-haired guy by the name of Fred D'Ambrosi was hired as news director. He had been out of work when Allan Horlick, the general manager, hired him to run the WUSA9 newsroom. Fred was in trouble from the start. Gannett, which was now Tegna, was moving toward a cost-saving multimedia journalist approach to news gathering. That meant reporters on the street, like me, would lose their camera operator. We would be trained to record and edit our own video, in addition to research, set up, interview, and drive to the assignments. The company in its marketing said it was a new innovative way of covering the news.

A rival news director who was trying to hire me said the entire industry was watching what Tegna was doing. If it worked, everybody would start doing it, he predicted. It didn't work.

I asked an executive producer what a news director would have to do to get fired. He responded, "They'll keep you around as long as they are convinced that you have one big idea left."

In January of 2014, Fred D'Ambrosi was about to launch his last big idea.

It was freezing outside and Fred decided that an anchor desk carved out of a block of ice and positioned outside in the circle in front of the station would be a hit with viewers. It wasn't.

It was 18 degrees outside. A company called Hot Ice was contracted to sculpt the masterpiece for its debut on the 5 PM newscast. Fred was a fan of one-hit wonder White rapper Vanilla Ice, so naturally the rapper's one hit "Ice Ice Baby" became the theme each time we showed the ice desk going into and coming out of commercial breaks; but also during two separate reports about the how the sculpture came about. We dropped a couple of hard news stories from the broadcast in order to showcase our new anchor desk in every newscasts. I thought the ice desk could set our weather segment apart from the competition, but it was overkill. Viewers were not impressed.

The newsroom can be a volatile place. Competition is fierce. Deadlines are nonnegotiable. People would sometimes snap and say the wrong thing.

Fred D'Ambrosi snapped at me one evening as I was trying to finish a script, putting a track down for an editor who was trying to make page. Get the story into the show where the producer has assigned its place in the rundown.

"Bruce, why don't you speak English?" He's coming at me and he's angry. I'm the most senior journalist on staff. I've written scores of news scripts, magazine articles, a couple of books! I'm a Black man and this tall, heavy White man is coming at me and attempting to put me in my place for all to see. This is a setup. He's baiting me. Why?

"'Why don't you speak English?'" Andrew McCarren, our veteran investigative reporter, repeated Fred's question, in surprise and disbelief. The rest of the newsroom staff had frozen in place. The usual banter was gone.

Fred's tirade followed a brief an unexpected conversation that he initiated at my desk. It was a strange request. He wanted me to call the mayor to inquire about a story idea he had. I said okay. But can it wait? He seemed to accept my response, headed toward his office at the front of the room, but then pivoted back to me.

"Bruce, Why don't you speak English?"

It sounded like a racial slur! I do speak and write in the acceptable vernacular. I get paid a lot for this. He was cutting me down to size for all the newsroom to see.

I had instinctively leaped to my feet, fists clenched. I was furious. Didn't he know I was raised in the projects? This was going to be a one-punch match and I had learned from my older brother's beatdowns to be the one to throw the first punch. Did his size advantage convince him he could talk to me this way?

Fred was now several feet away and that was a good thing. I was about to get myself fired. I didn't have the words to retaliate in such a hateful manner. I had never exchanged angry racial insults with a White person or anyone.

In the end I didn't take the bait from Fred. I didn't retaliate, as a young Bruce Johnson would have said a simple "Fuck you."

It was as though I was hearing my mother's voice in my head. She was a fighter. But she was telling me, *Don't move, uncurl your fists but don't sit back down cause it will look like you're backing down. Don't say anything.*

I finished my work assignment and marched upstairs to the general manager's office.

The GM, Mark Burdette, offered me a seat. "I'm going to quit, I can't work for him anymore!" Burdette summoned D'Ambrosi to his office. What Fred said to me and where it was said was never in dispute, but Barnett never got an explanation for why it was said, and I never got an explanation from Fred nor an apology. I had calmed down. This isn't really my problem, its Fred's! No way was

I letting him have that kind of power over me. I was hearing my mother's voice when I stood up and said, "Okay, I have to go." I reached out and grabbed his hand and shook it. He seemed surprised. Nobody had asked me to do that. After we shook, I left the room. I still don't know what Fred meant when he said "Bruce, why don't you speak English?"

Bill Lord replaced D'Ambrosi. Lord packed a lot of news and management skills, and Mark Burdette seemed quite pleased with his new hire. Lord had been news director and station manager at WJLA (ABC). He was forced out by Sinclair Broadcasting, which bought the ABC7 station. Gordon Peterson and Maureen Bunyan were also part of the exodus.

There were no more gimmicks under Lord, which was a welcome change for me. He wanted to cover the news which sounded a lot like what we did when Jim Snyder brought me here from Cincinnati. Good content, great video, and of course, exclusives stories! Lord put me on the 6 PM anchor desk and created a 7 PM show "Off Script with Bruce Johnson," which allowed me to cover stories and bring people on set for live inadept interviews.

Bill Lord was news director at Channel 9 for only two years. The ratings improved. Gannett broadcasting split from Gannett newspapers and became Tegna Incorporated.

The new company doubled down on its approach to multimedia journalism. Every anchor and reporter was required to bring an impressive social media following.

Some of the young African American hires were straight out of the Black Lives Matter protest mode. A few, like sports director Darren Haynes, came with their own firsthand accounts of police brutality. Darren appeared one evening on my screen in a BLM demonstration. I wasn't sure if he was reporting or participating in the march. It should have been made clear.

If the Black Lives Matter protests have run their course, if White people and Black have returned to what had been their norms at least this much has changed, Black people seem more willing to discuss the impact racism has had on their lives and more White people seem ready to listen without either side feeling they're being judged.

I am reminded of something Oprah Winfrey said to me outside the Museum of African American History and Culture back in September of 2016. She had given me an exclusive interview arranged by Oprah's best friend and my former mentee at WUSA9, Gayle King. Oprah and I talked as part of the museum's grand opening, but we found each other again while touring the Slave and Jim Crow exhibits. We talked about the toll systemic racism was taking on Black people and why it was important for White people to hear us out. She said "In a family, if somebody is hurting and you don't acknowledge that they're hurting, you don't acknowledge their pain, you don't say that I can see that you're hurting, I want to do something about your hurting, you end up with total chaos and dysfunction."

Was the unanimous passage in the Senate of a bill making Juneteenth a national holiday a start? Perhaps.

Maybe Mitchell McConnell could explain and while he's at it, help Americans understand why his and my home state of Kentucky waited until 1976 to approve the 13th amendment, which freed the slaves.

I'm hopeful that the more important dialogue will take place at work, across the backyard fence, or maybe in a chat room—minus the anger.

In March of 2014, Dave Lougee, the Tegna CEO who is White, handed a Black attorney in a business suit a valet ticket after the two had sat at the same table at a business luncheon. Lougee was clearly embarrassed and apologized. Most people who worked for him at Tegna didn't hear about the incident until years later when that same Black attorney withdrew his name from consideration for a seat on Tegna's board of directors. Attorney Adonis Huffman wasn't going to win the seat. He was part of a hostile takeover bid that failed. My response and what I wanted to talk to Lougee about was how powerful that personal valet ticket story would have been had he revealed it.... First! Shared the incident with the rest of us in a powerful constructive conversation about race.

Dave's response was that he couldn't talk about it further. He sent an email to Tegna employees explaining what happened after the story was published in the *Wall Street Journal.*

Black Lives Matter jump started the conversations about race and commitment to equality on every front. Police, politics, socio-economic conditions, health disparities. I plan to put a lot of my retirement time into continuing the dialogue and the progress. But talk without action is just that. You've heard this expression, "If we are now running a race at the same speed, it doesn't mean it's a fair race if you were given a ten yard head start." I can never make up for the centuries of legal and illegal advantages that have been given to you. To fix what is ailing this country racially will require some courageous and unselfish decisions from White people in power. Those entitlements that I wrote about that White protestors have come to expect will have to be shared. There should be enough opportunity to go around in this great country. Competition can be scary for people only concerned about their own self-preservation. My grandchildren's success shouldn't be considered a threat to your children.

As a Black man, I no longer carry a resentment for the harm done to my ancestors. I don't have a right to complain or room to hate. They've paid my fare to be here. My role is to do the best in the time I have left to honor my mother, great-grandmother, and the others' legacy. And to Black people and their progressive supporters, how bout we not rush to judge people in matters of race?

I'm reminded that in May of 2019, many noted Blacks and Whites wanted to force Virginia Governor Ralph Northam out of office because he may have appeared in Black face while a medical student. It was never confirmed that a picture was in fact Northam. An old Black man in Virginia told me at the time it would be a mistake to force the governor out. He said, "Bruce, there is personal racism and there is policy racism. A lot of White men grew up racist but learned better." My friend who was in his eighties said Northam is not a racist now, and his policies are certainly not racist. He was right. Governor Northam's policies have proven to be very good for African Americans.

It's hard to judge what a heart is capable of doing. That's God's work!

ACKNOWLEDGMENTS

THIS BOOK BEGAN WRITING ITSELF in February of 1972 when I walked into my first television newsroom in Cincinnati, Ohio. But it would not have been possible without the behind-the-scenes skills and encouragement of lots of committed people to whom I am forever grateful.

My editor at Post Hill Press, Debra Englander, was on point from the beginning. Debby was encouraging and persistent. She reviewed every line. There were great questions and smart suggestions. Her awesome editing skills made this a better book.

Sha-Shana Crichton is my agent and the driving force behind getting my book to publication. Sha-Shana is a brilliant writer, attorney, and professor at Howard University Law School. Our first conversation lasted forever. She believed in my book before we had a title, chapter outline, or a plan on all that I needed to say in this book. Sha-Shana Crichton—through scores of long talks and lots of patience—was determined to bring my book to publication. She said the time was now! Sha-Shana, you rock!

Lynn Hooghiemstra, an editorial writer, I can't thank you enough for your early help with this book. Although living in a different time zone, you were always available to take my calls and add some structure to my project.

Marita Golden, noted American novelist, you are everything other writers have said about you. "An amazing read" is how you described my book. It reached that point after your critique. It helped immensely that you lived through the times and some of the experiences that I write about.

Jonetta Rose Barras, I can't thank you enough for being there again when it came to nailing down some political history that few Washington journalists are able to appreciate.

Ronald Baker of Solid Images; one of the best commercial photographers in the country and the cameraman the biggest stars trust. I'm grateful for the time you took to create the images that are on the cover and inside pages of this book. Your work is awesome. Our private conversations, inspiring.

The late Jim Snyder, Post–Newsweek vice president and news director who hired me at WTOP-TV (CBS), which eventually became WUSA-TV (CBS). Snyder took a chance and then reminded me that white men with no journalism experience and no college degrees had been given the same journalism opportunities for years.

Over the years in Washington, I begged my mentors, Max Robinson, Jim Vance, Ed Bradley, Gordon Peterson, JC Hayward, Lee Thornton, Maurine Bunyan, and more to write their stories. I'm not sure I could have handled the kind of inside and outside pressures they faced. My book is partial payment on what I owe them.

Al Schottelkotte, the late VP and news director at Scripps WCPO-TV in Cincinnati, is owed a big thank you. From the day he gave me my first newsroom job as desk assistant, I let him know I needed to finish undergrad school and more. He made a path for me. There was no one else who looked like me in his newsroom. By the time I left Cincinnati, I had a college degree from Northern Kentucky University and a Master's degree from the University of

Cincinnati. After his retirement, Schottelkotte visited me whenever he came to Washington.

I should thank the good priests at Sacred Heart seminary in Cincinnati. Those two years of high school away from my neighborhood in Louisville might have saved me from an entirely different life.

I retired from WUSA-TV in D.C. at the end of 2020. The coronavirus pandemic helped in my decision to move on. It was time after almost forty-five years. I left behind some talented and dedicated journalists.

Executive Producer Samara Martin Ewing and I went through some battles. Two trips to Rome to cover the installation of a couple of Cardinals. We worked twenty hours straight on the day and night that Pope Francis was elected. We were the only major market TV operation that didn't send a second crew to share the workload. Thanks Sam! We did some great work. I earned twenty-two Emmys! Your name is on several of them.

Stephanie Wilson, a senior producer, is the colleague you want to go to war with. Dakar Senegal was one assignment. Her knowledge of the DC news market is unmatched. Stephanie and chief video editor Larry Sindass put together a month-long sendoff on WUSA9 to mark my more than four decades at the station. Larry edited some of my best feature stories including tributes to the legendary Chuck Brown, the father of DC Go-Go music. Thanks Steph and Larry.

Richard Dyer, the president and general manager at WUSA9, presided over an awesome sendoff for me at Channel 9. It lasted through the November sweeps period. I wanted to leave on a high note. It was all that and more. Thanks, Richard.

James Brown, CBS Sports anchor and longtime friend. Thanks JB for being a living example.

Glenn Brenner, the late sports anchor and my good friend, thank you. Earl Casey and the late Walt Swanston and Pat Casey, thanks so much!

Lois Dyer, a walking encyclopedia on everything Washington, thank you!

Mark Seegar, Jody Small, Meredith Resnick, Sheila Jack, thank you.

There is no way to single out all the great film and camera operators, editors, and studio staff who tirelessly, courageously, and creatively followed me into the streets and halls of power on assignments.

Kline Mengle, Greg Guise, Kevin King, Mike Trammel, Mike Murphy, Mike Fox, Dion Wiggins, Bill McKnight, Keith Williams, Dave Chater, Mark Boss, Frank McDermott, Tad Dukehart, Bruce Bookholtz, Paul Lester, Denny Bly, Dave Goulding, Tom Hallor, Tim Duluca, Hal Hoilland, Bill Thompson, and Dave Moubray, Peady Shiflett, Brooks Meriwether, Earl Dunmeyer, Leo Pitts, Britt Arrington, Julius Brown, Douglas Johnson, Tom Chessman, Vanessa Kooloff, Bill Clemmons, Wayne Meyers, Bill Moore, Dave Ewing, Carrol Bush, Al Calogero, Gerry Gordon, Larry Sindass, Mary Lou Donahue, Judy Fitterman, Lori Werner, Charlie Balkin, Calvin Turner, Bob Oberlander, Jim Suthard, Tom Buckley, Danielle Gill, and my longtime reporting-anchor friend, Delia Gonsalves.

I thank all the reporter and anchor colleagues. Gayle King at the CBS Morning News, thank you. I was a mentor to Gayle when she was a reporter trainee at WUSA-TV. Lesli Foster and I anchored the 6 PM news for years. She remains one of the best journalists in

Washington. Terri Okita was a weekend co-ancho Debra Alfarone and I teamed to anchor weekend news with Howard Bernstein holding down the weather desk. Topper Shutt, Jan Jeffcoat, Darin Haynes, Frank Herzog, Ken Mease, Cari Hernandez, Derek McGinty, Erica Grow, and Kristen Berset. Thank you.

And to the former TV program director who sent me all over the world on assignment, Sandra Butler-Jones, thank you!

Dave Roberts, senior vice president at ESPN, thanks for challenging me while recognizing the importance of the work. Bill Lord, a former news director once heard me complain, "You're abusing me by having me anchor and report every day." Bill responded, "I'm not trying to abuse you but I am trying to take advantage of you!" Thanks Bill.

I want to thank the citizens of Washington D.C. and beyond; on TV and social media at every level you've trusted me to tell your stories. Many people gave me confidential information, sometimes at great risk to their careers and safety. I never betrayed a news source. I so appreciate your trust!

Virginia Ali, the founder and owner of the famous Ben's Chili Bowl restaurant in Washington, DC, I can't thank you enough for the love and encouragement from the beginning of my time in the Nation's Capital. You've placed my image on the Wall of Fame on the side of your iconic restaurant alongside national figures, including President Barack Obama and First Lady Michelle Obama. I'll spend the rest of my years trying to be worthy.

I want to thank my loving wife. Lori, you have been my partner and best friend. There would be no me without you. To my adult children and grandchildren, thanks for the patience over the years while I tried to cover every big story.

To my late mother, Mary Johnson-Marbry, and my late great-grandmother, Millie Buckner-Bell, you have been my rock. Thank you for the life, the lessons you gave me.

Surviving Deep Waters is now part of your legacy.